# DOWN NORTH

*Ciarán de Baróid*

**Ogham Press Belfast**

Published 2010 by Ogham Press
5-7 Conway Street
Belfast BT13 2DE

Copyright © Ciarán de Baróid 2010.

The right of Ciarán de Baróid to be identified as the author of this work has been asserted by him according to the Copyright, Designs and Patents Act 1988.

All rights reserved. This book is sold subject to the condition that it shall not, by way of trade or otherwise, be lent, resold, hired out, or otherwise circulated without the prior consent of the author/publisher in any form or binding or cover other than that in which it is published and without a similar condition including this condition being imposed on the subsequent publisher.

ISBN: 978-0-9566166-0-9

## Contents                                           Page

1. Pass The Parcel .................................................................. 1
2. Whatever Ya Say, Say Nathin' ....................................... 21
3. Down Springhill Way ..................................................... 37
4. A Free State Bawstard ................................................... 54
5. The Bombing Of Kelly's Bar ......................................... 65
6. Glaslough And Social Times ........................................ 72
7. Ceasefire .......................................................................... 85
8. In The Woods Of Truagh .............................................. 97
9. Resistance ..................................................................... 112
10. The House That Jack Built ........................................ 122
11. The Umbrella ............................................................... 130
12. The Bike ....................................................................... 139
13. The Suit ........................................................................ 144
14. The Summer Of '73 .................................................... 151
15. A Scary Joint ............................................................... 157
16. The Gloves ................................................................... 167
17. Dublin ........................................................................... 170
18. The Year Of Collapse ................................................. 176
19. The Dutchies ............................................................... 182
20. All In A Month ........................................................... 187
21. Living Off The Land .................................................. 199
22. Harry Comes To Town .............................................. 203
23. The Year Of The Feuds .............................................. 211

# Acknowledgements

As always, anything that relates to that remarkable district at the foot of Black Mountain owes much to its inhabitants. The stories recounted here are the legacy of the times created for myself and Cora – and for so many others of our friends and families - by the people of Ballymurphy. To them we will always owe a great debt – in terms of the richness of the experiences we shared, and the generosity of person and spirit from which Cora and I benefited, and which was always available to anyone who came along as a friend.

Special thanks must go to Liam Stone for his helpful reminders of times past, and to Liam's mother Ann who also prodded my memory and was so much a part of those early years. Thanks must also go to all those who helped the community and human rights efforts of our various projects during the early Seventies. Some are named in these pages. Some are not but they will know that they have our gratitude and remain in our fondest memories. South of the border, we remember those who came and gave unselfishly of their time and their homes, and that stalwart group of Cork people – Martin Thompson, Isobel O'Shea, Mary O'Donavan, Tom Marshall, , Patricia Brown, Gerry McCarthy and his youth group, my old friend, Tony O'Connor, our Niall, my father, Críostóir and my mother Máire who, along with Gearóid MacAllister from Dublin, Jimmy Doherty from Belfast and Harry Bellingham from Derry, fought our corner all the way and defended the rights of defenceless people on all sides when they needed it most.

Thanks also to Eibhilín Glenholmes for being my first reader and for the helpful suggestions she provided. Gura maith agat arís. And to Roisin McAuley and her team at L-S-D Books who prepared the final copy.

And finally, thanks to Cora. Without her, much of what was achieved would never have seen the light of day. She was the rock of 42. A tough woman from Ballyphehane with a heart of gold and a generosity that matched that of the people of Ballymurphy – no mean feat.

Ciarán de Baróid
Belfast, July 2010

**To Cora**

# Chapter 1
## Pass The Parcel

*'There is a tide in the affairs of men,*
*Which, taken at the flood, leads on to fortune;*
*Omitted, all the voyage of their life*
*Is bound in shallows and in miseries.*
*On such a full sea are we now afloat;*
*And we must take the current when it serves...'*

~ William Shakespeare (Julius Caesar)

If the *Sunday Press* hadn't come into the house that morning, I have no idea where I'd be today. But one thing is sure: I'd never have seen the ad that changed it all.

March 5$^{th}$ 1972: the *Press* led with the bombing of the Abercorn Restaurant in Belfast the day before. Two women were dead; 136 others were injured. There were photos of the wounded being led away, and reports of body parts strewn all over Castle Lane. Nobody had admitted responsibility, but everyone suspected the Provisional IRA: a commercial bombing gone horrifically wrong. Like so much that had happened since the outbreak of the Troubles, the bombing brought a sense of powerless dismay.

Not so long ago Cora and I had been levitating our way along the Hippy Trail, bound ultimately for Australia. Out there in Asia Minor, with no access to newspapers, radio or TV, it was all love and peace. None of us had a care in the world. If it wasn't happening in our line of vision, then it wasn't happening at all. That was until the Bangladesh War brought tens of thousands of troops to face one another with tanks, artillery and warplanes along the Indo-Pakistani border and put a stopper on the Australia plan. Without sufficient funds to fly over the war zone, we'd been forced to turn back from Kabul. A long homeward journey via Pakistan and the Persian Gulf delivered us back to England on the morning of January 31$^{st}$ 1972. That was the day after Bloody Sunday, when British paratroopers had shot dead thirteen civil rights marchers on the streets of Derry, fatally wounded a fourteenth and put high-velocity bullets in thirteen others. We were on a London tube when

# Chapter 1

we saw the headlines on the back of someone's paper. Then the small print: they were all bombers. Of course. Weren't they always? It was a bad homecoming - the love and peace of four months blown out a tube window on the Picadilly Line. Sitting on the train, I thought of my great-grand-aunt Maggie, the old republican who lived in Cavendish Street off Belfast's war-torn Falls Road, and great-grand-aunt Josie who had St. Vitus' Dance and agreed with Maggie all the way. Like so many people in Ireland, I and they had connections to generations of conflict.

Maggie and Josie were the aunts of my mother's father, Gerry Anderson. Gerry had fought in Belfast with the IRA during the Tan War, and in Cork on the republican side during the Civil War. His grandfather, William John McStocker from out Randalstown way, had been a member of the Irish Republican Brotherhood and was somehow linked away back to Betsy Gray who died with the United Irishmen at the Battle of Ballynahinch in 1798. I had in my possession at home John McStockers' silver pocket-watch, passed down from first grandson (Gerry) to first grandson (me). Gerry's wife - my grandmother, Lily Herbert - blew up a bridge in Cork during the Civil War, carrying the bomb on her lap as she sat on the carrier of a bicycle, pedalled by IRA Volunteer, Richie Noonan.

My father's father, Jack Barrett, ended up in the trenches of the Somme after being forced from his work in Pre-Independence Cork because he had joined the Gaelic Athletic Association. Driven out of the country by unemployment, he'd gone to look for work in Wales where, unable to locate any alternative, he'd joined the Welch Fusiliers. A spell in India led to the Somme, and mustard gas and a piece of German shrapnel that cost him three years in hospital. On his return to Ireland, he married Hannah Donovan who hailed from a west Cork townland called, ironically enough, Ballymurphy. A cousin of Hannah's was a young man called Bat Falvey. As an IRA section commander, Bat was killed in action at Upton in 1921. And, if all that wasn't enough, there was old Maggie in Cavendish Street.

'Youse all abandoned us after Partition,' she told myself and Michael Kenneally when we passed through Belfast in 1967. I was sixteen at the time and very upset at having abandoned anyone back in 1921. Keen to redeem myself in Maggie's eyes, I joined the Republican Movement at age seventeen, and was ready and able a year later when the Troubles broke out. But there had since been the republican split, and the two successive trips along the Hippy

Trail during which all that peace and love had made the war at home grow a faraway face. In the bazaars of Bandar Abbas and the *chai-khanas* of Kandahar, nobody knew much about the bother in Ireland and nobody much gave a damn. So a kind of calm had settled. Then, one headline on that London train, and I could hear a rampaging gurgle in my throat, which escaped in a loud hissing *'Bastards!'* sound. Cora advised me to shut up or I'd get a kicking from John Citizen; but all the serenity was gone. So much so that, when we landed in Cork on February 1st, I was only sorry that we were too far away to give the upstanding citizens of Dublin a hand as 30,000 of them burned the British Embassy to the ground. All I could do was apply sympathetic magic and roar support through the telly.

Two months had since passed and I was now looking for a job, something that would befit a chap of my standing, with two overland trips to Asia under his belt. Belfast had gone back to being the war on the telly until I turned to the employment section of the paper. And there it was. The only ad not boxed, it ran scrappily down the right-hand side to the bottom of the last page like a mistake. 'Youth Leader Belfast', was the post-title. Ballymurphy Tenants' Association was looking for a 'Community Centre Youth Leader (male)' to work with its youth development group. Salary: £1,070 to £1,620, with a 'responsibility allowance' of £250. Apply to the chair, Frances McMullan by March 14th. I read the ad several times and, failing to realise that 'responsibility allowance' meant danger money, decided to apply. It would be my third job application since coming home: the other two involved street work with small homeless-support groups that had splintered from the Simon Community in Dublin.

To say that Cora wasn't overjoyed would be to miss the point completely.

'You're a nightmare!' she said, when I turned up in her house in Ballyphehane with the news, 'I never know what's coming next! After four months together, it's hard enough living separately again [Catholic Ireland 1972], without you heading off to the other end of the country to get yourself shot dead or blown to bits!'

'It would only be for a year,' I promised, 'In the meantime, we can both be up and down, and I'll be back before you know it.' *Put me on a boiled egg*, I should've added.

'A year!' she said, 'Do you know how long it takes to get shot?'

'We could get married at the end of the year...' I said. Cora looked

# Chapter 1

at me with an element of disbelief.

'Gimme a cigarette...?' she said, '... and, by the way, that's the crappiest proposal I *ever* heard.'

A week past twenty-one, I went back home, put pen to paper (ommitting age), and dropped my CV in the post on Monday morning. For relevant experience, I had to dig deep. In my late teens I'd been involved in the committee of a rather rowdy version of a youth club at St. Anthony's Hall where I'd met Cora. Details I didn't include entailed the occasional slide to affray and a near miss outside the door one night when the lad next to me was shot in the thigh. The projectile that shot him was a 'banger' invented by one of our friends who'd stuffed gunpowder into the case of a .303 bullet salvaged from an IRA training camp. When he lit the fuse and dropped it on the ground it started to spin, and the guy who got shot hadn't run fast enough.

I had also organised a small group of my peers into a thing called Action Now, which went around the tenements of the inner-city, decorating the homes of pensioners. To raise funds, I'd organised a related, 30-mile charity-walk - for very limited returns - that crippled the entire gang. Then, during my final year at Coláiste Chríost Rí, I'd played a minor role in a school fund-raising project. This saw us bring a piano into Patrick Street in the city centre so that classmate, Cathal Dunne, a nephew of Irish Taoiseach, Jack Lynch, could hammer out an impressive repertoire while doing what my good friend Tony O'Connor called, 'making shit of the piano'. The rest of my CV involved a stint installing fume-cupboards for a British company in the new science block at Cork University, a couple of weeks navvying on the roads of Berkshire, a few months in the Shipyard at Cobh, and the two trips along the Hippy Trail, best not elaborated upon when trying to impress anyone who didn't fully appreciate the finer nuances of hippy culture. That was about it.

'You have a hell of a neck,' Cora said, 'Looking for an interview with that.' She then wished me all the luck in the world. 'You're going to need it,' she said, 'With the application. With the interview, if you get one. And with bloody Ballymurphy if you ever get there.'

I'd never been to Ballymurphy, but by early 1972 it was an Irish household name, synonymous with the Troubles. Right through the second half of 1970 this once-obscure, working-class neighbourhood had been the scene of fierce nightly riots between young Belfast republicans and the British army, until the riots were displaced by gun-battles. With the introduction of internment without trial in August 1971 and an accompanying spate of military killings, the district had gone on to become a virtual no-go area for the British army, whose new problems came chiefly from the Provisional IRA, the larger of the two IRAs to emerge from the split of December 1969. Applying for a post in Ballymurphy was not generally considered the soundest of ideas around Cork; but as it turned out, it was the best decision I would ever make in my life.

In the last week of March I attended an interview for one of the Dublin posts for which I'd also applied. When I got back home that night, I found a reply to my Ballymurphy application from Frances McMullan. Would I come to Belfast for an interview on the second Saturday in April?

'They're dying to see the eedjit at the other end of the application,' Cora assured me.

I took the train north a week later and was met in Great Victoria Street Station by Alain Gogarty. Alain, a little younger than me, was the son of a friend of my father's who'd invited me to stay with the family in Fort William Park, close to the Shore Road where my interview was due to take place the following day.

Greeting me with the authoritative air of a tour guide, Alain welcomed me, hoped I'd had a good trip, and asked after my parents. Commending the paucity of my luggage - a small square bag of Moroccan leather dangling from my right shoulder – he then led the way out into Great Victoria Street. I'd been on that street three years earlier with Cora, heading for Scotland. Then, it had been like any other city centre artery: shops, offices and busy footpaths of friendly people. Now, it was a blitz zone of blackened buildings and rubble. People hurried about their business and there seemed to be less traffic than before. To our left, two armoured Land Rovers came racing along the pavement, part of a British effort to curb the activities of a rejuvenated IRA. The IRA, meanwhile, appeared to be uncurbed, bombing its way from shop to shop, and robbing its way from bank to bank to cover the costs. As we crossed the street, it felt as if a big black crow was hovering overhead, its wings spread across the entire city.

'You get used to it,' Alain said, 'There are bombs nearly every day.' He then filled me in on the latest news as we made our way around to the City Hall to catch the Shore Road bus. While Alain talked about shootings and bombings I walked alongside, gaping in every

## Chapter 1

direction like a man who'd landed on Mars in an ice-cream van.

On the bus down Royal Avenue, as we passed the British army's city headquarters in the commandeered Grand Central Hotel, Alain let me in on some eccentricities of the accommodation out in Fort William Park.

'The house has been attacked a few times by loyalists,' he said with a smile that was counter-intuitively scary, 'We kind of live on our nerves a lot of the time.'

'Where do the loyalists come from,' I asked, hoping he'd say China.

'Mount Vernon,' he said, 'The big loyalist estate at the back of the house.' I watched for a nervous twitch or the sign of a joke but there was nothing.

'Oh…' I said. But what ran through my mind was: *Are you all out of your shaggin' heads!* However I said nothing and the bus droned on out the Shore Road, a delightful spot bedecked with loyalist flags. The passing walls screamed *Fuck the Pope* and *Kill all Taigs,* and called on people to join the loyalist UDA (Ulster Defence Association) and UVF (Ulster Volunteer Force).

'What are *Taigs*?' I asked Alain.

'The likes of me and you,' he told me, 'Anyone who might be deemed a Catholic.'

'Oh…' I said and mulled this over.

When we disembarked from the bus at the bottom of Fort William Park, I had that sudden feeling of having been washed ashore on some unmapped spike of land where anything could lie behind them there bushes.

'Your first Belfast souvenir,' Alain said. He handed me an Irish 10-pence piece that he'd just got from the busman, still legal tender in the North at the time. 'Turn it over.'

Face down, the coin showed the Irish harp. Face up, it was embossed with the usual leaping salmon, but the salmon had been punched with the letters UDA. Alain wasn't doing anything to make me feel better.

'Isn't that about as sectarian as you can get?' he said, 'It doesn't take a lot of brains to do that, but it takes a bit of effort.'

We weren't long away from the bus stop when we ran into Alain's mother. Jacqui Gogarty had been shopping. A gentle, fair-haired, elegantly-dressed woman in her mid forties with the most perfectly white skin, she welcomed me to Fort William Park in a strong

French accent.

'What are you doing coming all the way from lovely Cork to Belfast?' she wanted to know, 'Do you prefer the weather? It could not be any love of the British.'

'It's the weather,' I joked.

'You know,' she said, 'I grew up in Marseille, and lived through the Nazi occupation, but I never saw such a concentration of military armour and military arrogance as I have seen in Belfast.'

'Oh...,' I said. Lots of *Ohs* had run through my conversation since the first hello from Alain.

'But, we must be careful now,' she warned, nodding towards the block of high-rise that towered up behind the bus stop, 'They are waiting...' That did not sound promising.

'Jesus!' I whispered to Alain, looking towards the flats, 'Is *that* Mount Vernon? Right *there!*'

'Unfortunately yes.'

'And where's the house?'

'Around the corner and a hundred yards up the hill,' he said as we turned from the Shore Road into Fort William Park, 'It virtually backs on to Mount Vernon...'

Alain's voice trailed away and, for the first time since we'd met, worry colonised his face. I followed his stare to find a group of burly men heading our way across some open ground from the direction of the nearest tower-block. When they reached a slight rise in front of the flats they stopped and began to hurl obscenities at the three of us: seven or eight grown men ranging from early twenties to late forties shouting the likes of *Fuck the Pope* and *Fenian bastards*! From any angle they didn't look good - too many heavy boots and cans of beer. Not to mention the large back-up I assumed to be on ready call. *Sticks and stones*... I tried, but it didn't work. I looked behind, but the bus was well gone.

'Ignore them,' Jacqui said, 'They are just being territorial.'

Despite a reasonably streetwise childhood in inner-city Cork, I was taken aback. Initially, by the hatred in the voices. But more so by the fact that Jacqui Gogarty was calmly walking past, as if the ranting lads posed no more of a threat than a dog piddling on a lamp post. At the same time, I could see how easily the Gogarty house could be attacked: you could do it without ever leaving Mount Vernon. I could also not escape the awful feeling that it was about to happen again – *tonight* when I was there! As for the why? Well, that

## Chapter 1

had to do with Alain's father, Frank.

Frank Gogarty had been the first chair of the Northern Ireland Civil Rights Association. NICRA had been agitating since mid 1968 for basic civil rights for Northern nationalists. It had staged countless marches that had drawn down the wrath of loyalist mobs, the firebrand, anti-Catholic fundamentalism of the Reverend Ian Paisley, and the clubs of the Royal Ulster Constabulary. In the spiralling violence, sectarian riots and pogroms had reduced whole streets to ashes. Attacks by loyalists, the RUC and the British army had left a growing tally of dead. And the IRA had re-formed and retaliated, gradually engaging the British army in a war of attrition. As far as the loyalists were concerned, the NICRA part had turned Frank Gogarty and the other civil rights leaders into Public Enemy Number One. A dentist by profession, Frank had been a fearless, inspirational organiser, absolutey commited to the civil rights cause. More recently, that commitment had extended to the outright nationalist revolt that had followed the introduction of internment. For his pains, he had also been arrested and jailed. Witnesses saw him being battered by several paratroopers. However, by the time the case came to court, Frank, despite being a relatively small man, had assaulted half the Parachute regiment. He got the mandatory six months for 'riotous behaviour'.

This holy terror, a dapper man in his mid forties, with black hair, greying at the temples, met us at the door of the Gogarty home.

'They're at it again,' he said, 'You get used to it. But, we'd better go inside in case they get too serious.'

That was the beginning of the strangest evening of my first 21 years. Inside, I was introduced to the rest of the family – studious Lonnan, the oldest in the family of boys, and the younger, cavorting Ultan and Francis. (Fintan, the second son, was down in Cork where he'd become friends with my brother, Niall.) Apart from the eerie feeling of a siege being blanked out, all was normal. The boys chatted away, wanting to know all about my plans. Frank showed me to my room. I showered, washed the shirt I was wearing, and changed. I re-joined the family downstairs and, given the limitations of my CV, got down to business.

'Do you know much about Ballymurphy?' I asked Frank, 'It would be good to have a few pointers before tomorrow.'

'It's between the top of the Falls and the foot of Black Mountain,' Frank said, 'Lots of social problems over the years. It's a tough place, but with good people. And it's been out front in taking on the British army since early last year. I don't know a lot of people up there; but if you like, after we've eaten, we can take a run over to the Falls. I know some people there who might be able to give you more information.'

'What about the Association for Legal Justice?' Lonnan suggested.

'Exactly what I'm thinking,' Frank said.

While Ultan and Francis watched TV and Jacqui made dinner, Frank, Lonnan, Alain and I sat in the living-room, surrounded by polished antique furniture and family memorabilia. As the conversation moved from Ballymurphy to the state of the world, flute music filtered through from the direction of Mount Vernon and the siege was on again.

'Is that *The Sash*?' I asked.

'It's the local kick-the-Pope band,' Alain informed me. I had never heard of a kick-the-Pope band. But the image of the Pope charging down Fort William Park in papal cloak and mitre, with an entire band trying to kick him up the arse seemed funny.

The conversation then drifted over to my recent journey to Afghanistan, and from the wilds of the Asian steppes back to the terror of Bloody Sunday.

'They shot 27 innocent people in cold blood,' Frank said, 'There were seven teenagers among the dead. Two other marchers were run over by the British army. Five of the wounded were shot in the back. This was mass murder by the state. And the lies we've had to listen to since! When all this started back in 1968, I used to believe that we could bring about change through exclusively peaceful means. We thought the state might react violently, but we never expected this. Now, I believe that there's only one viable future – drive the British out of this country for once and for all.'

Frank had been one of those civil rights leaders who had approached the IRA leadership in Dublin in the civil rights movement's nascent days to ask if it would be able to protect nationalist areas in the event of a violent knee-jerk by the state. The failure of the IRA to do so during the anti-nationalist pogroms of August 1969 had been a considerable factor in fomenting the divisions that had given rise to the Provisional IRA in December of that year.

'The IRA had no choice in the end but to split,' Frank said, 'The Goulding faction had let us down badly. They promised protection but left vulnerable areas to the loyalist mobs. And once the shooting had started, the war took on a life of its own. You can't turn back

## Chapter 1

the clock.' He then told me that he'd recently had a narrow escape himself when he was shot at as he arrived home from work. 'Come out till you see this,' he said.

'I was lucky,' he said, as he showed me the hole in the back of the driver's seat of his car, 'The bullet came in through the back window, hit the tubular steel frame of the seat, and was deflected upwards at a 90-degree angle and out through the roof.'

'The guy who fired that shot will be scratching his head for years,' I said and we all laughed. Mine was a kind of hollow gallows laugh.

The more Frank, Lonnan and Alain talked, the more I felt like some fool who'd unwittingly joined Custer on Last Stand Hill, expecting Crazy Horse to show up with the tennis rackets. While I had to admire the extraordinary courage of the Gogartys as they staunchly held the Maginot Line, I also wondered how wise it was, Frank being a figure of history not too in favour with the people out the back. Listening to a distant rendering of *Dolly's Brae* and looking up at the lights of Mount Vernon, David and Goliath came to mind. In the absence of anything more solid, that analogy gave some small succour, but not a lot. One petrol-bomb, and we could *all* be figures of history.

'Back to tonight,' Frank said eventually, 'Do you know the Falls?'

'A little,' I said, 'I have connections there?'

'Of course,' he said, 'Your grandfather was a Belfast man...'

'That's right, I confirmed, establishing some credentials, 'My mother's father. He fought with the Third Northern Division during the Twenties. I still have two great grand-aunts living in Cavendish Street. But I won't call tonight: it would just spook them. They'd worry about me for the rest of the week.'

'We can drive over,' Frank said. Immediately, bullets through back windows sprang to mind.

'But, only if we can get back again in one piece,' I kind of joked, 'I have my interview tomorrow morning.'

'No problem!' Frank said. *No problem*, I assumed, meant something else in Belfast.

* * *

The Falls Road, translated from the Irish *Bóthar na bhFál* (road of the hedges) cuts from Divis Street in the city centre to Andersonstown. Originally a country lane, it saw a huge population explosion in the 19th century with the arrival of the linen industry and the large mills that attracted waves of migrant workers to

Belfast. Rows of red-bricked, back-to-back houses, two-up and two-down, had quickly fanned out into a maze of narrow streets, to become the major nationalist enclave of the city. Ironically, many of the growing area's street-names commemorated the British role in the Crimean War of the 1850s: Raglan Street named after the man who led the British forces, Sevastopol Street after the Siege of Sevastopol, Balaclava Street after the Battle of Balaclava. By the 1960s, the area had fallen into considerable decay and the lower end was demolished and replaced by the horrible prison-like complex of Divis Flats.

Historically, the Falls had been to the fore of the nationalist struggle of the early 20$^{th}$ century. As a predominantly working-class community, it had enjoyed a strong socialist tradition. Irish socialist leader, James Connolly, one of the seven signatories of the Irish Proclamation of Independence, had lived for a while in a house at the bottom of the Whiterock Road – which now led up to Ballymurphy.

Since the birth of the civil rights movement, it had again been to the fore of Belfast's nationalist struggle. In August 1969, the lower end had been engulfed in loyalist/RUC pogroms that left 150 nationalist homes gutted, six people dead and another 150 wounded by gunfire. Then, in July 1970, a British army curfew of the Lower Falls had resulted in heavy gun-battles between 3,000 troops and units of both the Official and Provisional IRAs. While the small, tightly-packed houses were systematically destroyed by the troops and residents were battered, four civilians were killed and another dozen wounded by gunfire. Eventually, after two days of terror and confinement, the people of the Lower Falls were reprieved by a march of women from further west in the city. Carrying food and milk, three thousand of them barged through General Ian Freeland's troops and broke the curfew. The Falls Curfew was widely regarded as the event that brought an end to the British army's honeymoon with the nationalist community in the North. Seen by many as saviors when they came in and lifted the RUC siege of Derry's Bogside in August 1969, they had now taken on the mantle of the Unionist state.

At about nine o'clock Frank and I left Fort William Park and drove across a city centre totally deserted apart from military checkpoints and convoys of military vehicles. After about twenty minutes, we arrived in the Lower Falls, still 'shared' between the

## Chapter 1

Provisional and Official IRAs. With republican, loyalist and British assassins patrolling the nights, few ventured out on the main arteries after dark. As a result, a chilling stillness hung over the streets and buildings. Not so long ago I had also walked down this road with Cora. It was a bright and cheerful place with trolley-buses and shoppers and daylight. Now, it was dark and menacing, with blacked-out streets (where the street lights had been shot out by the British army to deter snipers), barbed wire barriers, and the shadowy figures of vigilantes dodging car-lights at street corners.

'Wait till you see this,' Frank said, turning into one of the back streets and manoeuvring around a makeshift barricade. Immediately, the car was surrounded by men in heavy coats, with hoods over their heads.

'*Óglaigh na h-Éireann* [Irish Volunteers],' one of them called as he stepped up to the driver's window. Frank wound down the glass. 'What about ya Frank?' the man said, 'Watch yer tyres on the broken glass.' He then waved us on into a landscape of devastation where the lights of the car swept across an area of redevelopment and demolition that resembled Berlin at the end of World War II.

'This was what I wanted you to see,' Frank said, 'The housing here was of such an appalling quality that the state has been forced to pull it all down.'

'Who were those guys?' I asked, my interest in poor housing sideswiped by the casual encounter with the vigilantes.

'Here? Probably Officials. The lower Falls, the Markets and Turf Lodge would have a strong Official IRA presence.'

'How did people choose sides after the Split?' I asked.

'Different reasons,' Frank said, 'Sometimes, it was a case of follow-the-leader.'

'And in Ballymurphy?'

'They mostly went with the Provisionals.'

After driving around for a few minutes, we returned to the main Falls Road and parked close to a school that had its lights on. We stepped from the car into an empty, silent darkness.

'Who's that?' a man's voice asked from somewhere to our right.

'Frank Gogarty,' Frank replied, 'With a friend from Cork.'

'On you go Frank,' the voice instructed. We never saw the man.

Frank led me into the school. Inside, the hall had been taken over for the night by the Association for Legal Justice, established to monitor and record human rights abuses linked to the conflict.

At a number of tables, women were taking statements from people who'd been brutalised by the military and the RUC. Some victims had broken limbs. Others were heavily bandaged. Frank led the way to one of the tables and introduced me to a middle-aged woman whose name I've long forgotten. She was volunteering for the night. She sat wrapped in an overcoat against the cold of the hall and looked tired.

'It goes on day and night,' she said as Frank stood to one side, 'They beat the crap out of anyone they can get their hands on. These ones here are the lucky ones, who weren't charged with 'assault'. Otherwise, they'd be away for their tea, doing six months. People come in here with gunshot wounds and broken arms and broken legs and broken heads. They busted a baton over some wee lad's head not so long ago.'

'Ciarán is down from the Free State,' Frank explained, 'He's going for an interview tomorrow. For a job in the community centre up in Ballymurphy.'

At this the woman looked me up and down, like someone viewing a horse at an auction, and considered her verdict. Meanwhile, I was standing there, very unsure about the introduction. For one thing, as far as I was concerned, everything to the north of anything was *up*, not *down*. So, I had come *up* from Cork. However, I now appeared to have come *down* from Cork. If this was true, then I was down North which didn't make sense. Secondly, I understood that the Irish Free State had ceased to exist in 1949 when the 26 liberated counties of Ireland had been declared a republic. (I had yet to glean an understanding of how Partition had trapped language. As far as Northern nationalists were concerned, the South may have been proclaimed *a* republic, but it was not *the 32-county Republic*, and was therefore still the 'Free State'.)

'God bless you son,' the woman laughed, having eventually come to a verdict, 'You'll *never* last. You know, don't you, that the last man in that job, Paddy McCarthy, was killed during Internment Week and they haven't been able to fill the job this past seven months. This is Ballymurphy you're talking about, son. If you were into taking advice, you'd get the train back to Cork.'

'He comes from good stock,' Frank assured her, 'His grandfather was a Belfast man.'

'Oh,' the woman said, 'That's different. Why didn't you say so in the first place...'

# Chapter 1

'Don't let this put you off,' Frank laughed, 'For all the troubles of Ballymurphy, you'll find the people are the salt of the Earth.'

'If you live long enough to get to know them,' the woman laughed.

On the way back to Fort William Park there was heaps to mull over.

\* \* \*

The next day's interview made no mention of how the Ballymurphy post became vacant, nor why the interview was held on the far side of the city. Otherwise, it went as well as could be expected. I was met at the Star of the Sea youth club on the Shore Road by Frances McMullan and Billy Caldwell of the Ballymurphy Tenants' Association (BTA), Dr. Paddy Conlon, chair of the Star of The Sea, and Paddy McDermott who was an inspector with the Department of Education's youth service. Frances McMullan chaired the panel. An elegant, but tired-looking, woman with greying hair and dark circles rimming her eyes, she asked several questions that ranged across all my areas of 'experience' while I made the best of the little I had. Dr. Conlon, a big affable, balding man in a beige suit who looked every inch the village family doctor, wanted to know if I thought I could run a *big* youth club, and would be OK about managing the community centre.

'Yes,' I said, but had no concept of what big meant in terms of youth clubs. Then Paddy McDermott, a small, beaming, middle-aged man in a grey suit, whose every gesture was designed to make me feel at ease, asked why I'd travelled to Asia, fairly unheard-of behaviour in those days.

'To see a bit of the world,' I told him, 'Since I had very little money, Asia was the cheapest because there were no seas to cross. I was trying to get to India.'

'And did you?'

'No. The first time I went with a friend who turned back from Istanbul because he was low on money. I had £50 left so I went on. I'd been planning to go on to India and sell my passport on the black market, but I got sick in Kabul and had to turn back with amoebic dysentery - and £15 in my pocket. The second time, my girlfriend and I had to turn back because we got caught up in the Bangladesh War.'

The four interviewers looked at one another. Selling passports. Travelling with girlfriends. Catholic Ireland. *Oopsy-daisy*, I thought, *I've blown it*.

'What did it teach you most?' Paddy McDermott asked.

'A lot about people and a bit about me. And how people organise in tribal settings.'

'Well, that last bit will come in handy here,' Paddy laughed.

Billy Caldwell, a silver-haired man in his mid fifties, quiet as a mouse, had only one question. More of a joke, under the circumstances.

'Have y'ever had a gun aimed at you?'

The whole panel laughed.

'Twice,' I said, which took them by surprise. 'By desert tribesmen in Afghanistan. And both times, I thought they were going to shoot.'

I could tell by Billy's big smile that he was happy with that.

'Well Billy,' Paddy McDermott said, 'There's your answer.' Everyone laughed again. The conversation then moved on to the matter of salary.

'The advertised salary,' Paddy McDermott explained sheepishly, 'is for a *qualified* worker. Someone with a third-level qualification would start at £1,070 per annum – but you don't have a third-level qualification.'

'No,' I said, feeling my heart sink.

'That would mean a salary of about £800 a year,' Paddy said, 'Along with the responsibility allowance. But, there might be a training course in Youth and Community Work starting at the Polytechnic in Jordanstown in the autumn. It would be an in-service course - you study as you work. Would you be interested in doing a course like that if it was to come about?'

'Yes,' I said, 'I would've done a course like that in Cork if it had been available.'

'Then, of course, you wouldn't be here,' Paddy said and everyone laughed again. It was turning into a great-laugh interview.

\* \* \*

Frank picked me up after the interview and I wondered again why it hadn't taken place in Ballymurphy.

"Maybe they didn't want to take the chance,' Frank shrugged, 'Sometimes it can be tricky getting into the area if there's a riot or a gun-battle.' Indeed, I agreed, that would be tricky.

From the Shore Road, we drove to Duncairn Gardens where Frank had his dental practice. Now, if Frank's house was not ideally placed, you should've seen his dental practice! Sandwiched between the republican New Lodge and loyalist Tiger's Bay, Duncairn

# Chapter 1

Gardens was one of the most violent interfaces in Belfast. Just driving up the street posed a risk, which made me conclude there and then that Frank was a victim of poor locations. After a quick nip into reception to collect a mould for a gold tooth that he was going to complete at home that evening, we continued around to the nearby New Lodge Road, an area of older narrow streets with red-bricked houses, dominated by several tower-blocks, built in the 1950s. Frank gave me a quick history lesson as we parked the car at the lower end of the main artery that cut through this staunchly republican area.

'The New Lodge was bombed by the Germans in 1941. After the war, lots of people moved out to the new housing developments like Ballymurphy, Glengormley and Rathcoole. Then, in the 1960s, after the towers were built, many families who had lived in Sailortown in the Docks moved to the New Lodge.'

'Since the Split and the reorganisation of the IRA, the area has been a stronghold of the Provisionals' Third Battalion. As you probably know, it's seen its fair share of the riots and gun-battles - with the British and with the loyalists. And, of course, McGurk's Bar was in the New Lodge - in North Queen Street. [Three months earlier, a bomb had exploded in the doorway of McGurk's, collapsing the building. Fifteen people, including two children and three women, died. Seventeen others were injured.]

'Who do you think bombed McGurk's?' I asked. The British were claiming it was an IRA 'own-goal'.

'Everyone knows who bombed it,' Frank said, 'The UVF did.' (Many years later the British would apologise for blaming the IRA when they knew full well it had been the UVF.)

'The area is particularly vulnerable to loyalist attacks,' Frank said as I walked with him towards O'Kane's Starry Plough bar, 'Especially drive-by shootings. They say that the junction of the New Lodge and Antrim Roads is the most dangerous spot in Ireland. Don't ever stand there.'

'No Frank,' I said, 'I will never, ever stand there.'

In O'Kane's it was Saturday afternoon and the small bar was busy. Without thinking I walked in first, me and my Moroccan shoulder-bag. The result was silent, freeze-frame panic. Talk stopped and every eye in the bar locked on the bag. Then Frank walked in behind and an audible sigh was followed by unnatural joviality.

'Fuck me,' one of the men at the bar said, looking speculatively from Frank to the bag, 'Is there a banger in there?' Neither of us, I noticed, issued a denial. Then, safe again, the bar resumed its Saturday afternoon buzz and somebody bought us a drink. Talk flowed eagerly and we were drawn in as if we belonged to some large extended family and had turned up just in time for Christmas. But the events under discussion were seriously alarming. Stories of gun-battles and bombings and sectarian murders, of people shot in drive-by shootings, crossfire and random military killings.

Tommy McIlroy had been shot dead by the British army in Ballymurphy in February while working on his car close to an army base. Seven people had been killed in a bombing in Donegall Streeet. Bernard Rice had been murdered by the Red Hand Commandos while walking past the shops in Ardoyne. A couple of kids in a stolen car had been shot dead by the RUC on the Falls Road. Two soldiers were blown up by a booby-trapped car on the Grosvenor Road. Four IRA men were killed in February by their own bomb when it went off prematurely. Four more in March. IRA explosives were a thing to watch, I was warned - unstable. And everyone in the bar seemed to have had a narrow escape of one sort or the other. All in all, it was a picture of dangerous chaos and confusion.

In the bar, however, there seemed to be an overriding sense of clarity and purpose. Everyone was on a mission, all linked to the war. Huddles of men sat in corners. Others were leaving to 'go up the road on a wee message'. Many probing, half-joke comments were made about the bag that now sat at the foot of the stool on which I was making my way through a line of donated Guinness and being welcomed to Belfast by all sorts of people. (I even got a kiss from an old woman who had left her false teeth at home - 'Look,' she said, 'Not a bar in the fuckin' grate.') Gradually, although nobody mentioned it, the bag was becoming pregnant with possibilities. Maybe there was a bomb in there? Or maybe a gun? Or maybe some highly-classified IRA documents come up from the South? A half hour into the Guinness, and I myself was beginning to wonder the same when a voice behind rose above the general din of conversation.

'So, you're a Free Stater and yer goin' to work in Ballymurphy?'

I looked around and found myself facing a short, fat, unshaven man of about forty who was dressed in a baggy pullover and jeans. With eyes that half-reminded me of a barn owl, he was giving me the once-over from under a grimy old spogger. Clearly more than a

## Chapter 1

little refreshed, he was grinning like a skinless skull.

Now, I was still having a problem with the *Free State* thing. The problem was that I'd now noticed myself being described as a Free Stater more than once. Up north, where they hadn't apparently given any great validity to the happenings of 1949, people from south of the border were referred to as Free Staters. Down south, Free Staters were those who'd accepted Partition in 1921 and opposed the IRA in the counter-revolution that we called the Civil War, people my grandfather and grandmother had fought against. Armed and equipped by the British, they had defeated the IRA which had then gone underground waiting for another day. Now, that this other day had seemingly come, the term had an even more unwholesome flavour to my southern ears. However, I held fire and listened for whatever was coming.

'I'm a Murph man meself,' came the next sentence, 'I'm just over here on a wee message. Whass yer name?'

'Ciarán,' I said.

'Pleased ta meet ya. I'm Jimmy. Put yer hand there.' We shook hands as others leaned over to pick up on the conversation. Jimmy took another enormous gulping swig from a pint of Bass.

'You know the fastest game in the world?' he asked.

'No,' I admitted, 'Haven't a clue.'

'Pass the parcel in a Belfast pub,' He said. He then slapped his cap on the bar and howled with laughter. Others around joined in. I smiled in confusion more than mirth. Three months after the bombing of McGurk's Bar, how could anyone make a joke like that? I then realised that all those people, drinking away merrily, lived with the constant possibility that whoever next opened the door could also toss in a bomb. (The pub was in fact levelled by a bomb in 1977.) One of the ways of dealing with horror is to drown it in humour on a Saturday afternoon.

'You wanna hear anorr joke?' Jimmy asked. Whether I did or not, I was going to get it anyway.

'Paddy the Irishman gets shipwrecked away out in the ocean an' gets washed up on this island. It's all full o' jungle an' he's lookin' aroun' him when outta the trees pops this tribe o' cannibawls. Bones through their noses. Feathers in their heads. Bows an' arrows. The heap. "Fuck me!" Paddy says, "I'm in big shit now!" Anyway, he gets hauled off till the village and stuck in a big pot. The cannibawls light the fire an' just as the water starts bubblin', the big chief comes along an' decides he'd like to know where his next dinner come from. "Where ya from?" he asks Paddy the Irishman. "Ireland," Paddy says. "Whereabouts?" the chief says. "Belfast," Paddy says. "Oh," the chief says, "Is that right? What part?" "Ballymurphy," Paddy says. "Fuck me!" the chief says an' he throws a bucket o' water on the fire, "Dya know our kid?"'

Again, howls of laughter. Haw-haw-haw! And much slamming of the bar.

'One more,' Jimmy says and by now I'm beginning to like him. 'This Englishmawn goes intill a bar in Belfast an' orders a pint. He sits there drinkin' for a while, then he turns till a wee mawn next to him. "Paddy," he says, "This is a karate chop from Japan." An' he whacks yer wee mawn an' knocks him flat out on the floor. After a while, the wee mawn gets up an' sits back on his stool. "Paddy," the Englishmawn says, "This is a kung-fu kick from China," an' he sends the wee mawn on the floor again. So the wee mawn gets up an' sits back on his stool. "Paddy," the Englishmawn says, "This is a tae-kwon-do punch from Hong Kong an' he knocks the wee mawn on his arse again. This time, the wee mawn gets up an' goes till the toilet. Five minutes later, the Englishmawn gets this fuckin' almighty whack on the back o' the head and he's knocked out cold. Kapow! Out fer the fuckin' count! The other punters at the bar look around an' the wee mawn is standin' there. "When he comes around,' he says, "Tell him that was a fuckin' crowbar from Ballymurphy". Haw-haw-haw.'

'Right,' Frank said at this juncture, 'We need to go, before Jimmy here scares the hell out of you and you get back on the train to Cork and never come back again.'

Leaving O'Kane's that afternoon, as darkness closed in and a chilly wind blew down on the city from the 1,200-foot-high Black Mountain, I had the distinct feeling that only Belfast people of a certain persuasion would get away with jokes like that. Mostly, they had to come from Ballymurphy.

Back in Fort William Park I sat with the Gogarty family while they did family things - had dinner, did home work, watched the day's News. I marvelled at the calm of such a vulnerable household in a city patrolled by sectarian assassins where thousands of nationalists had already been burned from their homes. Over in Mount Vernon they were pounding on drums.

'Lambeg drums,' Lonnan said, 'War drums.'

# Chapter 1

'For our benefit,' Jacqui added with a becalming smile. 'You know,' she said, 'It is ironic. When the plans were being made to build social housing at Mount Vernon, there was big opposition from the people living around in the expensive houses. We were one of the few families who argued that the people had a right to the homes. Frank went to many meetings to support that view. Now, *they* want to drive *us* from our home.' She then got up and put on a vinyl album of Irish folk music by *The Dubliners*. It was scratched from regular use. Later, Frank showed me how to make a gold tooth, but through lack of practice I don't think I could manage it now.

On Sunday morning I took the train back to Cork and as I crossed the border to the south of Newry, I felt as if I'd just had a terrible dream. For two days I'd lived in a world that couldn't possibly exist a mere 264 miles from Cork. How could I describe the Gogartys' existence, or the vigilante-patrolled back streets of the Falls, or the columns of armour moving through Belfast's bombed-out streets, or the crowd in The Starry Plough, to anyone back home. And I hadn't yet reached Ballymurphy which was taking on mythical dimensions of all the wrong kinds. Even if I didn't get the job, I was thinking of going back, if I could find some way to make a few bob.

For the next few days I waited to hear how well or poorly my interview had gone. Then, in one single day, two letters arrived. The first was from Dublin, offering me one of the posts I'd applied for. The second was from Belfast. My interview had, it transpired, gone better than I could have expected. The only other applicant, I later discovered, was another poor innocent like myself - from Dublin - who decided on the spot that he was no longer interested when he heard the 'unqualified' salary scale. So I got the job by default. 'It has been the unanimous decision of the interview panel...' my letter from Frances McMullan began. Delighted by this commendation, I declined the Dublin post and decided to set off for Belfast immediately though the job didn't start for another two weeks.

'At least,' they said at home, 'if you die in Ballymurphy you'll have a clean shirt on.'

They all thought that was very funny.

April 1972 was coming to a close. If anyone had told me then that Belfast would still be home four decades later, I would've advised them to double up on the medication.

# Chapter 2
## Whatever Ya Say, Say Nathin'

I hadn't seen Cathal Dunne - who'd anchored that fund-raising bash down in Patrick Street with his dashing derring-do on the piano - since we'd both walked out the front gates of Coláiste Chríost Rí back in June of 1969. Cathal and I would've always got on well. We shared a bit of the hippy optimism of the Sixties which meant a perennial battle against vigilant parents and the school principal, Br. de Salles, over the trappings of that genre. In our final year, both of us grew our hair but had to devise all sorts of schemes to make it appear to be actually *not* growing. We also darkened the bum-fluff above our lips with a light dab of black shoe polish to give a cool moustache touch, but had to remember to strike it before facing for home or school. Any slip-up on either front meant a haircut or shave.

When we parted back in 1969, Cathal was one of the few people who thought that Tony O'Connor and I had a half-decent chance of getting to India on the first of the trips along the Hippy Trail. Cathal himself wanted to study music, also not a greatly appreciated goal in those times. Everbody else wanted to be a scientist or doctor.

'Ciarán!' I heard as I made my way along the corridors of the early Dublin-bound train, still sitting at Kent Station. It was the morning of Monday, May 1$^{st}$ 1972 and I'd been in nostalgic mood, thinking of how, when we were kids, steam trains ran through this station, and how we'd all gone down to see the first of the diesel engines – *the silver bullet* we called it – when it came into service. And of the times we took the train to Dublin to All-Ireland football and hurling finals. And the riotous parties on the way back when drunks would pull the emergency cord because they were passing close to home and wanted off. I was even wondering why Engine No. 36, dating from 1847, was sitting on two short lengths of rail in the booking hall, and how the hell its likes could ever have ferried passengers from Cork to Dublin.

'Back here!' Cathal shouted. He was at the door of one of the compartments: I'd missed him as I passed. I about-turned and joined him, grateful for the company as I left home and Cora for my year in Belfast.

## Chapter 2

'What are you doing with yourself?' he asked, 'I heard you were at university for a while, but that you left after a few months and went off again to somewhere in Asia.'

'Afghanistan and Pakistan,' I said, 'I was trying to get to India again, but the Bangladesh War broke out and myself and Cora had to turn back.'

'Where are you off to now?' he asked.

'Belfast,' I said, 'I've just landed a job at a community centre in Ballymurphy...'

'Belfast...?' he said, 'That's a bit mad.'

'That could be the truest thing you ever said...'

Over the coming hours, Cathal and I shared our stories. He was, as he'd always wished, studying music in Cork University and was happy in it. Two more years and he'd be through. But, what about Asia, he wanted to know, and was all agog when I recounted tales of desert sunsets, Afghan bandits, camel trains, hashish dens, and semi-naked women in shop windows in Istanbul.

"You've lived a pretty full life in three years,' he said in the end, 'You're also bloody lucky to be still in one piece. What's the plan for the longer-term?'

'To travel again as soon as I get the chance,' I said, 'And yours?'

'To become a singer and musician,' he said.

Some four hours after leaving Cork, we parted in Dublin city centre and wished one another all the best in our respective aspirations.

'Some time when you're back in Cork,' Cathal called after me, 'look me up. And try not to get shot in Belfast...'

'I will,' I called back, 'And good luck with the music. If anyone should make it, you should, after that performance down in Pana.'[1]

'Thanks,' Cathal shouted.

After leaving Cathal, I made my way to Connolly Station in Amiens Street and boarded a second train for Belfast. With a mixture of excitement and trepidation, I spent the next three hours staring out the window as the spring countryside passed me by. At 21 years of age, I had just been landed with an enormous responsibility, running a community centre and a youth club in what was essentially a war

---

[1] Pana was the name given to Patrick Street by everyone who lived in Cork. On Saturdays and summer evenings it witnessed the Pana Patrol when young people wandered up and down to view 'the talent' of the opposite sex.

zone. As the wooded hills of the border came into view, it sank home: in this I was on my own, although I had already made a friend on the train.

His name was Garry, a big tall lad with long blond hair who came from a working-class area of East Belfast. He was, he told me, a member of a loyalist Tartan gang, hence the scarf around his waist. At the time, Tartan gangs on both sides of the political divide were fighting it out on the streets of the North, but some of the loyalist gangs had gone a step further and linked their activities to the sectarian murder campaigns of the UDA and UVF. Nevertheless, Gary and I got on well and he gave me his address.

'Call over some time and I'll show ya around,' he promised, 'But you'll have to keep yer bake closed. Even though I know all the Boys, that accent could get ya shot stone fuckin' dead.' I really did think about that offer in the months to come, but my diary seemed to always get too plumb full. Consequently, I never did get to wander around the loyalist back streets of East Belfast among Gary's club-wielding friends in their balaclavas and combat gear.

I landed back in Belfast in the middle of that afternoon, arriving in Great Victoria Street station to find the platform lined with British paratroopers - all aiming rifles and sub-machine guns at our chests as we disembarked. This was my first real contact with the war in the North, and despite my previous visit, it seemed fully surreal. Part of me felt like laughing at the barking-mad figures in front of me, who reminded me of Nazi footage from World War II. The other part remembered the Derry massacre. This was the same regiment. Along with the other male passengers, I was spreadeagled against the station wall, and searched and questioned.

'What's your name?' one of the soldiers asked.

While greatly resenting being questioned in my own country by a foreign soldier, I told him.

'Keyraw the what-what? He said, 'Got any I.D. mate?' I handed him my passport.

'What's your name in English?' he asked after checking the name in the passport.

'What's yours in Mandarin?' I asked, trying to put his question into perspective.

'Oh, a fucking smartass,' he said loudly, 'See how long *you* fucking well last.' I noticed other people looking at me. Some were scowling. Some were smiling. The line in the Belfast sand.

## Chapter 2

The soldier handed me back my passport and told me that if I had any sense I'd 'fuck away off out of rifle-range'. As I left the station, I felt delighted at having needled the enemy and struck a blow for Ireland. Now all I needed was to find my way to Ballymurphy.

In the city centre, which looked even more bombed-out than last time, I approached a Citybus inspector.

'Excuse me,' I said, 'Where can I get a bus to Ballymurphy?'

He stared at me with slowly widening eyes, as if I'd just asked if his wife was doing anything later.

'They don't *run* any buses to Ballymurphy!' he snarled, 'They *burn* all the buses in Ballymurphy!'

From then on, I only asked older women with walking-sticks until I was directed around to Castle Street, from which point a bus ran up the Falls Road to the lower end of Ballymurphy. In Castle Street, I stood at the head of the queue with my rucksack for three consecutive buses. This was because I was well brought up and people who've been well brought up respect the order of the queue. However, each time the bus stopped, the queue of mainly women would disintegrate into a column of wind and storm the platform, bashing me aside and leaving me behind in a crumpled heap as they sailed off up the Falls. On the fourth attempt I asserted myself and elbowed my way furiously on board. This caused great offence. 'Do you *mind*!' came a raucous chorus from the gentle petals of the Falls Road. Ostracised like the unclean, I stood at the back of the bus, absorbing the heat. Ten long minutes later, I got off at the bottom of the Whiterock Road.

With no accommodation arranged and no word to anyone in Ballymurphy that I was on my way, I walked up the Whiterock Road with my rucksack on my back. Facing me, as I crested the first hill, was the brooding hulk of Black Mountain, rising up behind the housing estates to its twelve hundred feet. On my left, I had the grey stone wall of the City Cemetery. In there, among the 'better' graves, lay Lord Perry, responsible for the building of that Belfast icon, the *Titanic* - the most famous ship that ever sank on its maiden voyage. Further up in the cemetery, a nine-foot-deep underground wall, built prior to the opening in 1869, separated the Catholic and Protestant dead. On my right, the red-brick housing estate of Whiterock. Then St. Thomas's School. Then finally, beyond the school, Ballymurphy itself. Nothing told me that it was Ballymurphy: I just knew. As if, all my life, I'd been meaning to arrive at this very spot.

I remember listening to the birds as I continued up that hill, and thinking that this could be any working-class area in Ireland: rows of identical houses with roughly-plastered walls, tiled roofs and exposed gardens - some well tended, others in poor shape. I even considered sleeping that night in the cemetery if I was stuck. It seemed impossible just then that a guerrilla war was being fought on these ordinary streets. Yet, the city was in pieces and the streets were full of military vehicles and jumpy troops, and there was all that TV footage down in Cork. Tellingly, there were no soldiers on the Whiterock Road. Nor was there anybody else. But behind the net curtains and Venetian blinds, the eyes were watching. There was a stranger on the road. And there never was a stranger, like a stranger in Belfast, in those days. Suddenly, I began to feel like some tourist who had stumbled, all unawares, into the middle of no-man's land.

It was then that I started to notice the bullet-holes.

\* \* \*

As I had no actual point of arrival, my plan was to find the home of Frances McMullan, who had signed that lovely letter. She might, I thought, have some suggestions on where, other than the graveyard, I could stay the night. But finding her wasn't going to be easy. I knew that she lived in Glenalina Road; but the street signs had all gone - ripped off the walls to confuse military raiding parties - and there was nobody about. So, wading through the broken bricks and glass of the most recent riot, I turned into a street opposite a large, rectangular, red-bricked building. That, I figured, had to be the community centre. Instantly, hope rose. Three little girls of about six or seven were playing around one of many burnt-out cars that littered an area of waste ground above the community centre. When they spotted me, they came running.

'Here mister,' one of them shouted, 'What d'they call you?'

'They call me Ciarán,' I said, 'Do you know where Mrs. McMullan lives?'

Silence.

'She works with the tenants' association,' I tried again, 'in that red building over there.'

Silence again. Then they looked at one another, looked back at me blankly, slowly shook their heads and melted away. With no way of knowing it, I was at that moment directly outside Frances McMullan's door. But no seven-year-old in Glenalina Road was

# Chapter 2

about to tell *me* that. However, I was rescued by a call from behind. A small, middle-aged man with a sallow complexion, dark sticking-out hair and an unhealthy wheeze was heading my way.

'Are you Keern?' he puffed, 'I'm Tommy Crooks. I'm on the tenants' association.'

'That's me,' I said, 'Ciarán.'

'I *knew* it was,' Tommy said, 'You must be starvin'.'

Minutes after my arrival in Ballymurphy of the notorious reputation, I was seated to an Ulster Fry in Tommy's house at the corner of Glenalina Park, surrounded by Tommy's family, while his wife, Sarah, a small woman with black curly hair streaked in threads of grey, explained to me my encounter with the kids across the way.

'Whatever ya say, say nathin'! That's an ould Belfast saying,' she enlightened me.

'Aye,' Tommy said, 'You'll get nathin' outta the kids around here. They know not to open their bakes for *anyone*.' I took it as some kind of advice for the future.

Sarah then called to one of her sons. 'Tony! Away out an' get the houl' of Mrs. Mac an' Big Ellen an' Ann Stone an' Big Alice.' Across the street, I noticed, all the houses were back-to-front: there were no living-room windows to be seen, only the front doors and the frosted glass of the bathroom windows.

'How come those houses are back-to-front?' I asked Tommy and Sarah.

'Nobody knows,' Sarah said, 'They think it might have somethin' to do with gettin' sunshine in through the livin'-room, but it's a bit weird. Ya see it nowhere else.'

By the time I'd finished the fry, the Crooks's house was full of men and women, most of whom seemed to be in their mid to late forties. Half the tenants' association committee, including Frances McMullan, known to all as Mrs. Mac, had turned up to welcome me. I was introduced to Big Ellen Cosgrove, an extrovert, matronly woman with a booming voice and brown hair tied up in a massive beehive; Ann Stone, dark-haired, bespectacled, energetic and wiry, who spoke with a strong Armagh accent and came across as a steel-willed and sincere woman; Big Alice Franklin, a tough-looking woman with a floppy mop of brown hair and a serrated Belfast accent who peered at me over the rim of her glasses; Wee Geordie Moylen who was older than the others, a small grinning man with thinning hair who was dressed in a suit and tie like a retired civil servant; and Hugh McCormick, a tall, thin, distinguished-looking man with a flourishing nose and thinning hair who was introduced as the former secretary of the BTA. Such an auspicious event as my arrival 'out of nowhere', everyone agreed, needed to be celebrated. A plan was drawn up for a visit to Casement Park Social Club in Andersonstown; and, while the banter flew about the room like crossfire, Sarah Crooks quietly slipped out the front door. When she came back ten minutes later, she had me a place to stay - with the second-next-door neighbour. His name was Billy 'Scrubby' Scribbons and his wife had died two weeks earlier.

'Billy is one of the last Protestants in Ballymurphy,' Sarah told me, 'Along with Mrs. Mac there and wee Rossie over in Ballymurphy Drive.'

Then, as the TV blared in the background, everyone happily gave a rundown of all the reasons why I would die in Ballymurphy. The British army. Assassins. The kids in the BTA youth club. And some guy called Jimmy McKenna. There was no end of possibilities.

'Don't you worry,' Tommy Crooks said in the end, 'We'll look after ya.'

At that, the door opened and a shy man in his late fifties with a light moustache and thin, slicked-back, greying hair, flattened to his head with Brylcreem, walked in.

'This is Billy,' Sarah introduced and we shook hands as Billy's eyes darted from mine to the floor and back again. My rucksack and I were then escorted two doors up, and for a fiver a week I became Billy Scribbons's lodger.

'The BTA minibus will call for you at half past eight,' Mrs. Mac said as she left.

\* \* \*

Billy Scribbons turned out to be a lovely, inoffensive man. His grown-up family - two daughters and two sons - had left the area when the Troubles broke out, but he and his wife, Thomasina, had stayed put. In August 1969, following the Belfast pogroms, they had worked with the hastily-convened Ballymurphy Welfare Committee and helped their neighbours provide for the great influx of refugees that had fled to Ballymurphy from the burnings of the Falls, Bombay Street and Ardoyne. Then, horrified, they had watched the News each day as barricades went up across towns and cities, and the North spiralled into sectarian warfare. However, with no interest in politics and bewildered by the violence that had broken around him, Billy had seen no need to flee. He and Thomasina bore nobody any ill; why should they be borne any? But Billy had been looking in the wrong direction. On Easter Monday 1970, the state in which he had believed sent a massive military column into Ballymurphy to attack his neighbourhood and neighbours with armoured cars, batons and indiscriminate clouds of CS gas. In June of that year, the riots came again and the military attacks and the gas became regular, supplemented by rubber bullets. Finally, on January 14$^{th}$ 1971, the army had come in and wrecked the houses. Gradually that night, the riot that followed the wrecking became a gun-battle as the IRA hit back. That was when the war, and the live rounds, had come. Early the next morning a soldier was shot in the area, the first in a long line.

Seven months later, during the awful days of the internment operation, the area was placed under a brutal curfew and attacked by paratroopers. Billy and Thomasina had listened in disbelief as word spread of the casualties: eleven civilians dead and an unknown number wounded. The dead had included a Catholic priest, a 50 year old mother and my predecessor, Paddy McCarthy. Throughout, Billy and Thomasina had given one another the strength to face the horrors that evolved around them. Now, since her death, he was alone. The company of the new arrival, the BTA committee figured, would do him good.

At first I had no idea what Billy was saying due to the strongest of Belfast accents coupled with the fact that Billy had what Tommy Crooks had described as 'fuck-all in the line of teeth'. However, through some careful lip-reading, I managed to grasp the gist of what he meant as he led me up to my new abode.

'This is your room,' I guessed he said, showing me into the rear bedroom which had a double bed and a small table. The walls were papered in a pale floral design and the floor was carpeted in red. Immediately my eye latched on to a gaping gash in the plasterboard ceiling. 'Sorry about the hole,' Billy went on (I guessed), 'The Brits done that. One of them was up searching in the glory-hole and he fell through the ceiling. Down on my wife who was sick in bed.' [She was actually dying of cancer.]

Looking up again, I could feel in my bones the gales that would blow down that hole from the mountain on stormy nights. However, I was delighted to have so easily found a place to stay and to have such great neighbours as the Crooks family. After settling in, I went downstairs and Billy and I had a cup of tea while we made one another's acquaintance. It was awkward again as I basically hadn't a clue what Billy was saying. Reverting to lip-reading, while nodding and grunting - and hoping I was nodding and grunting in the right order - I scraped through, hopeful that Billy was having similar problems with me and my Cork accent. At six o'clock I was saved by the News. Everyone in Belfast watched the News, I learned - every bulletin. When Billy switched channels to catch the News again, I excused myself and walked outside - and smacked my head into a memorably solid metal lamp post that had been bent at 45-degrees during the riots. *Welcome*, the lamp post said, *to Ballymurphy*.

At half past eight on the button, in the gathering of that bright May evening, silver-haired Billy Caldwell turned up at the door. Billy, who had interviewed me at the Star of the Sea, was another gentleman, soft-spoken as a ghost, and always willing to do anyone a favour.

'Are youse ready?' he asked as my Billy hunted for his coat and I threw on a jacket and cloth cap. Outside, I could hear the yahoos from a dented green minibus that was full of predominantly middle-aged men and women. I could see all the faces from earlier along with a few others.

'Hurry up Keern!' Alice Franklin's voice called 'Before we all die o' thirst!'

The great Ballymurphy party had begun. In defiance of the war, it was to run outrageously for the next four years. *Eat, drink and be merry, for tomorrow we die* was, I'm convinced, a slogan coined by the Spartans after a social encounter with the good people of Ballymurphy.

Driving up the Whiterock Road and up towards the neighbouring estate of Turf Lodge, I was introduced to Billy Caldwell's diminutive wife, Sarah, and Big Barney McGivern and ruddy-faced Frank O'Brien, and thin Mrs. Sheridan, all members of the BTA committee. Then the whole bus, bar myself and Mrs. Mac, broke into a song that I'd never heard before. It appeared to be called *The Fightin' Second Battalion of the Belfast Brigade* and began with the lines:

> *'Craigavon sent the Specials out to shoot the people down*
> *He thought the IRA was dead in dear old Belfast town*

## Chapter 2

> *But when they got to Ballymurphy they were seriously delayed*
> *By the fightin' Second Battalion of the Belfast Brigade...'*

On the way past Turf Lodge Social Club, Tommy Crooks stuck his head out the window of the bus. 'Stickie bawstards!' he yelled into the evening. He then pulled his head back in and chuckled loudly to himself. The 'Stickies' were the Official IRA, so called because the badges they used to annually commemorate the Dublin Easter Rising of 1916 were stick-on, whereas those sold by the Provisionals were attached by pins. 'The Stickies', I presumed, could be found in Turf Lodge Social Club.

'Tommy!' Sarah Crooks said, 'You're awful!'

There were hoots of laughter on the bus, although Mrs. Mac looked slightly reproachful in the front seat.

'Well Keern,' Tommy Crooks said when we reached Casement Park Social Club, 'Here's to yer new job and yer good health.' I hoped he wasn't alluding to the definite lack of good health of poor Paddy McCarthy.

'Thanks Tommy,' I said, as I surveyed the spacious, crowded smoky bar, 'By the way, it's *Ciarán*.'

From my arrival earlier in the day, I'd had trouble with my name. Ciarán is an old Gaelic name, pronounced like Keyrawn. But when I gave my name, everyone in Ballymurphy (apart from Ann Stone who had no problem), and now everyone in Casement Park, came back with *Keern*.

'No,' I'd say, 'It's Ciarán.'

'Och,' they'd all say, 'We say *Keern*.' and that was the end of that.

All together, they then told me the story of how Paddy McCarthy had died.

Paddy was a portly 43-year-old Londoner who'd spent eight years in the British army. He arrived in Ballymurphy, accompanied by his partner, Jan, on November 17th 1970. That was the day after the IRA had shot dead Alexander McVicker and Arthur McKenna, two petty criminals who had been terrorizing the area. The killings, the first fatal Ballymurphy shootings linked to the Troubles, had left deep shock throughout the area; yet, despite this, Paddy and Jan were welcomed with the same open generosity that had greeted me. They too had chosen to live locally, moving into a house on the Whiterock Road. A seasoned youth worker, Paddy had seen Ballymurphy as a personal challenge, and soon became a central figure in the developments taking place in the local social field. He had also been involved in defusing two unexploded nail bombs - the legacy of the previous night's rioting - before children could get to them in the morning.

'There were two wee lads in the area,' Ann Stone told me, 'who weren't lucky enough to have Paddy get to the nail-bombs first. They lost a hand each.'

Nine months after Paddy and Jan arrived, the internment swoops of August 1971 had triggered off a round of killings, carried out by British paratroopers, that had left five residents dead in the first 24 hours. Among them was Fr. Hugh Mullan, the first of two Catholic priests to be shot dead by soldiers in Ballymurphy. In response, Paddy McCarthy and Mrs. Mac began to organize an exodus of terrified children across the border to refugee camps established by the Irish army. This was on the morning of August 10$^{th}$, while young people attacked the local military base and barricades were erected to seal the area against further military incursions. Then, in the early hours of Monday, August 11$^{th}$, the British army launched a second attack.

Although the IRA had taken up positions throughout the area, the massive military incursion had forced the Volunteers into a defensive retreat while the civilian population was subjected to another round of army brutality and murder.

When the shooting started, there were some 30 people, many of them children, still in the community centre. At about three o'clock in the morning, Paddy McCarthy, who'd been in the centre since the morning before, tried to get the children out. He stepped outside with a Red Cross flag tied to a brush-pole, and had it shot out of his hand by the paratroopers, a splinter gashing his hand. Everyone who was there remembered what he said when he got back inside: 'Even the Jerries respected that flag'.

Later in the morning, Daphne Robinson, a Quaker woman who'd been helping to establish a knitwear cooperative in the area, heard about the plight of the Ballymurphy people. They'd been hemmed in without provisions for two days and were now under curfew. Loading up her car with crates of milk, Daphne drove across the city, took her car up through the graveyard to the wall beside the centre and handed the crates over to an exhausted Paddy McCarthy.

Paddy then got a trolley from the Pensioners' Chalet, loaded it up with the milk, and wheeled it across the Whiterock Road to

Ballymurphy, calling out, 'Milk for babies!' But he didn't get very far. He was stopped in an entry by the Paras and, while one stuck a gun in his mouth, the other kicked over a crate of milk, smashing most of the bottles. Paddy picked up the crate and put it back on the trolley and backed off, telling the soldiers that they wouldn't get the chance to shoot him in the back. He then started calling to houses that had young children.

When he got to Whitecliff Drive, he collapsed of a heart attack. While he was being carried into one of the houses, the Paras smashed every last bottle of milk, taunting the people who'd gathered to help. Paddy McCarthy was dead on arrival at hospital, one of eleven Ballymurphy residents who would have died by the end of Internment Week.

'I don't envy your job,' Hugh McCormick said when the story came to an end, 'Filling a dead man's boots is never going to be easy.'

'You'll get on fine,' Ann Stone assured me, 'Here's to your new job.'

Everyone raised a glass and the urge to run was temporarily quashed. We then moved on to stories of military raids and ambushes and gun-battles.

'I was just looking at you there,' Billy Caldwell said as we finished the second round of drinks, 'and from this angle you look the spit of Todler.'

'Who's Todler?' I asked.

'Tommy Tolan,' Billy said, 'He's one of the top Provies [Provisional IRA members] in the Murph. One of the 'Magnificent Seven' who escaped from the *Maidstone* prison ship in January there. The Brits have him on their death-list. Last month they shot the two Conways down by St. Thomas's School in mistake for him and Jim Bryson. Bryson is *the* top Provie in the Murph. He escaped from the *Maidstone* too.'

This was somewhat unsettling information which took fully a while to digest.

'Do I look like Todler from any other angles?' I asked.

*Ha-ha-ha!* everyone around the table went.

'Wait till ya hear this!' Mrs. Sheridan said, 'Anne's mawn, Billy, thinks Crossan's hardware shop in the Bullring sells the worst alarm clocks in the world. Every time he comes home, there's a different clock on the mantlepiece. What Billy doesn't know is that Bryson keeps comin' along and takin' the clocks and then buyin' Ann a new one!' More uproarious hilarity.

'When you were down in Cork,' Ann Stone said when the laughter subsided, 'I bet you never heard of Bo Gibson.'

'No, I didn't,' I admitted, 'Do I look like him too?'

'No you don't!' Ann laughed, 'Bo was a friggin' *dog*! He belonged to Herbo Gibson, who used to be one of Dunne's Guerrillas - about a dozen young bucks who used to fight the Brits like tigers... Herbo used to run about the place during the riots with a portable siren that he was always looking to plug into some light socket or other. And he used to make bugle sounds to go with the charges and retreats. And Bo was always at his side, always in the thick of it - you know we had a riot in Ballymurphy that went on for seven friggin' months! Anyway, whenever the young bucks was up rioting, Bo used to chase the stones that they threw at the Brits and bring them back again. Then one day there was a riot down in Divismore Park, near Murphy's entry, and someone threw a nail bomb at the Brits - and Bo took off after it...'

'You can imagine the goes of the young ones when they seen Bo grab the nail bomb. Herbo was running like the clappers of Hell, running for his friggin' life! He was bloody lucky that the nail bomb blew up before Bo could catch up with him! That night, a crowd of the young ones gave Bo a military funeral with a guard of honour - black berets, dark glasses, the heap! They even played *The Last Post* when they buried Bo in Herbo's back garden...'

As Ann finished this remarkable tale and I concluded that I'd arrived in some kind of madhouse, Mrs. Mac called me up to the bar. There, she introduced me to John Hume, a leading nationalist political figure from Derry.

'I met you before,' I said, 'In London last October. You were fasting outside Number 10, along with Bernadette Devlin, Austin Curry and a few others. At the time I was on my way to Asia with my girlfriend...'

'Oh ... yes,' John said, pretending to remember.

'We might need your help John,' Mrs. Mac told the big Derryman, 'Keern is coming to work for us at the community centre, but he's going to need a work permit because he's from the South. If we run into any trouble on it, I might have to give you a ring.'

'Sectarianism again,' John said, giving me an empathetic look, 'It's nothing personal. They have it in for all of us. If I can do anything for you, I will.' I suddenly felt included, part of the gang. Being picked on

## Chapter 2

by the vagaries of Unionism was clearly a plus. I thanked John for his support. I never mentioned that, after establishing the purpose of his London protest (against military brutality), Cora and I had continued on our way as there was no point joining a hunger strike for an hour.

'Here Keern' the diminutive Geordie Moylen asked me when I sat down again, 'When you were coming up from Cork, didja not notice that everyone else was going in the *other* direction?'

'I did notice a crowd of children in the railway station,' I said, 'But they looked like they were away on a school picnic.'

'Yer arse!' Big Alice Franklin interjected, 'That was no picnic. Them was refugees!'

'You'll have to forgive Big Alice,' the distinguished Hugh McCormick said, 'She forgets sometimes she's not out fightin' the Brits.'

'Tell him what your husband said!' Ann Stone called from the far side of the table, trying to drown out the din of the packed club.

'Shut you up!' Alice shouted back, but Ann wouldn't be silenced.

'Some fella came to the door and Alice's man answered. "Would you like to buy *The Voice of the North*," the wee fella asked – it was some paper that was doing the rounds at the time. "Buy it!" Alice's man said, "I'm friggin' well *married* to it!"'

'I'll knock yer head in,' Alice threatened but you could see that she didn't mind. I would soon learn that this was one of the milder anecdotes surrounding Big Alice Franklin. Once the laughter around *The Voice of the North* story had died down, Hugh McCormick moved over beside me. As former secretary of the BTA, he felt I should have some background history of the organisation.

'Frank Cahill got the whole thing going,' he said, pronouncing Cahill like *cackle*, 'Ballymurphy used to be treated like a leper colony. Nobody wanted to live there, and with everyone leaving all the time it was impossible to get any kind of steady tenants' association. Any family that could get out did. We had 12,000 families go through the place - 660 houses - in 14 years! Then we had all the bad propaganda. Coal in the bath. Breaking up the doors for firewood. That kind of rubbish. And almost anything that happened in the whole of west Belfast got blamed on Ballymurphy. We were the scapegoats. All the problems we had - poverty, money-lending, unemployment, bad housing - got turned around so that we got the blame.

'Then, a few of us got together to form the BTA in 1963, at a meeting in St. Bernadette's School. We got a 70% turn-out, and we elected 25 people to the committee. We just had to get up and fight back. So, we started with things like repairs to the houses, organising socials to give a sense of community, and fund-raising for a building that would belong to the people. Seán Mackle, the architect, gave us a design. Then he kept on giving us bigger and better designs until we ended up with this plan for a two-storey building that's going to cost £100,000. Since then, money has come from the government and what you seen earlier is the first stage. We also got a survey going with Tony Spencer from Queen's University; but that fell by the wayside when Frank Cahill got scooped and interned in Long Kesh.'

'Who is Frank Cahill?' I asked.

'You've heard of Joe Cahill,' Hugh said, 'He used to be the commander of the Provies in Belfast until he moved to Dublin. Well, Frank is Joe's brother. He was good at getting things going and building up contacts and things. You'll meet some of his sons around the community centre...'

The drinking then continued, with story after story of the war, until one o'clock in the morning, when we all sang a few songs. Mine was called *The German Clockwinder*, all about a man called Benjamin Fooks who wooed the women of Dublin's Strand area.

'Keern,' wee Geordie Moylen said when I'd finished, 'You're wired up to the Black Mountain. What kind of a song was that!'

As the night wore on, people from all corners of the club joined us to say hello to one or other of the company or to buy us a drink or to find out who the stranger was, and all the time I was struck by a tremendous sense of community. I had also felt it earlier in the Crooks's house in Ballymurphy, and during my previous visit with Frank Gogarty to the New Lodge. There was that same sense of purpose, of everyone travelling down the same set of tracks. People shared a bond, forged against a common enemy. Just as I'd experienced with Frank in O'Kane's in the New Lodge, arriving with the Ballymurphy people gave me an introduction to everyone in the bar. A friend of one was a friend of all. The flip side, I presumed, would also hold. Far too quickly, the night passed and it was time to leave.

At this juncture, we discovered that the minibus was facing the wrong direction and there was nowhere to turn. So, with Billy Caldwell reversing and Billy Scribbons shouting directions which mostly sounded like 'Whoa! Stop!' which Billy Caldwell always seemed to hear shortly after he'd crunched into the next vehicle, we pluckily reversed our way down the long driveway to the Andersonstown Road.

'Billy is rightly,' Mrs. Mac said to me, 'He shouldn't be driving.' *Rightly*, I sussed, meant legless.

'Right Billy,' Ann Stone said, 'Now, we need a friggin' chip!'

At one in the morning, we set off through the blacked-out streets and tangles of rolled barbed wire and broken bricks, with patrols of nervous British soldiers with blackened faces suddenly running out in front of us, and Big Ellen Cosgrove hanging out the window of the bus, while she and Ann Stone led the raucous sing-song, endearingly directed at the military, with lines such as:

*'We don't want to be defended by an army who surrendered*
*When the kids of Ballymurphy came to play'*
or
*'The boys of Ballymurphy, they led the way that night*
*When they showed those English bawstards how Irishmen could fight.'*

Then big deafening yahoos. You just knew you were in good company. We were then stopped by an army patrol whose members suffered all kinds of verbal abuse from the women on the bus - bar the sedate Mrs. Mac - before Big Ellen leaned out the window.

'Here son,' she asked the officer in a suddenly conciliatory tone, 'D'ya know anywhere where we could get a chip this hour o' the night?'

And thus was I baptised into my new home.

# Chapter 3
## Down Springhill Way

I woke up next day to morning light filtering in through the curtains of my first Ballymurphy hangover - and the sound of gunfire! At first I thought a car might have backfired. But then there was another. And another. Loud sharp cracks that seemed to be coming from somewhere nearby. Creeping across the bedroom floor on all fours, I raised one eye to the windowsill and tried to spy what was happening on the far side without making too much a target of my head. *Ciarán, I said to myself as I twisted into strange contortions, this might not have been such a good idea.* As I pondered on how the normality of yesterday was gone, Sarah Crooks's voice rang out through the gunfire.

'Billy! Keern! Yer breakfast is ready!' *Oh, it's OK, I thought, the gunfire isn't real: I'm just hallucinating.* Then Sarah called again and I heard Billy going into the yard.

'Is Keern up?' Sarah's voice said.

'No,' Billy said, and added something about drink.

'Ya better call him,' Sarah said, 'Or his fry will go cold.'

A minute later, Billy was back in the house and calling from the bottom of the stairs: 'Yer fry is ready!' I threw on some clothes and went down to investigate. There on the table, sure enough, were two Ulster Fries, similar to yesterday's. That peculiarly Northern institution requires at this stage a bit more celebration as it has probably reaped more souls than the Black Death. In the early Seventies, before cooking oil was invented, the Ulster Fry came from a pan of sizzling lard. Bacon, sausages, and black and white pudding were dropped into the pan and lovingly turned until crisp. An egg and a slice of potato bread were then added, so that these could absorb the flavours of the meats and a considerable dose of the lard. Then, finally, the *coup de grace* came in the form of a soda farl, sliced in two and dropped into the pan so it could soak up the remaining lard and any fat that might have seeped from the sausages and bacon. Doctors in Belfast called it *the heart attack on a plate*. One plateful provided you with all the saturated fat you'd ever need in several lifetimes. It was also, unfortunately, delicious after a night in Casement Park.

## Chapter 3

'How come Sarah made us our breakfast?' I asked Billy as he and I tucked in.

'Ever since the wife died,' Billy explained, 'Sarah's been cookin' my grub and washin' my clothes and I give her some money at the start of the week.'

This arrangement I had now automatically inherited. From now on, until Billy and I declared independence, we'd listen at mealtimes for Sarah's voice. 'Billy! Yer dinner!' or whatever, and one or the other of us would dart across next door's back garden and collect the food over Crooks's fence. On rainy days, we'd both go out, one of us holding the brolly for the other.

After the fry had congealed my blood, I decided to take a walk. The area, Hugh McCormick had explained, covered about a square mile. Ballymurphy estate was the nucleus, but Greater Ballymurphy began at the bottom of the Whiterock Road and ran clear to the base of Black Mountain, taking in the public-housing estates of Whiterock, Westrock, Springhill, Ballymurphy, New Barnsley and Moyard; and the owner-occupied Dermott Hill and Springfield Park. I'd have a look around, I told Billy, familiarise myself with the geography.

'Be careful,' Billy advised, 'Watch out for the Brits and the Provies.'

I thought this an odd piece of advice. If I was a perceived enemy to one, surely I was a friend to the other? I then recalled Billy Caldwell's story about the Conway brothers and how one of them had been shot by undercover Brits in mistake for someone who looked like me; and how the lad who looked like me - and his friends - might be a tad touchy about stangers who might be undercover Brits. I considered wearing a hat, then decided I was being ridiculous.

'Don't worry,' I told Billy, 'I'll walk in the middle of the street so nobody thinks I'm suspicious.'

'And stay off the Springfield Road!' Billy warned.

I left the house, gave the lamp a wide berth and made my way out onto the Whiterock Road. Wondering about all the burnt-out cars on the far side, I turned downhill, retracing my steps of the previous day. Close to St. Thomas's school, a woman, pushing a pram and hanging on to two shrieking children, came out of what I would later learn to be Ballymurphy Road. She gave me a curious look, said, 'What about ya?' and hurried past. When I looked back, she was staring after me.

Beyond the school, I passed MacRory Park, a small rough playing pitch bequeathed to the local community by a former bishop of Down & Connor. Immediately past the pitch, a narrow lane led down to St. John's Social Club. Beyond the lane, I was surprised to see a small farm I hadn't noticed the day before. A horse nuzzled a metal gate and whinnied. In amongst all the housing developments and a war, it seemed fully incongruous. A little further on, I came to the first of two entrances to Whiterock estate and turned in so I could double back towards Ballymurphy. In each of the narrow streets, I came across windowsills with hand-carved wooden harps and Celtic crosses, and framed painted handkerchiefs, all bearing the name Long Kesh and proudly proclaiming a family member or relative incarcerated without trial in the prison camp outside Lisburn. (I had seen similar reminders on the Falls, in Ballymurphy, and in Turf Lodge.) Ten minutes later I was out the other end and in Westrock, an estate made up entirely of painted aluminium huts, many corroding at ground level. At first glance, Westrock looked like a hastily erected squatters' camp; and I wasn't far out. The huts (and similar ones in Taughmonagh in South Belfast) had been put up after World War II as temporary accommodation, but temporary had run on. With their scattering of dumped rubbish, they looked cold and dreary, like the internment huts at Long Kesh, minus the barbed wire.

Passing out from Westrock, I arrived at Corpus Christi church, the religious centre of Ballymurphy where I would, over the coming years, attend many a funeral. A little further on, facing the church, Springhill Avenue ran up towards the Springfield Road. On the avenue's left hand side, small terraces of three-storey box-houses with corrugated metal roofs ran off towards Ballymurphy estate like half a herring-bone. Later, when I got to know them better, they seemed to change colour with the weather. On a sunny day they looked pink. In bad weather, they looked grey. In either weather, they looked grim. On the right hand side, the wall of Corry's timber yard ran from the Springfield Road to the lower end, where a few more terraces gave shelter to Mary's Shop, set a little back from the avenue. As I passed the shop, a stockily-built teenager with collar-length, fair hair came out through the door with an ice-cream. When he saw me, he stopped dead.

"Bout ya mucker!' he said, 'Are you the new worker in the centre?'
'What makes you think that?' I asked.
'Either that,' he laughed, 'Or you're a Brit! But if you were a Brit,

## Chapter 3

walkin' about like that, you'd be dead by now. Therefore, I must conclude my friend, that you are not a Brit.'

'Definitely not a Brit,' I said, 'Please spread the word...'

'The word, the word...!' he laughed, 'First there was the word...'

'I mean it,' I stressed.

He laughed again. 'See ya at the centre mucker!' he said, 'By the way, you call me Stevie, Stevie Mallon.' He then shook his head slowly as if to say *poor bastard*, and went on. I smiled inside. I felt good. I felt safe. Little did I know: in time Stevie and I would feature prominantly in the inglorious Battle of Castle Street.

Leaving Springhill, I turned right and was back again on Ballymurphy Road. A short distance on, I swung off along a narrow entry and came out into what I now know to have been Divismore Park. Suddenly, I found myself staring at one end of a massive fortified structure of corrugated iron and Gulag-style watch-towers that loomed over the bottom of the street. What had once been the Henry Taggart Memorial Hall was about 150 yards away on the far side of the Springfield Road. Abbreviated to 'the Taggart', the former Protestant church had been a military base since the early days of the Troubles. Having heard, three weeks earlier in The Starry Plough, how Tommy McIlroy had been shot dead from one of those towers while working on his car, I didn't hang about. I turned up Ballymurphy Drive and made my way towards the centre of the estate.

By now, I'd noticed several wrecked houses scattered throughout the area. These were later confirmed as casualties of war: some had belonged to suspected IRA Volunteers and had been destroyed by the British army; others had been abandoned by families who'd fled the area. The shells were used for IRA ambushes one day, and torn apart in military searches the next.

A few minutes from Divismore Park, I arrived at a circle of grass and mud in the middle of Ballymurphy estate where four streets met: the Bullring, the focus of so many stories of the night before. Gun-battles, riots, they all happened here. On the side that backed onto the mountain, a row of grubby shopfronts, plastered in graffiti, were topped by two storeys of flats. All but one of the flats (the still-functioning welfare office) were derelict. Behind the grilled window of the butcher's shop, sides of mutton, beef and pork hung on hooks. Outside the grocery shop there were boxes of vegetables, stacked up against its grilled window. I smiled at everyone I met and said hello, and wanted to explain that I was from Cork and harmless.

From the Bullring, I made my way up to the Springfield Road, the main artery that cuts Greater Ballymurphy in two. On the far side, the neat, red-brick homes of Dermott Hill rose in a series of stepped streets on one side of what Billy Scribbons had called 'the mountain loney'. On the other side, the homes of New Barnsley looked pretty much like those of Ballymurphy. Further down the Springfield Road, several blocks of maisonettes climbed back towards the lower slopes of Black Mountain. These, I took to be Moyard. And further still, beyond the Taggart, I could see the last estate, Springfield Park, curling up towards a fortress of grey flats with Union Jacks fluttering from their roofs and sniper-slits cut into their gable walls. This, I concluded, was loyalist Springmartin. Further up the Springfield Road, in neighbouring republican Turf Lodge, similarly vacant flats also had sniper slits cut into their gable walls. Standing in this line of fire gave force to Billy's warning to stay off the Springfield Road. Head down and heart thumping, I darted to the far side.

Another hour of wandering, and I arrived back in Ballymurphy estate and went looking for home. As I attempted to make sense of the nameless circular streets that all looked identical, a car came cruising towards me. Inside were two men in their early twenties. The passenger was slim, with shoulder-length hair and a biker moustache. The driver was a heavy set man, with dark hair and a broken nose. As they passed they glared out at me. As was custom for 21-year-olds from inner-city Cork, I glared back. Although an odd encounter, I thought no more of it. Then four spaced gunshots rang out. In the silence that followed, I made my way through an entry out onto the Whiterock Road. More shots rang out, and this time I could see the guns and the men firing them.

On the far side of the road, beyond the burnt-out cars that lay above the community centre, three young men in Bay City Rollers skinners, out in the open and in broad daylight, were firing rifles at stand-up targets. Over the coming months, I would regularly see target practice taking place in the same spot. Other IRA Volunteers in the cemetery would fire handguns at tin cans lined along the wall, the military presence in the Taggart causing not the slightest concern. I also learned that the metallic graveyard was the final resting place of vehicles used in barricades, or burned to destroy forensic evidence after IRA operations.

## Chapter 3

The war between the IRA and the British state which was to last 27 years, is one of the best-documented conflicts of modern times. The pivotal role played by Ballymurphy in that war has been well acknowledged elsewhere. Suffice to say that, in early 1972, the war was at its height and its effects were everywhere to be seen in Greater Ballymurphy.

A campaign of civil disobedience, initiated as a protest against internment without trial, was in full swing, with nobody paying rent, rates, gas or electricity. Simultaneously, the community had taken control of housing, the 'licensing' of drinking establishments, the conversion of the Northern Ireland Housing Executive's property into community facilities, and the development of local industry. On top of this, a great many families had unofficially swapped houses. Other houses, vacated by those whose nerves couldn't hack it any more, were occupied by squatters. In Moyard, whole blocks of bullet-riddled maisonettes lay vacant as they were in the front line, facing loyalist Springmartin and the Taggart.

During the first few months I spent in Belfast the sound of rifle and sub-machine gun fire became a constant to which I would become virtually anaesthetised. It was like passing cars: you didn't hear it any more unless it was punctuated by something unusual, like a screech of brakes or an exploding grenade. But on that first day, when I wasn't used to it, it was very disconcerting. It got no better in the afternoon.

Following the stroll through the area, I had gone on to the community centre to check out my new working environment. It wasn't that impressive. The completed part of Seán Mackle's grand plan was no more than a big rectangular barn of bare red brick and steel girders, with adjoining toilets and a small office. To create separate spaces, you turned the heavy, moveable stage-sections on their sides and used them as partitions. There was also a 'Pensioners' Chalet', a wooden pre-fab painted turquoise-blue, where the older folk held bingo and other such harmless social events. They also hid guns under the floor but that was a bit of a secret. As for equipment for a youth club?

'Well,' Mrs. Mac explained as she showed me around, 'There are two table-tennis tables, a couple of footballs and a small snooker table...'

I tried to imagine fifty or sixty war-hyped young people being impressed by that little package but it eluded me. (I hadn't yet realised there would be hundreds!) As Mrs. Mac explained how it all worked when Paddy McCarthy was there, and how it would all come good when the second phase of the centre was finished, a tall, young, pregnant woman walked into the hall. She was in her early twenties with long fair hair parted to one side of a high forehead, and was wearing the shortest of maternity dresses from which strode two of the longest legs on planet Earth. With a sunbeam of a smile, she came over to where we stood and looked at me.

'Hello,' she said in an English accent, 'I take it you're my new neighbour.'

'This is Jenny Quigley,' Mrs. Mac said, introducing us, 'Jenny lives across the street from Scrubby's.'

'Ciarán de Baróid,' I said and we shook hands.

'Yes,' Jenny said, 'I live across from you in Glenalina Park. My husband, Seán, is a local teacher, and I'm involved in a few community projects. I heard that the new centre-worker had arrived last night and was wondering if you'd like to come to a meeting this afternoon of Springhill Residents' Association? It's around in 123 - Fr. Des Wilson's house in Springhill Avenue. You'll have a chance to meet some of the people involved in community work in Springhill and Westrock.'

'That sounds great,' I said.

We arranged that Jenny would call for me at Billy's house at two o'clock. I was looking forward to meeting Des Wilson. The Ballymurphy priest, an outspoken critic of British policies and actions, and a thorn in the side of the Catholic establishment, had become a leading community and human rights figure in Belfast. His house, Jenny had explained, was a local people's base. It was May 2nd, and though I can't remember now what that meeting was about, I will never forget it, or the walk to Des Wilson's house.

We first called by the back of Corry's timber-yard. The massive yard, with its entrance on the Springfield Road, backed onto Springhill and the aluminium huts of Westrock. (I had passed it earlier in the day.) We arrived on the Westrock side to find a group of IRA men tossing fire-bombs and blast-bombs over the wall. They had, apparently, taken a deep dislike to the stacks of lumber used as army sniping positions. (Later, in July, they would turn up with a home-made Roman catapult to lob containers of petrol into the yard, resulting in 60-foot flames that caused £250,000 worth of damage and accidentally gutted two local homes and the community centre.)

## Chapter 3

After the visit to Corry's wall, Jenny and I proceeded to Des Wilson's house as heavy gunfire, triggered off by the attack on Corry's, erupted around us. A gun-battle had broken out in Springhill and Ballymurphy estates between the British army and the IRA. I considered this a dangerous escalation. This was nothing like the gunfire that had woken me up that morning: this was continuous firing, coming from several directions, which made me awfully aware of ricochets and mistaken identity as we speed-walked for the safety of Des Wilson's house. Nevertheless, Jenny seemed only mildly bothered.

'Sometimes, you get a lot of shooting like this,' she said as she opened the unlocked door of the priest's house at 123 Springhill Avenue, 'But nobody gets injured.'

Inside, in Des Wilson's living room, a dozen or so people from Springhill Residents' Association had already started their meeting. Jenny introduced everyone to me and we took our seats in an atmosphere that again mirrored that powerful sense of community that seemed to be everywhere. I was disappointed that Des Wilson wasn't there as I'd hoped to meet him. *Next time,* I thought. A couple of minutes later, all comfortable thought vanished as the gun-battle began to close in and the meeting went into disconcerting denial. While the shooting intensified, the members of Springhill Residents' Association were, incredibly to me, deeply engrossed in some minor detail of last month's all-important minutes! With rifles and sub-machine guns blazing and blast bombs exploding, the people in the house continued their discourse with an imperturbability that would have done the Buddha proud. Gradually, I was beginning to think that there were two possibilities here: either Billy Scribbons had slipped me an almighty Mickey Finn, or everyone else was stark-raving bonkers. Then, the battle was in the alley outside. There were IRA men with rifles at the far side of the garden wall to our left, firing past the window. Still, nobody broke a sentence. Then it was the turn of the British army, who seized the garden and were firing over the wall in the opposite direction. Not a whit of a sentence suffered.

'Is everybody happy with the minutes now?' Jim Donnelly from Westrock Drive asked. Everyone nodded thoughtfully. Then a blast-bomb landed outside in the garden and the soldiers fled.

'This is a right Laurel and Hardy act!' a disgusted Jim muttered as we all funnelled out the living-room door to the safety of the hall.

Then, to crown the farce, a young boy ran in from the garden.

'It's OK!' he shouted, 'It's only a *wee* bomb!' The meeting was back on track again while I knew full well that, any minute now, I was going to wake up in bed with a frightful start.

Eventually, the meeting finished with A.O.B. and date-of-next-meeting. Jim Donnelly then peered out the front door to check that the coast was clear, and the members of Springhill Residents' Association filed out one by one in orderly procession as if nothing related to guns had ever happened.

\* \* \*

Apart from the insanity of the actual meeting, what was happening that day in Des Wilson's house was of great import. Although I wasn't aware of it that afternoon, it was part of a working-class social revolution that had been sweeping nationalist areas of Belfast since August 1969. Rising from the ashes of the pogroms, a vast plethora of self-help organisations had become intent on supplanting the state that had long neglected their communities. Running on twin tracks of militancy and self-determination, perhaps best illustrated in names such as the Ardoyne People's Assembly, they drew a broad and determined membership from the huge body of unemployed people in those communities. Institutionalised sectarianism had resulted in families who had been unemployed for generations, within which existed a vast reservoir of skill and ability just waiting to be tapped. The Troubles had delivered purpose.

Ballymurphy, long a sink estate for Belfast Corporation, had woken up one day in August 1969 to find refugees pouring in from the burnt-out streets of the Lower Falls and Ardoyne. Left to its own devices, the community had organised accommodation, food, clothing, trauma-counselling, registers of displaced people, medical support, rescue-transport and defence, and had not been found wanting. Within days, a community that had been little more than a transit camp, had been transformed into a cohesive unit of collective action that had shone where the powers-that-be had miserably failed.

When the conflict finally reached the area in Easter 1970, this network was further strengthened. Since then, some of it had gone to war. The remainder had gone on to establish entities such as Des Wilson's community house and Springhill Residents' Association.

Just as I was about to follow the Residents' Association members out the door – on the grounds that it must've been safe as none of

## Chapter 3

them had yet been shot - Jenny called me back.

'Not so fast,' she said, 'Before we leave, we'll go and see if Des is about. You can introduce yourself.'

I followed Jenny out into the hall and up the stairs. I was delighted: meeting Des Wilson would complete the day. Half way up the stairs, I could hear voices which grew louder as we reached the landing. 'In here,' Jenny said, opening one of the closed doors and walking in.

In a bedroom that was now an office, we found 47-year-old Des Wilson, recognisable from his head of swept-back, wiry hair. Wearing a loose sweater and dark trousers, he had his back to us and was punching out a letter on a small portable typewriter.

'Does this sound right?' he asked, running the last sentence past a thin woman with short greying hair.

'Sounds fine,' the woman said in a Dublin accent. She then turned towards myself and Jenny.

'Well, hello Jenny,' she said, 'And who have we got here?'

'This is Ciarán from Cork,' Jenny said, 'He's taking Paddy McCarthy's place at the community centre.' The woman straightened up and smiled.

'Come in! Come in!' Des said, 'Come in old man of the road!' He got up and shook my hand vigorously as Jenny continued the introductions.

'And this is Noelle Ryan,' she said, 'Noelle has been here since the end of last summer.'

'Grab a chair! Grab a chair!' Des said and we sat ourselves down.

There was then some small talk about the gun-battle that had moved about the front garden.

'It's a good job the bomb didn't go off,' Des concluded, 'It would've broken all the windows...'

*The windows!* I thought, *Who gives a shite about windows!*

'So you're going to come and work with us,' Des said, getting back to the topic of me, 'Sit down and I'll get you a cup of tea, while Noelle tells you how *she* ended up here.'

Noelle then delighted in explaining how she'd outfoxed the local Parish Priest who was not, I gathered, a figure of great love around 123.

After five years as a Parish Worker in Liverpool, Noelle had come home to Dublin and become involved in a holiday scheme for Belfast children. She was so moved by the spirit of the young people, and the horrors they'd lived through, that she wrote to Bishop William Philbin of Down and Connor, saying that she'd like to work in Belfast. The Bishop suggested she go to Ballymurphy. The Parish Priest, 59-year-old Canon Pádraig Murphy, who welcomed no intrusions on his patch, was pushed to agree under the circumstances. It would be a month's trial, he said, although he could see no possible role for a Parish Worker, and a woman to boot!

'The month, however, has become eight months,' Noelle concluded, 'And by the time the PP got around to telling me last week that I had to go, I just found I couldn't, now could I? And there's not a lot he can do. I've managed to find myself a part-time job and I'm here for the long haul.'

Noelle had dug in at 123 and she and Des were working together on developing the 123 project. At the time of writing, Noelle still lives in Springhill, sharing the community house with Des Wilson.

'You wouldn't have come across our Pádraig Murphy,' Noelle said as Des came back with the tea, 'But you will.'

'It will all come to a head one of these fine days,' Des said, 'The hierarchy must realise that *they* are not the Church. If it wasn't for attitudes like the one that tries to prevent someone like Noelle from contributing here, I would probably still be working from the Parochial House. But the events of 1969 put an end to all of that! And indeed, the events that came prior to 1969.'

Des then went on to explain. He had been living in St. John's Parochial House on the Falls Road when the pogroms broke out. Already sickened by the state's cumulative response to the demands of the civil rights movement - climaxing in the killings and burnings of August - he now found himself almost as disturbed by the response of the Church. Although the people of Ballymurphy had opened their doors to those who had been burned out of their homes, the models of authority within the Church prevented the Parochial House from doing likewise. There had also been deep resistance to opening the schools to the fleeing families, so that people in many instances had to kick the doors in.

'Yet they had seen this coming,' Des said, 'Or at least had been told by others with better vision, but they did nothing to prepare. Instead, we just stood there helpless, and watched the flood of destitute people pour past our door. But, we shouldn't have been surprised at the Church getting this wrong. There was already a pattern of very deliberate activity aimed at undermining the whole people's movement that had been growing up around the civil rights and the struggle for democracy. That had been another example of the Church getting it wrong.'

He went on to outline how, in 1968, in the early days of the civil rights agitation, Bishop Philbin had instructed the clergy of the diocese not to allow any Church property – which meant most of the public buildings in nationalist areas – to be used for any meetings convened by the executive of NICRA. This led directly to a clash between Des and the hierarchy when Michael Farrell of People's Democracy addressed a meeting in St. Bernadette's School in Ballymurphy. At the next clerical briefing at the Bishop's house, Monsignor Mullally, Vicar-General and the Bishop's second-in-command, made reference to 'such people as Michael Farrell being allowed into Church property in some parts', whereupon Des Wilson was at pains to point out that Michael Farrell had *not* been allowed in: he had been *invited* in.

'Then there was the awful issue around the welfare committees. Immediately after the pogroms, once the initial pressure had been relaxed, representatives of the welfare committees that had sprung up across nationalist areas of Belfast decided to organise a central coordinating body so that maximum use could be made of all resources in the event of further emergencies. When word of the move reached the Bishop's ears, he immediately set a parrallel operation in train which undermined the welfare committees by installing clergy in key positions until the movement became little more than a clerical front.

'The Citizens' Defence Committees became the next target. These had been set up to defend nationalist areas against further attack. This prompted another briefing at the Bishop's house. This time, it was announced that part of the clergy's task in their respective areas was to take over the CDCs. This was an appalling situation. There was no way you could stand by and let this happen without making some attempt to prevent it.'

However, despite the dissenting voice of Des Wilson – who pointed out that defence organisations might well become weapons-procuring organisations, and that the clergy would then be in control of weapons-procuring organisations, and that it was up to the people themselves to decide on whatever defensive measures they felt were needed – the clerical plan went ahead. Clergy, or those whom they'd introduced into positions of power, took control of the working-class defence organisations, eventually rendering them impotent.

Although Des ommitted to mention it that afternoon – and would often cite it later - there had also been the Vere Foster Affair. This had become folklore in Ballymurphy and would eventually be described to me by Bill Rolston, who found himself in the eye of that particular storm and would later become a colleague and friend in battles to come.

Prior to the riots of 1970, New Barnsley and Moyard had been predominantly loyalist. However, the riots had prompted a loyalist flight from the two estates. This meant that, overnight, Vere Foster state school was stripped of its clientele, placing it in the front line of a turf war between the state education system and the Catholic Church.

In September 1970, nationalist parents arrived at Vere Foster to enrol their children. In the Six-county context this was an unusual move as education was generally segregated: the state provided for Protestant children; the Catholic Church, through its 'maintained' schools system, providing for Catholics. What the parents arriving at Vere Foster failed to realise was that they were encroaching heavily on a core Catholic principle. The Church believed that religion should permeate the entire atmosphere of the school, not simply be another subject as would be the case in a state school such as Vere Foster. One of the parents, Bernadette Savage, later described how, at an emergency meeting called by one of the local curates immediately after the enrolments, the Vere Foster parents were told that if the children remained at the school they wouldn't be allowed to make their Confirmation or Communion. To traditional Catholic parents, the refusal of the sacraments was a serious threat.

As a result, some parents withdrew their children. But the parents of 218 children decided to fight. The Church was arguing that proper religious instruction would not be provided at Vere Foster. The parents countered that it was the duty of the clergy to make good the shortfall, that a Catholic teacher should be sent into Vere Foster by the Down and Connor Maintained Schools Committee. But the Church wasn't budging. The parents were told that their only option was to withdraw their children from the school. This would have led to the closure of Vere Foster and its probable sale to the Catholic Church.

The parents approached several retired teachers and asked if they

## Chapter 3

would fill the gap, but they were afraid of losing their pensions. By December defeat was looming. Then, out of the blue, 24-year-old Bill Rolston, an ex-seminarian who'd returned from New Hampshire in November, wrote to the school, offering to provide religious instruction. As Bill wasn't qualified to teach, he couldn't be employed by the school authorities. Nevertheless, the principal put him in touch with the parents' committee. Although Bill was willing to work for nothing, the parents decided that they would employ him, raising the funds through a weekly collection.

Bill's intervention turned the tables. Despite the Bishop's refusal to meet the parents - Philbin claiming that there was nothing to discuss! - the Church was losing the battle. On March 10th 1971 the parents of children due to be confirmed were asked to bring the children along to Corpus Christi Church that evening. To their surprise, the Diocesan Inspector was waiting to examine them. Bill wasn't invited, but he turned up anyway - and was completely ignored. However, the Church had conceded. Five days later it was announced that a Ms. McKenna was being seconded from St. Bernadette's School to teach religion at Vere Foster.

Immediately after Easter, a delegation of three clergymen, including the Diocesan Inspector, turned up at the school to establish Rome's position. They also wanted to sack Bill, who had to patiently explain that they could hardly fire when they hadn't hired in the first place. All of this had added more fuel to the fire under Des Wilson's skin.

'The growing gulf between what the Church did and what the Church was supposed to do had by now led myself and [Fr.] Hugh Mullan to the belief that we needed to move out into the community. Hugh was keen on developing a second-hand furniture depot and establishing a credit union that would undermine the illegal moneylenders who were plaguing the area. I was interested in the whole area of adult education and social action. But always, we faced the same problem: despite the fact that the Catholic Church owned schools, halls and the Parochial House, we could never get the uninhibited use of any of these buildings. In the end, the only conclusion, as we saw it, was to find an independent space, however small, out in the community. By early 1971 we had decided it was high time to move.

'After managing this time to secure the approval of the Parish Priest, we applied to Belfast Corporation for a house in Springhill, which was granted without hesitation. But, just as we were about to move, the minutes of the Corporation's meeting were published and the news reached Philbin and word came back that the move wasn't to be. I heard it from a curate. He heard it from the Parish Priest who in turn heard it from Philbin. These were the kind of mystical channels we had to deal with. Eventually, Hugh accepted the decision, but was later allowed to move into Springfield Park, [one of the few owner-occupied areas in the parish] where a house was bought for the purpose. I decided to hang on to this house and see what happened.'

A few months later, on the heels of the first internment swoop in August 1971, Hugh Mullan was to leave his house in Springfield Park to die suddenly and violently in a hail of British bullets. Meanwhile, Des Wilson established the community house at 123 in a move that marked the beginning of a long war.

When Des had finished his story, Jenny and I thanked himself and Noelle for their time and the tea and got up to leave. But not before Jenny - in an act of complete lunacy as far as I was concerned - promised that we'd be back for the next meeting of Springhill Residents' Association to check again those all-important minutes.

\* \* \*

'Now,' Jenny said when we got outside, 'Would you like to meet Jan McCarthy, Paddy's wife?'

'She's still living here?' I asked.

'Indeed she is,' Jenny said, 'She lives around the corner from us.'

As soon as Jenny knocked on her door on the corner of Glenalina Road and the Whiterock Road, Jan McCarthy answered with a flourish. A big, round-faced woman with a sweeping personality, short blonde hair, square-framed glasses and a polished English accent, she greeted us as if she'd been expecting the call for years.

'Come in!' she gushed, spreading her arms in a wide welcome, 'I heard on the grapevine that a Corkman was coming!'

She led the way into the living-room where a tomcat the size of a panther rose from a harem of lesser mortals, arched its back and glared at us. From the narrow green slits of its eyes, it was clear that we were not welcome.

'Oh Flea!' Jan purred at the black monster, 'Don't be so anti-social now! Say hello to Jenny and Ciarán.' Flea hissed, flicking the tip of a bushy tail that looked like a python with the pip.

'Careful there are no cats in that hole in the settee!' Jan shrieked as we were about to sit down, 'Tess Cahill squashed one of the kittens to death last week.'

I had a vision of flying cat-guts as I carefully placed my arse on a corner of the settee and Jan went off to the kitchen to make a cup of coffee.

'We've just been around at Des's house,' Jenny called to her from the living room, and began to recount the story of the gun-battle.

'I heard all the shooting,' Jan said as she came back in with the coffee, 'I thought it was coming from the Taggart direction.'

'You should've seen Jim Donnelly's face,' Jenny said, 'when the wee lad came in and said not to worry...'

'I can just *imagine*!' Jan howled. She then switched tack. 'Felicity [one of my co-workers at the community centre] and I have been talking to Fred Bass about the summer play-scheme,' she told us in a loud excited voice, 'There are about twelve students coming from England this year. They're going to use this place as a base and we'll get them billeted around the area. There are activities planned for the streets and for all the community centres, and there's going to be a number of bus-runs to places like Cronulla beach...'

Jenny and I stayed for an hour and there was never a mention of Paddy McCarthy's death. Just Jan waltzing about the living-room, chatting jovially about this and that, and hooting with laughter at bizarre anecdotes of life in Ballymurphy.

'You heard the one about the kids - six and seven-year-olds - over in Divismore Park, throwing stones at the tins around the Taggart? Well, in the end Lily Quinn couldn't take it anymore so she chased them. "I've had enough of this!" she shouted after them, "I've been putting up with it for a week now!" "Missus," one of them shouted back at her, "We've been putting up with it for seven hundred years"!'

But despite Jan's effervescent joviality, she had a serious side that I would encounter many times in the years ahead. Mostly, it was roused by the need for justice. I would often come across her in the street, intervening in some military outrage against some defenseless civilian and facing down British guns along with the other fearless femmes of Ballymurphy. She never mentioned Paddy, but Paddy was deep in Jan's heart. As were the cowards who'd caused his death.

That night, back in Billy's we watched the News again and heard about the afternoon's battle in Springhill and Ballymurphy. It had not been one of Jenny's injury-free days. During the course of the afternoon a soldier had been wounded in Corry's as was 17-year-old William Robinson, an employee at the timber yard; and in Ballymurphy Drive, 14-year-old John Armstrong had been shot in the back by the very kind of stray bullet that I'd had on my mind.

Watching TV that night was very strange – I felt like I was sort of involved in the News.

# Chapter 4
## A Free State Bawstard

There had been more gunfire during the night, the IRA apparently laying siege to the Taggart. It had woken me up but I'd managed to drift off again, despite the sporadic shooting. By morning the shooting had stopped as everyone who'd been involved was away to bed. After all, you had to sleep sometime, Billy explained, a good time now to go for a stroll or around to the shops.

It was now Wednesday. Two nights and a day had passed since I'd first arrived. As I had nothing better to do, I decided to go to work, although my post didn't officially start until the middle of the month. I walked over to the community centre, where Mrs. Mac was on the office phone, and announced my intentions.

'Settle yourself in there,' Mrs. Mac smiled, pushing a chair in my direction. With strands of greying hair falling in her eyes, she looked like she'd run a mile. 'Big Alice will be here soon,' she added, pointing to a third chair, 'To do the complaints. And Donal and Felicity will be here this afternoon.'

Twenty-three-year-old Donal Fagan and twenty-eight-year-old Felicity McKerr were my part-time colleagues at the community centre. During our drink at Casement Park, Mrs. Mac had explained that they ran sessions in the afternoons and evenings for young people up to the age of sixteen. Since Paddy McCarthy's death, there had been no activities for the older age group. These, I had to remind myself, were aged seventeen to twenty, and I had just passed 21 at the end of February.

I heard Big Alice long before I saw her. The voice was at full pitch and I could imagine her striding through the reception area, up the steps and into the main hall, then turning right towards the office, the glasses perched on the thin nose and the eyes darting from side to side as she took in the details of the familiar surroundings.

'Them Brits was out of order yesterday,' Alice was complaining, 'Firin' at anything that moved. But the Boys gave 'em a run for their money.'

'That King's Own isn't worth a shite,' came the reply and I recognised the voice of Tommy Crooks who came tottering along beside Alice with the gait of a penguin.

'Och, hello!' Tommy said when he saw me at my desk two weeks early, 'What about ya? Are ya goin' to sing us a song or what!'

'Dedication,' Mrs. Mac said, 'He's volunteering his time until he starts proper.'

'I do the housin' complaints in the mornin',' Alice said, aiming the information my direction, 'So I use the phone.'

I was glad she wasn't asking *me* to make the calls as I wasn't used to the phone and it made me nervous. I never knew what to say when the person on the other end answered.

'Alice... Tommy...' Mrs. Mac said, 'I need to go and see Seán Mackle about the second stage of the building, 'Can youse look after things until I get back.'

'No problem,' Alice assured her, and off went Mrs. Mac. Alice then sat down, lifted the phone and dialled the Northern Ireland Housing Executive with the day's housing complaints. Alice was the conduit between the residents of the area and the organization that managed its public housing. As the Executive's number rang, she pulled her glasses down to the end of her nose for full effect. When the telephone was picked up at the other end, she embarked on what was clearly a morning ritual.

'Hillo-o-o,' she began in a most polished accent that seemed suddenly detached from the Alice of a moment ago, 'This is Aylice Frawnklin of the Bollymeffy Tenants Association. Could I speak to the Heysing Officer for Bollymeffy please?' It was a remarkably polished performance. However, things went rapidly downhill. Within four or five exchanges, Alice was apoplectic. On our side of the conversation, it went like this: 'Are ya tryin' ta friggin' well tell me that nobody got back in touch?' Then: 'What! Are ya callin' me a friggin' liar?' And finally, yelling into the phone: 'What did ya say, ya wee bawstard! Maybe yer friggin' ma didn't skelp yer friggin' arse enough when ya were a wee boy!' She then turned and looked at me aghast, the phone at arm's length. 'The bawstard!' she spluttered, 'He hung up...!' And back on the phone with her again.

'We can't let the Executive get away wi' that,' Tommy said, winking at me behind Alice's back. *Well*, I thought, *There goes the relationship with the Housing Executive and Alice's conduit-role*. But no! Not so. Because, the next day, and the next, Alice would be back again as if yesterday had never happened. And she always seemed to manage the job, albeit piecemeal through a string of Housing Executive employees.

# Chapter 4

When Alice had finished her calls, I walked with her to the door of the community centre, wondering when Felicity would arrive.

'That's very weird,' Alice said, coming from behind, 'For a second I could see Paddy McCarthy standing there. Ya know, this was the last place he left on the 11$^{th}$ of August, the day he died... Cheerio!'

'Cheerio Alice,' I said and felt a shudder traverse what was left of my spine.

Once Alice had left, I went back into the office, got some paper and a pen, and began to draw up a list of what would be needed to run the youth centre. It came to an impressive whole page. Then more shooting. The IRA was making another attempt to burn down Corry's. This time a truck was driven into the wall and set on fire, sparking the gun-battle that had just broken out. Later, we heard that a soldier had been wounded, and that there had been a sectarian riot at the Springhill/Springmartin interface, followed by the arrival of the RUC and military. To separate the combatants, the RUC talked the loyalists back up the Springmartin Road while the British army blasted the Ballymurphy people with rubber bullets. Before I could take it all in, I found myself helping to evacuate children from the back end of Ballymurphy where the double event, and those of previous days, had done for the parents' nerves.

Felicity arrived just before three o'clock. A calm, quietly-spoken woman with short fair hair, she told me that she'd been involved, along with Fred Bass, in organizing summer play-schemes in the area prior to taking up the community centre job. The summer scheme that Jan McCarthy had talked about was a follow-up to those earlier schemes.

'And don't take it personally,' she added, 'but I'll not be staying much longer. I've just been holding the fort here with Donal until the BTA managed to replace Paddy. So congratulations! The show is now in your hands.'

I never got to mention the fact that I wasn't officially starting for another fortnight, nor would it have made a difference. Felicity had handed me the reins.

'At half three,' she explained, 'we have the junior session – for the under twelves. So we can get the hall ready.'

There wasn't much to prepare. We pulled out the two table-tennis tables, a football and the small snooker table, and made two goals out of the stage sections as a raucous, ominous crescendo of child-sound built up outside the main entrance to the building.

'Ready?' Felicity asked.

'Ready,' I said and she opened the door.

Seconds later, she and I were swept aside as a great dam-burst surged through the door. The older kids, in bovver boots and half-mast skinners were followed by a long tail that passed through five-year-olds with babies on their hips until it trailed almost to ground level as the three year-olds brought up the rear. Screaming and howling, they fanned out across the hall and proceeded to run amok, many engaging in a game called *Japs and Germans*. The 'Japs' I gathered, were the Brits. Heaven knows who the Germans were.

'What we do now,' Felicity shouted, 'is make sure nobody gets killed.'

For the next two hours, we both paced the wooden floor, jumping left and right to pick up casualties, while some 200 children ran riot around the big rectangular hall until it was time for them to go. This, however, was when the real fun began. Each child had now to be individually apprehended and bundled out the steel side-door, while the growing mob outside took to kicking the door and hammering it with rocks and all the fervour of the excluded. At the same time they decided that my real name was either *de Bow-wow, de Boink-boink* or *de Barricades*.

'Hey de Boink-boink!' a mighty roar came as I briefly opened the door to eject another howling monster, 'Ya Free State bawstard! Gimme back the bricks my ma paid for or I'll knock yer melt in!' Peeking out fearfully, I found a seven-year-old girl attached to the sentiment. Eventually, however, we cleared the hall and the rain of rocks gradually petered out.

'The twelve-to-sixteens come in at seven,' Felicity grinned as she packed up to leave, 'Donal will be here by then. You and him should get along just fine.'

As she left, I sat down on one of the stage sections and wondered how in the name of all that was wholesome I'd ended up in such a predicament. I then went home for the dinner that Sarah Crooks had prepared, and Billy and I watched the News. At half six I went back for the evening session.

Donal and I did hit it off. Two years older than me, he wasn't long back from the United States where he'd studied in a seminary in New Hampshire (with Bill Rolston as it turned out). He now lived back in the family home in Andersonstown, a couple of miles away.

# Chapter 4

With a big laugh and a deep commitment to social justice, he had, since beginning work at the centre, come to identify strongly with the community of Ballymurphy.

'Whatever you do,' he warned me, 'don't get in the middle if there's a fight – especially between the girls – or you're liable to get your head, or worse, ripped off.' He then named a number of specific families whose offspring were particularly homicidal. 'Cross one,' he said, 'and the whole shebang is down on top of you like piranha in a feeding frenzy.'

'How did you end up working here?' I asked.

'I fell on my head,' he laughed. He then took out a pipe, tapped out some ash, filled the bowl from a plastic tobacco-pouch and put a match to it.

'I work here four nights a week,' he told me between puffs, 'Most other nights, I play bass guitar in my da's céilí band.'

'Do you sing?' I asked with an eye to the future.

'When the mood strikes and the company's good,' he said. 'And what about you? How the hell does a Corkman end up in Ballymurphy?'

'It's a long story,' I said. I explained all about ending up in Afghanistan and Pakistan and having to turn back because of the Bangladesh War.

Just then, Big Ellen Cosgrove marched in, chirping like a sparrow in spring.

'I'm here to start up the Minstrels again,' she announced, 'I used to do the Minstrels when Paddy McCarthy was here. The wee girls love it.'

That night, as the twelve-to-sixteens emulated their younger siblings and wrecked the joint, Ellen had a group of girls in one sectioned-off corner dancing to the strains of her voice singing, *Are You from Dixie?* Their faces blackened with shoe polish, they looked like waifs from a Second World War bomb crater.

'Youse'll have to come to the wee Social next Thursday night,' Ellen shouted to myself and Donal as we paced the floor and broke up fights, 'The craic is great at the wee socials.'

With the promise of the wee socials rising from the vortex of chaos, Donal and I took the decision to reopen the senior youth club at the weekend.

'Just to get some discussion going,' I suggested, 'So we have some idea of which way to go.' Donal suggested that I bring a flak-jacket.

The eviction of the twelve-to-sixteens was not that different from the earlier experience – same insults, same shower of rocks, same threats to take back their 'ma's bricks'.

'Chisel-chin!' they shouted at Donal's bold jawline, occasionally abbreviating it to 'Chisel'.

So there we were, de Boink-boink and Chisel, ready to change the world.

At half past nine, Donal and Ellen left. As I bade them goodnight at the door of the centre, we heard more shooting from the top end of the estate.

'That's a Garand,' Big Ellen said, 'The Boys are at it again.'

Later, I learned on the News that a military patrol had raced into Kelly's Bar at the Whiterock/Springfield junction, looking for a wanted man. When they found nothing more than the usual quota of bar philosophers, they left again and were immediately shot at from Dermott Hill and the second soldier of the day was wounded.

Once the shooting had died down, I went back inside to reflect on day one. I put on the kettle and was about to pour a cup of tea when an urgent knocking sent me running for the front door. With the pounding continuing, I drew the bolts to find a group of seven determined-looking teenage lads standing there. Without a word, they strode past and marched up to the main hall where they planted themselves along one of the stage-sections. Slightly confused, I followed and explained that the centre was closing for the night. They said nothing and sat on.

'Sorry to spoil the night,' I said, 'but I need to close up.'

Nobody moved. Nobody spoke.

'You really need to leave,' I tried, hoping the Cork accent would help.

Again nobody moved or spoke, but there were a couple of snorts. It was time for one of those career-defining moments.

'Get the fuck *out*!' I roared in finest youth work fettle, 'Or I'll shaggin'-well *throw* you out!'

The seven lads looked at one another. For a minute it was touch and go. Until they calculated that I was most likely a dangerous lunatic, banished from Cork for serial depletion of the mental health budget. One by one, they rose from the stage-section and trooped out of the hall. In the months and years that followed, I would come to know them all as good friends. I would also hear wild allegations that the same lads were members of 'B' Company, Second Battalion,

## Chapter 4

(Provisional) Irish Republican Army... Some of them would do time in jail. One of them would die just up the street from my home.

Two days later, as the sectarian clashes and small-scale rioting and gun-battles continued, a sniper wounded yet another soldier near St. Bernadette's school in an action that was typical of the period. The British army came in; the IRA engaged them; a soldier was wounded; and the military retreated. Two days after that, the troops again launched a lightning raid into Ballymurphy estate, this time to the Bullring. At the time I was standing at the shops, in front of which a young man, with an underpants draped over his trousers, was tied to a lamp post. Leaping from their armoured cars, the soldiers charged to the rescue only to discover that the victim, plastered in flour, lipstick and tomato ketchup, was undergoing a traditional Belfast pre-nuptial ceremony.

'Last year,' 15-year-old Paddy McBride told me, 'they came chargin' in on the 1$^{st}$ of April on another rescue. When they got here, they found that the tarred-and-feathered guy was a tailor's dummy, with a placard around his neck sayin' *April Fool!*'

\* \* \*

Donal and I opened the BTA's senior youth club the following week and, a couple of days later, I officially took up my new post. By the end of the week, my tot of the full membership across the three sections of the club came to eleven hundred! Apart from the addition of a small cassette-player and the sing-songs led by Donal and his acoustic guitar, we were still trying to function with the two table-tennis tables, the footballs, the small snooker table and a couple of wooden panels I'd removed from a truck that had been hijacked and partially burned close to the community centre. Whereas its cargo of stainless steel sinks had gone off to revolutionise the kitchens of Ballymurphy, I had organised a team of young people to cannibalise what was left. As it happened, Paddy McDermott, the Youth Service Inspector from the Department of Education who had interviewed me that day out on the Shore Road, turned up. He was just in time to witness my team moving between the overturned truck and the community centre like a squad of leaf-cutter ants. It was then or never that Paddy knew they'd picked the right man for the job.

Nothing in Ballymurphy was untouched by the war, least of all the BTA youth club. On the one hand there were military raids when we had to watch in powerless rage as the young people were spreadeagled against the walls, often over the heaters, and searched and questioned. On the other hand, young people who'd endured months of rioting and lived with daily gun-battles and regular killings on their streets could not be expected to play tiddlywinks in the aftermath, nor did they. With explosive energy, the younger ones went doo-lally. At the same time, since anyone who didn't identify with either the Provisional or Official IRAs was stateless, the senior sessions were tense stand-offs between members and followers of both factions who at that time were fairly evenly placed at our events. This gave rise to all sorts of misunderstandings, fuelled by a lingering hatred left behind by a brief feud between the two organisations back in 1971 that had a particular resonance in Ballymurphy.

The feud which had broken out in Belfast on March 8th had claimed the life of Charlie Hughes, a Provisional, who was shot dead in Cyprus Street by the Officials. A number of other men on both sides were wounded. That evening a truce was declared; but, several hours later, Tom Cahill, Ballymurphy Provisional and brother of Frank (who was credited with much work on behalf of the BTA), and of then Provisional IRA Quartermaster General, Joe Cahill, was shot while delivering milk on the Springfield Road. As he lay slumped over the wheel of his milk van, his would-be assassin put the gun to his shoulder and pulled the trigger, leaving him paralysed down one side of his body. The legacy of that shot hung over Ballymurphy like a thunderhead. Nobody on either side had forgotten. And it took little to rev up the emotions.

'I'm back, I'm back, I'm a sticky-back,' the Officials ('Stickies') would chant along with the then popular Gary Glitter song.

'I'm back, I'm back, fuck the sticky-backs,' the Provisionals would sing. Then someone would take umbrage... Guns would be brought into schools and ominous mutterings would circulate in dark corners.

A young Provisional took all this to heart and turned up to play pool one afternoon with a pistol in his belt.

'Here,' I had to say, 'Would you mind going home and coming back when you're properly dressed?' Which he did, albeit with a level of complaint. Some time later I saw him running hell for leather through the City Cemetery with two armoured cars of Paras speeding along parallel to the railings and spraying him with sub-machine gun fire. Miraculously, he got away. (In 1981, he was one of eight men who shot their way out of Crumlin Road prison in

## Chapter 4

Belfast.)

Then Sammy Donnan who was on the BTA committee ran in one day and grabbed a cardboard box that had been sitting on my office floor for a week. Running to the back door, he chucked it out into the waste ground behind the centre. Shortly afterwards the British army came along and detonated the box which exploded spectacularly! Given the instability of IRA explosives at the time, this was an unnerving moment. On another occasion, I walked out of the centre into the blacked-out night to find that two young members of the Officials had just been shot in the legs on the far side of the Whiterock Road. They'd been 'knee-capped' by their own side for alleged anti-social activities. The peculiarities of war! To avoid offence, the Provisionals and Officials each shot their own miscreants.

'Keern' one of them said, 'Hold my hand.' Kneeling down where he lay in a widening pool of thick dark blood, I held his hand until the ambulance came to take both lads away. Then I went home to Billy's and tried to sleep. Soon afterwards, the guns were found under the floor of the Pensioners' Chalet... If it hadn't been for the BTA socials, we might have all gone stark-raving mad.

\* \* \*

Having taken up Ellen's offer, I went to my first social with Billy Scribbons and his friends, Paddy Crane from across the street and Don Mulhern from Ballymurphy Parade. To my astonishment, the rather dull hall had been converted into a kind of passable speakeasy. The stage sections had become tables; chairs had been hauled up from the Pensioners' Chalet; and a portable 'counter' had been dragged from the back wall to the office door where it became the bar. Kegs, gas and bottles of spirits materialised and the BTA committee became barmen and barwomen. During a short visit to the office, I even noticed a couple of their more enterprising helpers emptying a few drams into little bottles of their own – presumably for 'afters'.

The night began with a game of bingo, with the numbers being read by Big Alice Franklin who ensured absolute silence by glaring over her glasses at anyone who as much as uttered a sigh. 'Number one – Kelly's Eye,' Alice would call, 'Two fat ladies - Eighty-eight...' Bingo was followed by Paddy Rice playing the accordion while people in varying stages of inebriation got up to sing. Among them was the sober Owenie Meehan who was in his mid twenties and had a learning disability but was nevertheless a fully integrated member of the community. Owenie's party-piece was a wild impersonation of Elvis Presley which earned rapturous applause. There was then a Glamorous Gran display, followed by the diminutive and puny Geordie Moylen stripping to his waist and rolling up his trousers to give us 'Mr. Universe'. Next came a short céilí of sorts during which Billy, Paddy and Don joined many others on the floor in a kind of céilí-meets-the-twist. We then got back to the accordion and, as the night wore on, the songs became more spirited.

By now, my ear was becoming attuned to the Belfast sounds, and I could make sense of much of what Billy said. Meanwhile Billy, a simple man at heart, was trying to make sense of the upheaval that had become life in Ballymurphy since early 1970.

'Keern,' he asked me to one side, 'Do you think there's any danger for me here, like because I'm a Protestant?'

'No, Billy,' I assured him and there was no greater truth.

'I just mind my own business,' he said, 'I have my own wee house and everyone around is my neighbours; and I don't see any why that I should move anywhere just because others is fightin' and killin' one another.'

'You're dead right, Billy,' I agreed, 'Everyone around here has the best of respect for you.'

'Thanks Keern,' he said, 'I'm glad to hear you say that. My wife loved this place.' Then Billy's eyes brimmed for his dead wife and the times that had changed; and it was a struggle to keep a dry eye.

'Billy' I said some time towards the end of the night, 'Why are people gathering bottles on their tables?'

'It's for a special song,' Billy said, 'It gets sung at the end.'

'Aye,' Paddy confirmed, 'We need to hold on to four bottles.'

'Or eight if youse want,' Don said.

At one o'clock in the morning, after we'd had *The Rifles of the IRA*, *The Broad Black Brimmer* [of the IRA], *The Boys of the Old Brigade* [of the IRA - regularly played on the Walton's Programme on RTE before such became seditious] and *Come Out You British Huns* (a variation of Dominic Behan's *Come Out You Black and Tans*), the accordionist lilted into yet another song I'd never heard before. After a few lines it reached the chorus:

## Chapter 4

*'Oh, go to sleep my weary Provo - let the time go drifting by-y-y-y...'*

At that point everyone in the hall gripped an empty bottle and raised it above the table in front.

*'Can't you hear the bullets humming that's a Provo lullaby...'*

The bottles came hammering down on the tables in a staccato of deafening rattle.

'It's the bullets hummin',' Paddy explained.

Then, as the whole hall stood to attention, the Irish national anthem was played and we all went home.

# Chapter 5
## The Bombing Of Kelly's Bar

Ten days passed. Felicity and I continued to maintain the line against the toddlers and babes-in-arms. Donal and I, supported by Jenny Quigley and Ann Stone, held the evening lines. The doors, though they took a hammering at the end of each session, stayed in their frames. Big Alice terrorised the Housing Executive. Big Ellen ran the Minstrels. Tommy Crooks kept us up to date with war developments. Seventeen-year-old Stevie Mallon, true to his word, turned up to help with the younger kids, as did his friend Brian Fegan and Brian's brother, Michael. So did Tommy and Sarah Crooks's 18-year-old son, Tony; Frank Cahill's 15-year-old son, Philip; Philip's friend, Chuck McKinley; and Emmanuel Sheridan whose mother was a member of the BTA. From the ranks of the young women came the highly motivated and energetic Maureen Gillen and Ann Feeney from Divismore Park - that street facing the Taggart - and Vera McLaughlin who lived in our street. Mrs. Mac told us we were doing a great job. Meanwhile, Felicity worked on with Fred Bass, Jenny Quigley and Jan McCarthy, organising the summer scheme; Billy Scribbons and I continued to improve our communication; Sarah Crooks fed myself and Billy; and the May weather was good. In fact, if it wasn't for the bombs, firefights and prowling assassins, everything was tickety-boo.

Behind the barricades, Ballymurphy was pretty much a no-go area for state forces. There were no regular patrols of any type. The only time we saw the RUC was when they dashed in under heavy military guard to deliver the odd summons. Locally – and among the Brit squaddies - they became known as the Royal Ulster Cowards. The Brits, on the other hand, engaged in the occasional daylight sortie; night ventures were less frequent. But in most cases, military incursions were short-lived and ended in retreat before IRA gunfire. However, that didn't prevent the gun-battles. Shooting in the area was almost continuous. During the day the Taggart, and an army post at Vere Foster school were under constant attack and ambushes took place all the time. At night, the British bases were placed under siege and gun-battles, marked on the British end by tracer bullets, were common around the cemetery and the open space above the community centre. In a perverse way, waking up to gunfire acquired the comfort of an abnormal continuum.

There were two notable elements to those gun-battles: first, although thousands of rounds were fired, there were very few casualties on either side; and secondly, the British army displayed an astoundingly fertile imagination. There were 'hits' right, left and centre. We were all amazed that there was anyone left in Ballymurphy. The bodies were spirited away, the Brits told us. But nobody is missing, we'd point out. *Them Fenians are crafty bastards*, the media would chime, *dead, spirited away, and not missing.*

'But,' I said to an alleged IRA Volunteer one morning, in an effort to glean any speck of truth in the vanishings, 'the Brits claimed that three men were seen to fall.'

'So would you,' he assured me, 'if someone was shooting at you.'

Meanwhile, children with stones launched themselves against passing British armour, the ice-cream man did the rounds and Larry Sloan sold fish from his barrow on Fridays.

But, despite the virtual no-go status of the area, arrests, interrogations and internment continued to take a toll. People were also being lifted and taken away in armoured cars to be beaten up and sometimes dropped of in hostile areas, and there had been a couple of mini-riots, one sparked off when – in front of my own eyes - soldiers fired rubber bullets from an armoured car at a group of toddlers playing in a sand-pit outside the community centre. (I think they called it 'winning hearts and minds': any subsequent attempt to lodge a complaint got the standard our - boys-wouldn't do that response.) And, there was the constant fear of assassins.

Across the city, despite the barricades, republican and loyalist squads, and undercover units of the British army, roamed the blacked-out streets at night, looking for people to kill. Every time you went to a pub or club, there was the danger of a gunman or bomber. You watched the door until the third pint and then the pints helped you forget you were in Belfast.

The extent of that danger was forcefully demonstrated on Saturday, May 13$^{th}$, while I was still getting used to the hole in Billy's attic. My local was Kelly's bar at the top of the Whiterock Road where I'd struck up a drinking partnership with Ballymurphy's barber, Rab Maguire. Rab was a big, burly man of middle years with a round, ruddy face, thinning hair and the gentlest of personalities.

'You've cut yer own hair,' he said accusingly the first time we met, 'That's what happened to Van Gogh: he cut his hair in the pub and chopped his ear off.'

On Thursday, May 11th, I'd met Rab up in Kelly's. Earlier that day two double-decker buses had been hijacked and set on fire on the waste ground above the community centre. Kids then gathered to stone the buses. A little later, after photographing the burning buses, I was having my dinner at the window of Billy's living-room, with a clear view of the action, when two armoured cars came to investigate. They stopped with their back doors facing Ballymurphy and the soldiers piled out. Just as I was sticking a forkful of fried steak in my mouth, the IRA opened up with Thompsons and rifles. Six soldiers were wounded before they managed to make a run for it in the armoured cars, fleeing down the Whiterock Road towards the Royal Victoria Hospital.

'Rab,' I said, after recounting my tale, 'I couldn't believe they could've been that stupid.'

'It's the King's Own,' Rab said, 'They keep doing the stupidest things. Todler uses them as target practice when he's training the young bucks.'

That name again...

'Are you coming up to watch the football on Saturday?' he asked, 'England versus Germany. Hope the Germans bate the crap outta them.'

Rab was of that common Irish ilk that supports only two teams - Ireland and anyone playing against England.

'Naw,' I said, declining on the grounds that I hated football.

'I'm working myself,' Rab said, 'Otherwise I'd be here.'

We were both lucky. At 5.17pm on the Saturday, Kelly's was crowded with people watching the match and listening to the racing results from the Curragh when a car bomb left outside the front door by the Ulster Volunteer Force ripped through the bar. Sixty-three people were injured in the blast and 19-year-old John Moran later died of his wounds.

Mick Clarke of the BTA, was sitting in the back room along with Charlie Tolan and Barney Vallelly when a 'whoof' sound brought the windows in on top of them. (Ever after Mick Clarke was grateful to fellow customer Sammy McHugh who, in the face of much jocular derision, had cross-taped the glass a few days earlier to stop it from becoming lethal shrapnel in such an eventuality.) At another table

## Chapter 5

Hugh McCormick was being bowled over by what he remembered as the strongest drink of his life. 'I had just put the glass to my lips,' he recalled, 'when the world went up around me!'

Once the initial shock had subsided those who had been in the back rooms rushed into the front of the bar where most of the damage had been done. Mick Clarke and the others began to work with the wounded in the chaos and rubble of the explosion. Mick Clarke would later describe the scene:

'One man, Matt Cassidy, looked pretty bad. I got out through the front door to the street, where a young lad was lying - young John Moran, a student from Turf Lodge, who worked part-time at the bar. By then a big crowd had gathered and the ambulances were starting to arrive. We got the wounded into the ambulances, but had a terrible job with John Moran who was badly injured. Then one of the ambulance men said to me "I think you should come along too". I had a nick in the head and was bleeding heavily but hadn't noticed. Before getting in, I called back to see if my 16-year-old son Gerard, who also worked in the bar, was OK. Gerard McGlade, who thought I was calling to him, answered "Yes". But, unknown to me, my Gerard was lying outside at the Whiterock end of Kelly's with a blazing motorbike on top of him. As we made our way down the Springfield Road in the ambulance, the shooting started.'

As the first casualties were being whisked off to hospital, UVF gunmen opened up from the flats on the ridge in Springmartin, scattering rescue workers and ambulance personnel, wounding a number of people, and sending two army vehicles scurrying for the safety of the Taggart. Within minutes word was out that Jim Bryson, Tommy Tolan, Micky Clarke (whose brother had just been badly injured in the bar) and a number of other IRA Volunteers had left the top of the Whiterock Road in a taxi and made for the centre of Ballymurphy. After a quick muster of Volunteers and weapons – 26 in all - the IRA began to return fire into Springmartin. Immediately, the military at the Taggart opened up on Ballymurphy, while other soldiers fired from the flats occupied by the UVF gunmen. Meanwhile, three buses had been commandeered and thrown across the Springfield Road to obscure the firing line from Springmartin while a young IRA Volunteer, who'd been accidentally shot during an arms training session in a local house shortly before the bomb went off, was taken to safety. At Kelly's itself, once the casualties had been taken care of, the remaining bar staff and customers began to mop up the debris and board up the windows as the gun-battle raged outside. And with true Ballymurphy stoicism, drink was again being served! The stoicism, however, would cost 50-year-old barman, Tommy McIlroy, his life. Tommy had his hand to the optic when a UVF bullet came through the window and shot him through the heart.

Gerry McGlade, who was the manager of Kelly's at the time, had been blown off his feet by the explosion, but was otherwise unhurt. Later he recalled two incidents, which to his mind demonstrated the UVF preparations for the attack, and the ease with which those preparations were executed.

'The night before, we had been sitting at a table near the window having a staff drink - it was about half twelve - when a shot came through the glass and buried itself in a mirror at the other side of the bar. We immediately turned off the lights, which, with hindsight, was probably a bad mistake. I reckon that they [the UVF] were just finding their range for the next day, and us turning off the light gave them their clue. Then, on the day of the bomb, an odd thing happened: shortly before the explosion a stranger of about fifty-odd turned up at the door and said that there was trouble down the Kashmir and we should get on down there. It was a very strange thing for someone to do and to this day I think that he was probably a scout for the bombers.'

The bombing was followed by a 24-hour gun-battle between the IRA on one side and the UVF and Brits on the other. On Sunday morning amid continuous heavy gunfire, the IRA mounted a Lewis gun on a coalshed close to the rear entrance of St. Bernadette's School in the heart of Ballymurphy and later moved it to another coalshed in Ballymurphy Drive. People said that Tommy Tolan and Jim Bryson were taking turns on the Lewis while a 17-year-old young woman whose name was locally prefixed by 'Machine-gun...' had full charge of changing the ammunition pans. Then, the bizarre side of Ballymurphy's war showed up.

As the Lewis gun moved about the area, large groups of children followed, singing republican songs. At one stage they became such a danger to themselves that Bryson took drastic action to clear them out of Springmartin's line of fire. Some 50 of them had gathered on a wall behind the Lewis, cheering at each burst, and refusing point blank to go home. In desperation, Bryson swung the gun around.

'Right!' he roared, 'Anyone not off that wall in two seconds is a

## Chapter 5

goner!' It worked admirably.

Over the course of those 24 hours, 32-year-old Robert McMullan was killed by the British army or UVF; 13-year-old Martha Campbell was killed by the UVF; and 22-year-old Corporal Alan Buckley, 1st Battalion, the King's Own Regiment, was killed by the IRA as was 17-year-old John Pedlow over in Springmartin. The IRA also accidentally shot dead 15-year-old Michael Magee, who was a member of *Fianna Éireann*, its own junior wing.

Just before dark on the Sunday, the battle ended in a fierce firefight between the 26 IRA Volunteers and 300 storming paratroopers led by Colonel Derek Wilford who had presided over the Bloody Sunday massacre in Derry. And, while the battle moved through Ballymurphy, spectators gathered at the end of each street. Against anyone's better judgement, I found myself joining Tommy and Sarah Crooks and the other neighbours at the bottom of Glenalina Park.

'Jesus!' Sarah Crooks was saying, pointing down towards the Bullring, 'Look at the flashes!' She then turned towards Turf Lodge. 'Jesus!' she said again, 'Look at the flashes there as well!'

Flashes to the left, and flashes to the right: we were right in the line of fire! Was it any wonder bystanders got shot?

That night, I lay in bed, thinking of how six people who were living yesterday were now dead and how a love of football could get you killed. The attack on Kelly's had targeted men, women and children. Although nobody had yet died in the bombing itself, it was the biggest bomb attack ever on Ballymurphy and a litmus-test of its vulnerability. Yet, it was considered a normal part of the life that had overtaken the community. A week or two later, I was struck again by that same bizarre normality.

It was a Sunday, and Billy and I had run out of bread in the middle of another gun-battle.

'I'll go around to the Bullring,' I offered.

'Mind yerself,' Billy warned, 'Watch out for the shootin'.'

Everything was fine until I reached the Bullring corner, beyond which sat the line of small shops. The problem here lay in the form of an IRA man who was firing from the butcher's doorway down Ballymurphy Road, away from me, at somebody who, presumably, was firing back at him. The grocery shop lay one door past the butcher's.

'Excuse me,' I said, 'I need to get to the shop.'

'Sorry boss,' the IRA man said and lifted the rifle so I could trot past. Then at it again went he until it was time for me to go back home again, whereupon he again held his fire. In the shop, the women of Ballymurphy were chatting away about everything under the sun - except the rattle of gunfire outside!

Later that night, when things had calmed down, the heavily-built man with the broken nose, with whom I'd had the glaring competition when I'd first walked around the area, ran past Billy's front window. He had a sub-machine gun in his hands and he was letting rip at a chopper in the sky. I realised there and then that I should probably avoid glaring at people.

'Keern,' Billy said to me in all innocence when the shooting stopped, 'Who the hell are the Provies?'

I remember lying in the street one other day for a full hour during a gun-battle, with bullets taking lumps out of a wall behind me. Finally, when the shooting trailed off, I got up to go on home. 'Here son,' a woman who'd been spectating from her doorway called to me, 'There's a big dirty line down the side of yer jeans from lyin' in that gutter!' No *Are you alright?* Or *Did you get shot in the head?* Or anything like that. Just *a big dirty line down the side of yer jeans.*

A couple of days after the bombing of Kelly's, I visited Maggie and Josie down in Cavendish Street. At first, they didn't recognise me, but once I'd reminded them of who I was the china came out and a cake was bought at the corner shop, and we talked about my great grandmother who'd died since my last visit.

'She was so worried that time youse called,' Maggie said, 'She was afraid the Orangemen would get you.'

When she heard I was now living in Ballymurphy, she was aghast that, at such a terrible time, any of her relatives in Cork would come north. Although Maggie had aged a lot in the five years since I'd last seen her, and had been badly shaken by waking up one night to find a soldier – one of a patrol that had broken into the house – in her bedroom, she was still the old unbowed republican.

'Things are changing now,' she said, 'People aren't lying down any more. If your granddad was here, he'd be very proud of the young men and women we have.'

When I was leaving, she gave me a big frail hug. 'You know,' she said, 'I don't know what makes a grandson of Gerry Anderson come back to Belfast, but it lifts my heart that it's happened. It makes a young girl's blood run through an old woman's veins.'

# Chapter 6

Glaslough And Social Times...

In early May, nobody could have known about the Glaslough camp, mostly because it didn't exist. It was no more than words on a piece of paper buried in the silent depths of Mrs. Mac's handbag. Access to the bulging handbag, famous as the legendary repository of all knowledge relating to the workings of the BTA, was on a strict, need-to-know basis. But Glaslough would out.

The BTA management committee had just finished its meeting - the first I'd attended – and some of us were back in the office having a cup of tea when Mrs. Mac began to recount some of the offers that had been pouring in from philanthropic souls the length and breadth of Ireland. One had come from Desmond Leslie of County Monaghan, offering the use of his estate for a young people's summer camp...

'Can I see the letter?' I asked.

Mrs. Mac gave me a funny look, as if she wasn't used to people wanting to delve into the contents of her bag.

'If I can find it,' she said.

She began to root about in a broad wad of envelopes as I hovered above like a sparrow-hawk over a field of corn.

'Is that it?' I asked when I spotted an Éire stamp.

Mrs. Mac pulled the bag to one side, then extracted the envelope from the pile. 'I do believe you're right,' she said and handed it to me. It was an offer of the use of some coach-houses at Castle Leslie in Glaslough, just south of the border. There was also a phone number.

'We don't have any money for a summer camp,' Mrs. Mac warned as I lifted the phone.

'Sure, the money will come,' I said and rang Glaslough.

'Oh yes,' Desmond Leslie said when I explained why I was ringing, 'Would you like to come and see the place?'

'Sunday?' I asked after checking if Billy Caldwell could drive me down as I had neither car nor driving licence.

'Sunday it is,' Desmond said.

Two days later, I was joined in the new venture by a fair and lovely neighbour who lived ten doors up from Billy's house. It was mid afternoon and I'd walked into the office to find her sitting on a table. Draped in long brown hair and a dark-green maxi overcoat, she was talking to Tony Crooks.

'This is Jean Campbell,' Tony said, 'The best-looking teacher down in St. Louise's. She wants to know if she can do anything to help here at the centre.'

'I pay him,' the woman laughed, but she didn't need to.

'Well,' I said, 'You can help with the evictions in a couple of hours.'

'Before you take her on,' Tony warned, 'You better hear what she said yesterday.'

'You be quiet!' Jean said, but Tony wouldn't be silenced.

'Well,' he said, 'She asked me, "What's this new guy like?" I said "He's from Cork and in his early twenties." And *she* said "He won't last *pissing time* here."'

Not bad. At least I was making a consistent impression.

As we prepared the hall for the afternoon invasion, I mentioned to Jean the encounter during my first stroll through Ballymurphy.

'I think I was in Glenalina Road when a car drove towards me, with two guys glaring out the window. I've seen one of them since running about with a sub-machine gun.'

'What did they look like?' Jean asked.

'They were in their early-to-mid twenties. One was a heavy-set guy with a broken nose and the other guy had dark hair and a moustache.'

'Bryson and Tolan!' she said, 'What did you do?'

'I glared back.'

'Oh Jesus!' she said, 'You *won't* last pissing time if you go on like that!'

'Have you ever heard of a place called Glaslough in County Monaghan?' I asked.

'No,' Jean said, 'Why...?'

On the way out at half five, we had to run the gauntlet of some of the recently evicted who'd pooled around the front door waiting for a last chance to threaten us with the withdrawal of their mothers' bricks. One lad of about ten, who had long fair curls, a freckled face and a button nose, wanted to also share his take on Irish history.

'Hey de Barricades!' he shouted, 'D'ya know what happened in Dublin in 1916?'

*The Easter Rising*, I thought, *which led to the War of Independence which led to Partition, which led to the Civil War*... But I was treated

## Chapter 6

to a startling revelation.

'Pádraig Piaro and the Provies bate the fuck outta the Japs at the GPO,' my informant explained, finger in the air like a preacher quoting holy writ.

\* \* \*

On Sunday, in the full bloom of May's cherry blossoms, Jean and I were driven down to Monaghan by Billy Caldwell in the tenants' association's mini-bus. Several other BTA members joined us. It was pleasing to see such interest in the potential of a summer camp.

After dodging barricades on the Falls, in Portadown and in Armagh, and passing through several military checkpoints, we crossed the border at Middletown. We then swung right along a winding country lane for a few miles until we came to a dead end. The dead end was marked by a grey stone gate lodge with stepped gables, attached to the collapsing wall we'd been following for a half mile or so. To the left, a wrought-iron gate led unmistakably to an outpost of the landed gentry. We presumed it belonged to the Leslies and that we'd arrived in Glaslough.

'We're away in here,' Billy Caldwell said as the minibus engine cut. He was pointing, not to the gate, but to the door of the Pillar House bar. At that, the entire BTA contingent tumbled from the bus and disappeared, leaving myself and Jean standing in the street, taking stock.

Having, as a teenager, been escorted to the edge of one or two towns by the forces of unreason, I had come to believe that some places were best avoided by young people. Glaslough looked exactly like such a place.

We were looking at a small sleepy village, well-kept, with many old stone houses (including a former barracks of the Royal Irish Constabulary) adorned with flower-baskets and verges of trimmed grass. At its centre, the village Diamond was dominated by a stone monument to Charles Powell Leslie MP who died in 1871. Flanked by large urns of flowers and backdropped by a semi-circle of mature yew, the austere, life-sized bronze face of Charles himself, with huge sideburns and benign gaze, stared out from the upper reaches towards the Emyvale road. Some five or six feet below, a small bronze dragon spewed water into a trough, from which horses might once have drunk. The monument was, according to itself, dedicated to Charles 'by his grateful tenants' who had survived the ravages of the Great Famine thanks to the benevolence of the Leslies. Swallows flitted through the air and, in the tall trees beyond the wall, a colony of rooks engaged in an almighty squawking. I tried to imagine a bus full of Ballymurphy teenagers spilling out here and it looked like the prelude to catastrophe.

'However,' I said to Jean, 'We can only assume that Desmond Leslie knows what he's doing.'

'Well,' Jean said, 'Only one way to find out.'

We went through the gate and I realised that I'd never before graced the home of anyone who lived behind a big wall. With mixed feelings, mostly dominated by the belief that no great estate should've survived Independence, Jean and I followed a tarred avenue that curved off to the right, passing an old stone 'hunting lodge' into which the average home would've fitted several times. A little further on we came to St. Salvatore's church, a private family church set back from the avenue. Built by the Leslies in 1763 and boasting the tallest Church of Ireland bell-tower in Ulster, it was surrounded by stands of yews and a small graveyard of headstones and crypts, weathered away by the elements. I suspected it was full of tyrants, maybe even vampires. Onwards, the path ducked through fringes of laurel and mature woodland ringing with the calls of finches, thrushes, blackbirds and wood pigeons. Another 300 yards and we arrived at Castle Leslie, a rambling, four-storey mansion of pink Dumfries sandstone and grey limestone, with several annexes, steeply-sloping roofs and tall chimneys. Overlooking a broad lake and surrounded by lawns and rolling parkland, it had that aura of aloof grandeur so despised by those who thought the nice guys lost the Civil War. Beyond the house, the lake was sprinkled in silver flakes of sunlight.

'An idyllic place for a camp,' Jean said. I think she thought we were getting the lawn.

A few minutes more and we arrived at a set of steps that led to a double oak door deeply recessed in an arched porch. Above the arch, 1878 was carved in the stone. We climbed the steps, beat away the flails of history and banged on one of two thick knockers that hung from angelic female faces with wings sprouting from their heads. The knocking echoed in the hollows beyond.

'The master has been dead for ten years...' I croaked.

'Uh!' Jean said, 'Someone just walked on my grave.'

A minute passed. Then footsteps on the far side, and a bolt being drawn. The wooden door slowly opened to reveal a big smiling man

## Chapter 6

with a mop of greying hair, not fully the landed ogre I'd expected. Fifty-one year-old Desmond Leslie, former World War II fighter-pilot and laird of the manor, greeted us with a handshake and the offer of a cup of tea.

'Delighted you could come,' he said in a half-English accent, 'Please come in.'

We followed him into the hallway to one of those moments when worlds collide – Desmond Leslie's and the one of poverty and conflict that Jean and I had just driven from. The hall was enormous. Square-shaped with a mosaic floor, wood-panelled walls and a panelled ceiling, it had doors leading in all directions and a fireplace set against one wall. Above the fireplace the family coat-of-arms stood centre place while the higher levels were covered in medieval armour, swords and sabres, and the stuffed heads of gazelle, deer and antelope. Two enormous African water-buffalo skulls, complete with serrated black horns, dominated the trappings of the Victorian African hunt.

'We're in here,' Desmond said, opening the door to a massive room that looked out over the lake through three large windows, flanked by heavy green velvet drapes. If the hall was a surprise, the room was a shock of obscene opulence. Where some might have a picture rail, a thick corbelled border of carved wood ran around the upper walls. Above the border, the ceiling was criss-crossed by a plaster ridge that made it look like an iced cake. Below, an old Persian carpet covered much of the wooden floor. At one end, a red marble shelf ran half the length of the wall, while the walls themselves were plastered with great oil portraits of the Leslie ancestors and other notables. Desmond led the way through a litter of soft chairs to a small oval table. Shortly, a real live butler appeared and took the order for tea. It felt like we'd fallen through some malicious Looking Glass.

'So,' Desmond said when we were seated on large padded armchairs, 'Welcome to the home of Josephine's bed, among other things. I take it you have a plan for the summer.'

'A six-week camp,' I said, 'catering for about 20 young people each week.' I didn't mention that there wasn't a brass penny to back the proposal.

'Very good,' Desmond said, 'And maybe my sons, Shaun and Mark, can give you a hand. They're not here at the moment, but they'll be home over the summer.'

'That would be great,' Jean said although it was hard at that point to imagine a less likely meeting of worlds.

'Do you know anything about the castle?' Desmond asked.

'No,' I said, trying to mask any looks that might betray negativity.

'Well, first of all, the house sits on about a thousand acres and has been in the family in various shapes for 300 years...' *Fight ya for it*, I said to myself. This sprang from a story told by my brother, Niall – about a guy who was walking along a riverbank one day when he was accosted by a landed laird who accused him of trespassing. 'And where did you get the land?' the guy asked. 'From my father,' the landlord said. 'And where did he get it?' 'From his father', and so on until it reached the original family owner. 'And where did he get it?' the guy asked. 'He won it in battle,' the landlord said. At that, the guy took off his coat. 'OK' he said, *'I'll fight you* for it now.'

'When you come down,' Desmond said, 'We'll show you around. It's full of all sorts of memorabilia that the youngsters will enjoy. And you mustn't miss the Red Room, of course.'

'The Red Room?' Jean said.

'Oh yes, it's haunted - by my uncle.'

This was a bit of sitting-up-abruptly news.

'Captain Norman Jerome Beauchamp Leslie was killed during the First World War. His ghost was first sighted by my grandmother. She was sleeping in the Red Room one night and woke up to see him at the foot of the bed. He was poking through some letters, but when he noticed that she'd woken up, he turned around and smiled. Then he gradually faded away. Ever since then, we've had all sorts of strange happenings - bells ringing in the dead of night and all sorts of apparitions wandering the corridors.'

'We might keep that one quiet with the Ballymurphy ones, if you don't mind,' Jean said.

'More tea?' Desmond said.

He then began to share with us some views of the world. To this day, I don't know how much of it was a wind-up, but I began to soften to the man. *Duine le Dia* [a person belonging to God] came to mind – which is an Irish term for someone who's clearly mad. Describing himself as a 'discologist', he told us that he'd written a best-selling book, entitled *Flying Saucers Have Landed,* back in 1953. This had been translated into 50 languages and had become a Bible of the New Age movement.

'I have never been able to reconcile with the scientific materialism of our times,' he said, 'The mysteries of our world have been far more enticing, far more intriguing. Just look at the lessons of ancient history, archaeology and philosophy, and you'll find all the evidence you'll need of the influences of sophisticated cultures beyond those created by our kind. Take for example the enormous etchings on the Plains of Nazca. They can only be seen in their totality from the air. What else can they be other than a giant blueprint left by ancient visitors from space for other visitors from space? Then look at the Egyptian pyramids – we can't begin to understand how they were constructed. The technology can't be attributed to the people of their times. Yet, they *were* built. How do we explain these phenomena? The beings who built the great citadels of the ancients were either super-human or from outer space. When you look at all the reports of UFO sightings and alien encounters, and combine them with the technological achievements of the ancients, you can only come to the one conclusion. The Flying Saucers *have* landed.'

'A balmpot,' I whispered to Jean when Desmond wasn't looking.

According to Desmond, the first space ship had arrived from Venus.

'This can be calculated to the precise year from the ancient tables of the Brahmins, who were exceedingly accurate mathematicians. The visitors came quietly and left us their advanced skills which allowed ancient humans to build such marvels as the Mayan cities being discovered today in the jungles of Central America...'

Desmond then told us that, to his eternal gratification, *Flying Saucers Have Landed* was denounced by all of the people he loved to annoy. Arthur C. Clarke co-writer of *2001: A Space Odyssey*, called it a 'farrago of nonsense' while the astronomer, Professor Bernard Lovell, thought it should itself become a UFO and be 'dumped overboard in space'.

'When you infuriate academia,' Desmond said, 'You're normally on the right track.'

'You can say that again,' I said, as I'd always found that a handy thing to say when you can find nothing else to say.

Decades later, after Desmond had passed away, I learned that he'd written several other books, with titles such as *Hold Back the Night*, and *The Jesus File*. And that the Leslies had a long line of writers in the family. When Dean Swift visited the castle at the turn of the 18$^{th}$ century he left behind some related humour in the visitors' book:

*'Here I am in Castle Leslie with rows of books upon the shelves*
*Written by the Leslies all about themselves.'*

During the course of that afternoon conversation, Desmond Leslie never once mentioned his wartime exploits, flying Spitfires and Hurricanes. Or the family legend that had him destroying several aircraft, mostly piloted by himself.

'More tea?' Desmond asked again.

'No thanks,' Jean and I both said.

'Very well then,' he said, 'Let's go and see the coach-houses and the camping site.' He led the way out through the front door, where the outside world seemed exceptionally weird without an alien in sight. We headed back along the avenue before veering off down a light-dappled dirt track bordered by sprawling oaks and elms. Gnarled and twisted with age, they spread their limbs over carpets of primroses, bluebells and flowering wild garlic, covered in bees. On both sides, cattle grazed on strips of meadow beyond which lay the sprawling woodlands of the estate. These, according to Desmond, formed part of the ancient woods of Truagh.

'The youngsters will love it here,' he said as we finally arrived at the accommodation being made available for the camp, 'The building used to be the coach-houses and grooms' quarters. They were built away from the main house, so you can make all the noise you want and nobody will mind.'

Jean and I looked at one another. It wasn't quite what we'd expected.

The coach-houses were set into a long grey stone building with a covered gate cut through the middle. On the far side we entered what would've once been a courtyard, onto which the six arched doors opened. All had long ago fallen into disrepair. The doors were hanging off their hinges and most of the plaster was gone from the outside walls so that the stone underneath lay exposed. The 'grooms' quarters' at the lower end was a fancy name for one of the coach-houses that had been infilled at ground-floor level between the arches and had windows added at random. Additional rooms, to which we had no access, were set above the coach-houses themselves. On cursory inspection, we could see that the lot was riddled with rot and woodworm.

'I'm one of the few people in the world who can actually trace his lineage back to Atilla the Hun,' Desmond told us as Jean and I

## Chapter 6

surveyed the rotting buildings.

I poked at the soft wood of the windows and tested the upper floors for collapse potential. The place was in atrocious shape. It would take a lot of effort to even clean it. But, once the initial shock had passed, the site exposed some charm. Solitude and peace. Nothing but trees and birds, just what any young person from the city would love. (How wrong we can be!) From the upstairs windows we looked down on the grassy courtyard where coaches would once have rumbled in.

'Ideal for tents,' Desmond said.

'What do you think?' Jean asked.

'Perfect,' I said, blotting out any real thoughts.

'Then let's get started,' Jean said, 'You know what they say: never put off till tomorrow what you can do today; because if you like it enough today, you can do it again tomorrow.'

Liking it wasn't the point.

* * *

During the remainder of May and all through June, as the war raged across the city and we lurched through the social and political upheaval that swirled around us, Jean and I worked on the camp. To solve the money problem, I wrote to numerous Southern newspapers, asking the public for donations, and the response was overwhelming. People from all walks of life wrote back, wishing us the best and inserting £1 notes and multiples thereof until we had enough to pay for the transport, buy some basic equipment and subsidise the holidays. We also organised a series of weekend work camps, and were joined by Tony Crooks, Vera McLaughlin, Stevie Mallon's brother, Billy and Jean's English boyfriend, Quentin Summerfield. Donal offered to work at the camp for five of the six weeks of its duration; and at the end of term, his older brother, Kieran, who was studying music in Manchester, arrived home for the summer and offered to do likewise. Like Billy the Kid from *Easy Rider*, he rolled into Ballymurphy on a burnished Honda 175, hair and beard billowing in the wind. Liking what he saw, he stayed.

Gradually, the Leslie coach-houses and grooms' quarters came to life as we put as clean and bright a face on the old buildings as possible. It was mostly paint and patches but, with the splashes of colour and the voices of people, the place took on a cheerful air and became functional. A small pool table, dart-board, fishing-rods and books added an activities base, and some wildlife posters covered the worst features of the interior walls. Then, in a tremendous morale boost, chairs, tables, gas cookers and small box-dinghies arrived up from Cork, provided by the *Association of Human Rights for the North*, of which my father was secretary. Since 1970 the Association had been highlighting human rights abuses linked to the Troubles and providing support and respite for families in the North, and was now only too happy to come in behind the camp with a tremendous trawl of Cork city at very short notice. At the beginning of July, we finalised the preparations when we managed to borrow two large tents from the Irish army, install chemical toilets, and fit kerosene storm-lanterns around the coach-houses and the old grooms' quarters. It wasn't exactly the Ritz, but we were ready to roll.

Back in Belfast, Jean introduced me to various social clubs around town, and to her friends, Viv Holmes and Jude Goldfinch from New Zealand, who were subbing alongside her in St. Louise's College on the Falls Road, and I attended my first Belfast party at Viv and Jude's flat in Windsor Avenue off the Lisburn Road. On the same night, Viv taught me how to drive, but not as others might have learned.

Donal, Jean, her younger sister Anne, and I had gone over to Windsor Avenue in the BTA minibus, with Donal at the wheel. At the end of the night, however, Donal was in no fit state to sit behind the wheel and Anne needed to get home. As it was too dangerous to walk, I offered to drive. Others, who also considered it too dangerous to walk, piled into the back of the bus when they spotted the chance of a lift to the west of the city. However, all but Anne fled again when Viv was noticed explaining to me the difference between the gear-stick and the handbrake. Now, don't get me wrong, I had driven motorbikes, but things were laid out differently in minibuses. Eventually I kind of got the hang of it and Anne and I headed off down the eerily still Lisburn Road. It was my first time crossing the city at the dead of night, and it was precisely that: dead. Nobody else was giving the assassins a chance.

'Direct me,' I told Anne, 'I don't have a clue where I'm going.'

Anne was good at the directions, to a point. The point came at the bottom of the semi blacked-out Donegall Road. Instead of saying 'You need to turn right at the roundabout', she said nothing until it was too late. What she then said very loudly was 'Oh shi-i-it! We're on the M1!' I must admit that, wary of gunmen, I was doing the excess of speed required to dodge bullets. This meant that I was two hundreds yards down the motorway before I managed to bring the bus to a halt. I then had a new problem. Neither Anne nor I knew how to reverse.

'We've got no choice,' I said, 'We're going to have to turn around and go back the way we've come.'

'Against the traffic!' Anne said, 'You can't go back against the traffic!'

'Traffic!' I said, 'There's no bloody traffic.' I was logic to the end.

The next morning, Donal woke up in Windsor Avenue with a thick head and no bus.

'He did *what*!' he said to Viv, 'But, he can't bloody well *drive!*' At about the same time, the BTA minibus was found at the wrong end of Billy Caldwell's street.

'The miracle in my view,' Donal said later, 'is that the minibus was found at all.'

Over the course of those weeks the gun-battles intensified in Ballymurphy and people were dying around us, despite rumours of a pending IRA ceasefire. On May 21st, the danger posed by loyalist snipers was emphasised when twenty young members of the Liam McParland Accordion Band were shot at as they gathered at the steps of St. Bernadette's School, well within the perimeters of Ballymurphy. Seventeen-year-old Ann McBride was shot in the stomach and Liam Thornton, also seventeen, was shot in the left hand. On May 23rd a British soldier was killed in Springhill Avenue. Five nights later, 21-year-old James Teer of Whiterock Drive was making his way home along the Springfield Road when he was shot dead from a passing car at the junction of the West Circular Road by the UVF. A second British soldier was shot dead in Ballymurphy on June 6th.

To avoid accidental death, Jean and I did much of our late-night planning (after the community centre had closed) on the landing-floor of her house, below window level, as the bullets whistled up and down Glenalina Park. On one of those nights a new gun sounded off somewhere down the street. The next day neighbours said it sounded like an automatic .303 going off in an oil drum. It was the first night out in Glenalina Park for Ballymurphy's Lewis gun, known to the IRA Volunteers as Big Bertha.

\* \* \*

Building a social life in the midst of this unsteady environment was fraught with potential mishaps. A few days after arriving in Ballymurphy, I was visited at the community centre by a young nurse named Carol. She lived in Camden Street, just south of the city centre, and brought with her a visiting French sociologist.

'You'll have to come over our way for a drink some time,' she said as she was leaving.

'Sounds wonderful,' I said and arranged to go the following Friday.

Carol and her friends were from up country and were immersed in a folly. It was only later, when I discovered that I shared it myself, that I was able to give it a name: it was called cognitive dissonance, a belief that the war was on TV. So they introduced me to a pub of the other side's where my accent elicited a piece of friendly advice from one of the barmen. It went something like his – *Don't you open yer fuckin' Free-state gob in here boss.* Later that night, following after-pub drinks at the flat Carol shared with two others, I set off for home on foot. Radiating a virulent mathematical inclination, I calculated that the shortest distance from Camden Street to Ballymurphy lay up the Donegall Road. This was correct. It was also, alas, the main route through the loyalist heartland of South Belfast, not a prime location either for a Free-state gob. Having no idea where I was going, I quickly found myself wandering around at two in the morning behind the loyalist barricades of Sandy Row which, even at that unearthly hour, were patrolled by men in balaclavas. Some, I had to assume, were enjoying a break from their other pastime of assassinating people like me. Eventually I had to break out over one of the barricades and pray nobody wondered why.

'You're a miracle,' Jean said when she heard the story, 'A miracle you're not dead.'

On other cognitive dissonance occasions I'd leave city centre pubs late at night and, to distant rattles of gunfire, walk up the loyalist Shankill Road. From the top of the Shankill, I'd cross through Highfield to climb over loyalist barricades at the West Circular/Springfield junction. A couple of hundred yards further up the no-man's-land of the Springfield Road, the pock-marked interface houses of loyalist Springmartin and republican Springhill faced one another in mute stand-off. There, I would climb over *our* barricades into Ballymurphy. In a time of nightly sectarian slaughter, it was a lunatic thing to do: had the Highfield barricades been patrolled on any of those nights, I would most likely not be writing about it now.

## Chapter 6

'You're young,' old Joe McMullan (Mrs. Mac's husband) used to say to me over at the BTA socials, 'That means you'll have a big funeral when the Huns (Loyalists) blow you away.'

The second time I called over to see Carol and her friends was the evening of May 10$^{th}$, when the Belfast Co-op building was bombed. I was walking up Great Victoria Street about five o'clock when a massive explosion shook the town. A crack like thunder was followed by a reverberating boom, and columns of smoke rising over the city. The following morning, as daylight broke, I stood with Carol and her friends down in York Street where we finished the night's beer as the remains of the Co-op building burned to the ground. Apart from ourselves, there were only the firemen and a few cops.

# Chapter 7
## Ceasefire

On May 29th 1972 the Official IRA called a unilateral ceasefire. It was widely acknowledged that the Provisionals were now under pressure to follow suit.

On May 28th, the day before the Officials' ceasefire took hold, a premature explosion in the Short Strand had killed four Provisional IRA Volunteers and four civilians and blown away half of Anderson Street. At the same time, the fact that the partitionist Stormont parliament had been prorogued by the British in March was presented by the Dublin government as a victory for nationalists. The Provisionals, they argued, were simply mad bombers bent on jeopardising that victory. This line was also pushed in the North by the nationalist Social Democratic & Labour Party (SDLP). By June 6th, the day 22-year-old George Lee of the Duke of Wellington Regiment, was shot dead in the street behind my digs, rumours of an IRA ceasefire were rampant, as the media and clergy argued that no support remained for armed struggle.

On June 13th the Provisionals held a referendum in the Bogside, Creggan and Brandywell areas of Derry to gauge support for the IRA campaign. The response was 87% in favour of continued hostilities. But, despite the non-compromising republican exterior, peace feelers were already in motion. The Derry referendum was simply an indicator that the IRA was negotiating from a position of strength.

At the beginning of June, at a press conference in Free Derry, Seán Mac Stíofáin, Daithí Ó Conaill and Seamus Twomey (the IRA Chief of Staff, the Vice-President of Sinn Féin, and the Belfast IRA commander), offered William Whitelaw, the British Secretary of State for the North of Ireland, safe passage into the IRA-controlled section of the city to discuss the terms of a truce. Whitelaw refused the offer.

John Hume, my old pal from that first night in Casement Park, then intervened. He asked if the IRA would allow him to carry out further negotiations with Whitelaw. The republicans agreed, and discussions began between Hume and the Northern Ireland Office. Behind the scenes, Hume told Whitelaw that negotiations towards

## Chapter 7

peace were possible if the British agreed to two preconditions: first, the demands of IRA prisoners who were on hunger strike for political status, would have to be met; and secondly, Ballymurphy man, 24-year-old Gerry Adams, already a key member of the Republican Movement, would have to be released from internment to take part in the negotiations.

The release of Gerry Adams presented no real problem for Whitelaw. The fact that the British had initially lifted all the wrong people and were suffering the unsavoury publicity surrounding internment, had meant that 550 internees, more than half of the total held, had already been released while the British worked on an alternative method of achieving the same end. One more release wasn't going to create any undue ripples.

However, the granting of prisoner-of-war status to the IRA prisoners (a status automatically granted to the internees in the Long Kesh cages) would have long-term consequences for any future attempt by the British to criminalise the war. But Whitelaw and Maudling, the Home Secretary, argued that the only way forward was to negotiate with the IRA. Political status was accordingly granted to both republican and loyalist prisoners on June 20th 1972.

The IRA ceasefire came at midnight on June 26th after one of the most violent days of 1972. Jean and I were working on the landing again - and listening to the gunfire and explosions that had been continuous all day.

'That's a hell of a lead-up to a ceasefire,' Jean said, 'Do you think we've got the date wrong?'

In the 24 hours leading up to the truce, the North was rocked by IRA attacks: bombings, gun-attacks, hijackings, and bank robberies. Down in Castle Street, three 'nuns' robbed the Allied Irish Bank. An RUC man was killed in Newry, a soldier was killed in Derry, and at a minute to midnight, a second soldier was killed in Belfast. Then midnight, and silence.

'I suppose,' Jean said at one minute past twelve, 'that it could be safe to move back down to the living-room again. Seeing as the war is over.'

\* \* \*

Next morning the first death of the ceasefire took place on the Whiterock Road. There was a burst of gunfire, followed by pandemonium. The IRA had shot dead 38-year-old Bernard Norney of New Barnsley Crescent at a checkpoint designed, ironically, to protect us all from loyalist assassins. He had failed to stop and a jumpy Volunteer had taken him for an enemy. It had been a terrible mistake; but Bernard Norney was no less dead.

Following the killing, the IRA established a local HQ in the wrecked flats above the Bullring shops and set about erecting sentry posts at all entrances to the area. Armed men, who became part of the furniture, walked the streets. Quite independently, children built extra barricades and some Hoorah-Henry with a jackhammer cut a trench across the bottom of Glenalina Road which, I thought, was a bit over the top. To add to the new IRA presence, a commandeered jeep, emblazoned with a republican logo and the words *Óglaigh na h-Éireann* [Irish Volunteers], carried out mobile patrols. It had a single car-seat welded to its roof for a better view. When it wasn't raining, Tommy Tolan rode about on the roof, but my alleged lookalike eluded me again. Every time I saw the jeep the seat was empty. Owenie Meehan, who did the Elvis impressions at the BTA socials, was also at the IRA checkpoints, complete with mask and toy pistol. Apart from Owenie, you'd have to guess who else was on the checkpoints as everyone had now taken to wearing masks. Jean used to get particularly perplexed about this. I was in her car late one night when we were stopped on the Whiterock Road.

'Is that so-and-so?' Jean asked, trying to see through the mask.

'No, it's not. And never you mind,' came the answer, heavily disguised as some dialect of Swahili.

'It's not?' Jean persisted, 'Then is it such-and-such?'

'Jean, will ya for fuck's sake please stop asking me who I am,' came the plea from the deadly IRA man.

At the beginning of the truce, despite the shocking killing of Bernard Norney, a strange peace reigned inside our protected perimeters. The arms raids and swoops were over, and the gun-battles had come to an end. The Brits had agreed to stay out of the estates, their only presence being an occasional drive by on the Whiterock Road, during which they and the IRA sentries called one another ugly bastards, arseholes and thick shites. Such was the optimism that a clean-up of the streets was organised by myself, Jean and Donal, assisted by dozens of young people with brushes and buckets. For some long-forgotten reason, this was carried out at night! At the same time, the unsinkable Mrs. Zimmerer, a large, retired German woman who wrote for the Vatican newspaper and lived a few doors up from Billy Scribbons, had her house soundproofed. Having been

## Chapter 7

drawn to the area by the conflict, and raised funds for the BTA, the painfully posh Mrs. Zimmerer was not beyond making demands on the recipients of her benevolence. The preservation of her sanity in the face of child-noise was, she explained, the responsibility of the BTA which boiled down in the end to the ever-obliging Billy Caldwell.

'There's even talk about negotiations and a Brit withdrawal,' Donal said a few days into the truce.

I was delighted.

'That would mean that old Maggie down in Cavendish Street would see the island united again,' I said. I explained a little about that particular situation. 'She'll be over the moon.'

Steve Pittam, a 22-year-old Quaker volunteer, who had just completed a degree in Social Administration at Nottingham University and now lived up in Moyard, wasn't so sure.

Although not of that culture, Steve looked every inch a hippy. Of slim vegetarian build with long fair hair and a sprightly spring to his step, he could have blended into any of a thousand locations between Belfast and Kathmandu. He also had the required laid-back attitude to life, and the quirky distinction of being one of the few people in the world to live in an entire block of flats, albeit abandoned, bullet-riddled and in the line of loyalist and military fire. The block next door, he told us, was the Moyard Working Men's Club.

'The only thing I have to worry about,' Steve said the first time we met, 'is that someone will break in and steal my camera. Once that happens, I'll have *nothing* to worry about!'

Eventually when it did happen, he just breathed a hippy sigh of relief.

Steve had first set foot in Belfast (and Moyard) in the summer of 1971 when he was 21. Arriving as a medium-term volunteer working with the Voluntary Service Bureau, he was asked to do the preparatory work for an international workcamp that was going to operate in the brand-new Moyard Community Centre for three weeks. He was then to lead the workcamp and stay on for a few weeks afterwards. Having completed the second year of his degree course, there was an expectation that he'd engage in a social action project during the summer holidays, and he'd heard about the Moyard opportunity from friends, Bob and Ruth Overy - Ruth was working for VSB at the time.

'We had a fantastic group of students that year,' he later recalled,

'We operated the play-scheme from a maisonette in what became known as the 'Welfare Block' in Moyard Crescent as well as from the new Community Centre. To add some more value to the effort, four students stayed on after the workcamp, but we all know what happened in August 1971. [The Internment killings.] One of the four was the renowned Ali Khilleh - the Palestinian refugee from Copenhagen, after whom there was talk of re-naming Corpus Christi Church as St. Ali's following his and my efforts to bring out the body of Fr. Mullan in the battle that followed the introduction of internment.'

Steve became so involved in the community that he was on the point of asking for a year off university; but after internment, and the destruction of so much of the positive community development work in which he'd been engaged (which included building an Adventure Playground in New Barnsley) he decided to complete his degree instead. During his final year he talked to the Quakers in Nottingham, and they offered to support him if he decided to go back to Belfast. He had returned in June 1972 to lead the VSB workcamp in Moyard & New Barnsley again, but this time he was on a more permanent lease.

'It will be great if the ceasefire works,' he said, 'But it seems there's a lot to be sorted out. And there's no telling how the loyalists will react, whether or not they'll go along with whatever comes out the other end.'

'Then the Brits will have to face down the loyalists,' I said.

'I'm not sure they will,' Steve said.

Steve's doubts were well founded. The loyalists didn't like much of what they saw. In fact, they went berserk. Instead of being granted the full onslaught against nationalist areas that they were demanding, they now saw republicans - the avowed enemies of *their* state - openly carrying guns on the streets, and the British army *pulling back* from nationalist areas. A leaflet distributed in Ballymurphy and Andersonstown, announcing that the IRA was assuming full control of 'law and order' in republican areas, sent them into a further frenzy. While paramilitary groups warned of Armageddon, and Paisley threatened the state, William Craig, former Stormont Minister and leader of the right-wing Vanguard movement, stated that, 'If the security forces do not discharge their duty in apprehending the IRA terrorists, the loyalists will have no option but to clean them out themselves and take such action as is necessary against the republican community.'

I remember watching the ranting Craig on TV and he reminded me of Hitler. I also remember how vulnerable West Belfast felt, faced with the prospect of another round of loyalist pogroms, with the loyalists better armed and organized this time around. In the community centre, it was clear that the experiences of August 1969 had left a shaky legacy.

'The Brits will just stand by again like they did in Bombay Street,' Tom Farrell, one of the quieter members of the BTA said, 'and the IRA won't be able to stop them either.'

'The IRA will do alright,' Big Barney McGivern said, 'As long as the barricades are maintained.'

'What if the Brits bulldoze them away?' Tom said.

'In the name of God!' Mrs. Mac said, 'Is there no optimism left?'

But optimism was hard to hold. During the next two weeks gun-attacks on nationalist areas, riots, mass intimidation of nationalists out of all remaining mixed neighbourhoods, and a string of assassinations punctuated the truce. In Belfast huge sections of the city were barricaded off and patrolled by armed vigilantes. If there had been access to artillery, we could well have ended up with a Bosnia.

As it was, fifteen people died in sectarian killings between June 27th and July 9th and three others were shot dead as they crashed through IRA roadblocks. Among the dead was 19-year-old English student, Paul Jobling, who'd been staying in the block of maisonettes inhabited by Steve at the top of Moyard Parade. Paul had come to visit a friend of his called Bob, a mature student from the Co-operative College in Loughborough who was part of the VSB workcamp. He had then gone to London for an interview with Voluntary Service Overseas, and was on his way back when he was abducted. Having only ever been in Belfast for a day or two, he'd tried to get back from town up the wrong road. On July 1st he was found shot dead on waste ground in loyalist Ballygomartin.

'He wasn't even a member of the workcamp,' Steve said, 'He was just staying with his friend Bob.'

By the beginning of July, the optimism was all gone. On Monday, July 3rd, amid rumours of imminent loyalist invasions, we were again evacuating children from the community centre to the refugee trains that would take them across the border. Word had come that the UDA was massing on the Springfield Road for what looked like a pending invasion, intent on penetrating the republican no-go areas. In the community centre there were different assessments of the situation.

'The Brits are on the Springfield too,' Tommy Crooks said, 'There's hundreds of them, with Saracens and heavy machineguns. But, you watch, they'll let the UDA through.'

'Don't you worry none,' Alice Franklin said, 'We'll bate the crap outta them all.'

Mary McMahon, a younger woman from South Armagh who was associated with the Officials' camp, thought we should listen to Mrs. Mac and be a bit more optimistic. Mary, through her own tireless work in the community, had become a good friend of Mrs. Mac.

'In the meantime,' she said, 'Just in case, let's get the children a holiday.' Mary's was ever the practical view.

By seven o'clock 8,000 uniformed UDA men singing *The Sash* had gathered on the Springfield Road, facing the British army with guns, cudgels, iron bars, riot shields and bin lids. By half seven, a quiet foreboding had descended on Ballymurphy. We were all glued to the radio, scanning the channels for the crackle of RUC messages and any sign that the UDA had broken through the military lines.

But they didn't. Instead, the two sides came to a friendly arrangement.

It turned out that the UDA call-up had in fact followed an earlier confrontation between some of its units and the British army after an attempt had been made to seal off another loyalist-controlled area. This time, however, the area was of strategic interest to the military, and the soldiers Tommy Crooks had seen, supported by a heavy convoy of armoured vehicles and Browning machine guns, had been sent out to prevent the barricades from going up.

To defuse the situation, Whitelaw and General Robert Ford, GOC Land Forces, went into talks with the UDA. Four hours later, it was announced that joint UDA/British army patrols would be conducted in the Lower Springfield, and checkpoints between the Springfield and Shankill would be similarly controlled. The Brits and the UDA both hailed the outcome as a victory. As the late News told of further attacks on nationalists in Bangor and Carrickfergus, we sat in the community centre and wondered just how many more victories the truce could handle.

Over the next week, in the build-up to the 'Twelfth', hooded and masked members of the UDA, UVF and Tartan gangs attacked

## Chapter 7

nationalist homes and business premises while assassinations and sniping attacks were stepped up. At the end of a fine tether, Tommy Tolan eventually decided to strike back directly at the UDA's Springmartin club. He and another Volunteer drove across from Ballymurphy with two rifles, ran from the car and kicked in the club door. As they did, two powerful arms wrenched Todler's rifle from his hands and the door was kicked shut in his face. Both Volunteers had to flee for their lives!

But, even as an IRA delegation, including the freed Gerry Adams, was flown to London on July 7th to meet secretly with representatives of the British government, the truce was doomed. It collapsed in West Belfast two days later, on Sunday July 9th. With the benefit of modern technology, we were able to watch it all on TV.

A number of nationalist families, granted tenancies in Lenadoon, had arrived with their furniture in the mixed estate on Friday afternoon as the London meeting was under way. A contingent of the UDA had also arrived to prevent them from occupying the homes. The situation had been one of stalemate until Sunday, when the British army decided on a show of force - against the nationalists. As tension rose in Lenadoon, young men from many parts of West Belfast began to converge on the estate. Standing on the Whiterock Road, I watched a truck leave Ballymurphy with dozens of men – including many of the area's IRA Volunteers – on board.

'Here Ciarán!' one of them shouted, 'Have ya got a couple of hours to spare?'

It was the last sentence I associated with the 1972 ceasefire.

In the afternoon the Brits and the UDA blocked a furniture van that was attempting to unload in front of one of the vacant units in Lenadoon. A Saracen rammed the truck and triggered off a riot. CS gas and rubber bullets were fired at the nationalists. IRA leaders, Seamus Twomey on the spot, and Daithí Ó Conaill in Dublin, attempted to have the troops called off. Ó Conaill managed to get Whitelaw, who was in London, on the telephone. Whitelaw told him he would confer with his aides and ring back. But the phones must have all broken down.

At about five o'clock, as the Lenadoon riot continued, the first shots were fired.

'That's out of order,' Billy said as the fierce gun battle played out on the six o'clock News, 'We'll never have peace now.' And as the news continued to trickle in from Lenadoon, it became clear that the chance of peace had indeed been lost. At nine o'clock, the IRA Army Council announced that the truce was over and that all IRA units had been instructed to resume offensive action. Less than an hour later, on that bright summer's evening, the gunfire started in Ballymurphy.

There's a strong belief among the people of Ballymurphy that Derry's Bloody Sunday and the fact that the British army felt it could murder civil rights marchers with impunity was a result of them having already gotten away with it once. During the course of the two days that followed the August 9th Internment swoops of 1971, nine civilians died violently on the streets of Ballymurphy at the hands of the British military. Of the many others who were wounded, two more would die later, bringing the total to eleven. But there were no cameras and there was no outcry. Five months later, Bloody Sunday happened. Two massacres had given the military the idea it could do it again. On Sunday, July 9th 1972 it did.

I was in Billy's when the shooting broke out, but the ferocity of the gunfire brought everyone out of their homes to find out how on Earth the breakdown of the truce had somehow jumped from Lenadoon to our streets. Cautiously, small groups moved towards the location of the gunfire; and as we did, word came through that several people were dead in Westrock and that the Brits were firing into the houses from Corry's timber yard and shooting anything that moved. The best advice was to get back indoors as the IRA was taking up positions.

By the time we got back to our homes, the second most brutal attack by state forces on the civilians of Ballymurphy had already reached its bloody climax, although the gun-battles that followed would last for several days. What happened was later pieced together from the accounts of scores of witnesses.

Some time around 9.50pm an army sniper in Corry's had opened fire on two cars sitting in Westrock. One immediately reversed, the other tried to take cover among the estate's aluminium bungalows. As the occupants of the cars tumbled out, the sniper fired another burst, hitting 19-year-old Martin Dudley in the back of the head and leaving him seriously wounded. Three minutes later, Paddy Butler, a 38-year-old married man with five children, went to get a priest for Martin Dudley. As he left, Brian Pettigrew and John Dougal, both seventeen, ran towards the wounded Martin Dudley. But, no sooner had they broken cover than a second sniper opened

## Chapter 7

fire, killing John Dougal, a member of *Fianna Éireann*, and hitting Brian Pettigrew several times in the chest. Seven minutes after the first shooting, Paddy Butler arrived back at the scene, along with Fr. Noel Fitzpatrick and 14-year-old David 'Dean' McCafferty. After parking the car at Corpus Christi Church, the priest and his companions began to make their way towards the dead and wounded. Someone then shouted that a young girl had been shot and a priest was needed. She was 13-year-old Margaret Gargan who died in a fusillade of bullets fired by a third sniper positioned further down in Corry's yard. Fr. Fitzpatrick and Paddy Butler ran from the cover of a house. The first sniper opened up and shot the priest, the same bullet passing through him and killing Paddy Butler. Young Dean McCafferty attempted to drag the bodies clear of the line of fire and was shot to pieces by the same sniper.

In just under ten minutes five people had been murdered in Westrock by British army marksmen. Although the British army claimed later that night to have hit a number of 'gunmen' during a prolonged gun-battle with the IRA, it did not officially accept responsibility for the Westrock killings, and suggested that loyalists might have been responsible - that they could have sneaked into the yard during 'the general din'. The suggestion of loyalist involvement later gained some credence when it was discovered that, whereas all the dead were killed by army bullets, Brian Pettigrew had been hit by .22 calibre bullets of unknown origin. However, along with the sandbagged hide in the timber, reported by IRA intelligence, there was another army observation post in Corry's. If loyalist gunmen were operating from the yard (closed for the weekend) it is highly unlikely that they could have done so without the acquiescence of the military.

By the time the IRA Volunteers took up defensive position – most of them having to get back from Lenadoon - the slaughter at Westrock was over although the shooting from Corry's would go on and several other people would be wounded. Witnesses described how people were pinned down everywhere, in all the alleyways. If there was a target, the Corry's snipers shot at it; if not, they just shot into the houses. And when the ambulances came, they were shot at too. It was only under the cover of heavy IRA fire that the dead and wounded could be taken away. But, despite the IRA fire, Dean McCafferty's body had to be carried through one of the houses and hoisted out through a back window, while it took over half an hour to get John Dougal's body and the wounded Brian Pettigrew out of Pettigrew's garden where they'd lain since they were hit. People then had to cut a hole between the Pettigrews' house and Campbells' next door so the bodies could be carried under cover of the second bungalow to a hole in the wall of nearby Corrigan Park, and over on to the Whiterock Road to an ambulance.

What happened in Westrock was murder. Murder by agents of the state who well knew that the people they were shooting were civilians. Yet, as was the case in Ballymurphy during Internment week, and again on Derry's Bloody Sunday, nobody was ever charged. The community was left to deal with the trauma and the families were left to bury their dead and that was it. Tough shit Paddy. And, tell me Paddy, why did people join the IRA?

I still remember vividly the horror on Sarah Crooks' face when she came running up the street in convulsions that night.

'They're after killing Fr. Fitzpatrick!' she roared, 'And Paddy Butler! And the wee girl Gargan! What can we do against them – and they murdering priests and wee ones?'

Later, I sat in Billy's house, consumed by horror and anger at such random murder. It was a powerless impotent rage coupled with a waiting for the next News when you might learn that someone had hit back for the murder of defenceless people. Then the guilt of wanting someone else to do what you weren't about to do yourself. It was a feeling I would come to know well. It would surface when people were beaten senseless in the street or in military bases or in the back of Saracens; when children were shot to death by plastic bullets; when innocent people were cut down in cold blood; when homes were destroyed and families terrorised in the dead of night. There were many such times when it might have been easy to take up arms.

On Monday, July 10$^{th}$, as the newspapers reported widespread violence across the North in the wake of the ceasefire breakdown, and the guns blazed around the Upper Springfield, wounding several civilians and soldiers, the undertakers refused to come into Westrock so that the IRA had to bring in the hearses.

'It was the eeriest thing I've ever seen,' one of the Volunteers later told me, 'Just a single black hearse coming down a totally deserted street, Bryson driving and Todler riding guard with a rifle.'

'Bryson has the Lewis gun down in Springhill Avenue,' Billy said on Monday evening, 'Big Ellen Cosgrove says he's rakin' Corry's from the verandah above Mary's shop. Ellen says that Lewis gun

## Chapter 7

came down from Cork. Do you know if that's true?'

'I heard a rumour that it belonged to an old Fianna Fáil man,' I said. 'He's supposed to have had it from the Twenties.'

'What's a Fianna Fáil man?' Billy asked, 'Are they Provies too?'

And there were crazy stories coming out of Westrock, of how - when everything that moved was being shot - a young woman with a pram had walked straight through the middle of the gun-battle!

And of Bridget Maguire who would only smoke Gallagher's Greens.

On Monday morning, as the battle raged around her home, Bridget ran out. Some time later, after a heated debate in the house, her son, Martin, who was engaging the Corry's snipers, heard his name being called. He looked around in astonishment to find his sister-in-law, Ann, running from one bungalow to the next.

'Martin,' the awful request came, 'Would you ever give us some cover. Yer ma wants 20 Greens'!

Over the next six days the IRA hit back hard, killing eight soldiers and an RUC man and wounding many others. Cities and towns were blitzed while enormous landmines exploded in rural areas. And as the military carried out massive punitive raids, destroying nationalist homes, beating up residents, and arresting and torturing suspects, the flood of refugees to the South increased. By July 16th, 5,000 people had crossed the border.

I had left, with twenty-five teenagers, for County Monaghan.

# Chapter 8

## In The Woods Of Truagh

A week after the breakdown of the truce, we left Ballymurphy on a rented Ulsterbus coach with a jumble of cases, bags, food and equipment. An hour and a half later, we were disgorged at the entrance to the Leslie estate where Desmond Leslie was waiting. Beside him stood a smiling, bearded, dark-haired man in his early twenties, whom I assumed to be one of the two helpers I was expecting from Cork.

Desmond, flamboyant as ever, welcomed everyone. He asked about the journey from Belfast and whether or not we'd had any trouble with barricades or riots. He then introduced the man beside him as his son, Shaun; and while the young people flocked around Shaun, wanting to know where the castle was and did it have a ghost, Desmond turned to me.

'Are you alone?' he asked with a look of horror on his face.

'Oh no,' I assured him, 'Help is on its way from Cork and Dublin. I thought some of them might have arrived by now.'

'Nobody has arrived yet,' Desmond said, 'But if you're stuck, Shaun is happy to give a hand.'

Shaun, who was already helping to carry bags and cases, smiled.

'OK,' he called, 'Let's go!' I was amazed.

Like the Pied Piper, he led the way through the gate, followed by myself, Desmond, and a long procession of excited teenagers in their skinners and mini-skirts. Trailing bags and equipment, we looked like some kind of hurried evacuation from a disaster zone.

'Oh Keern,' one of the girls shouted as we caught sight of the castle, 'Is that where we're staying?'

I hated to disappoint her. But the question did trigger a thought.

'Has the army come with the tents?' I asked Desmond.

'No,' Desmond said, 'There's been nobody here with any tents.'

'That's half the accommodation,' I explained, 'But I suppose it's still early enough in the day...'

This was not good news. As we followed the long, tree-lined lane that led from the castle down to the coach-houses, and the young people shrieked that all the cows in one of the strips of meadow were 'bulls', I pondered that old Gaelic saying that translates

## Chapter 8

roughly into, *The day of the big wind is not the day to be tying your roof down*. I tried to imagine twenty-five teenagers and three or four adults stuffed onto the floors of the grooms' quarters and it wasn't working too well. Then, in the nick of time, the Cavalry arrived. We heard the sound of a motor and turned to see a military jeep trundling its way down the dirt track.

'Where do you want these?' one of the two soldiers asked when they reached the tail end of our procession.

'Just follow us,' Desmond said whereupon the jeep tagged onto the rear, adding to the impression of a disaster evacuation.

Down at the coach-houses, the soldiers dropped the tents in the green space allocated as the second accommodation-block. They then looked at the semi-derelict buildings behind and the surrounding woodland and profound lack of modern facilities.

'How long are you going to be here?' one of them asked.

'Six weeks,' I said.

'Back in the barracks,' he laughed, 'We'd call the likes of this extreme survival.'

Nowadays, if you brought young people to that particular site, they would probably agree, text their mothers, and call for a police rescue. But there was none of that when we arrived in Glaslough. In fact it was the opposite. The young people adapted like chameleons, throwing themselves wholeheartedly into the adventure, made all the more so by the lack of mod cons. In great excitement, bags were dropped and everyone ran off to explore the site and the immediate area. They then converged back on the grooms' quarters and we had lunch – sliced pan with cheese and ham, washed down by gallons of tea with powdered milk. And as everyone crowded around, Desmond again explained his relationship to Attila the Hun, and Shaun promised to lead a guided tour of the castle later in the week. It was then time to allocate the sleeping spaces in the house and erect the two ridge tents – one for boys and one for girls.

Just after three o'clock, when Desmond and Shaun had left, the first of the reinforcements arrived. A car pulled up at the site with the two Corkmen I'd been expecting. *The students are here!* rose the cry and the car was immediately mobbed. Inside, the driver and passenger sat rigid and stared out through the windscreen as if expecting to be overturned at any moment. *Hey mister*, the teenagers shouted, *What do they call you*, and *Youse sound just like Keern. Are youse from the Free State too?* At first I wondered if the reinforcements might flee. They had that unsettling look on their faces. However, they held their ground and gradually, gingerly, stepped from the car, to be instantly mobbed. It was great to hear the familiar accents. They brought succour and affirmation.

I can no longer remember what the two lads did in Cork. They might have been teachers but I wouldn't swear on that. But within minutes, you could tell that two better candidates for that particular afternoon could not have been found. Both were in their mid twenties, one with a big beard and a mop of long curly hair, on top of which sat a cloth cap that half covered his eyes, the other with jet-black, collar-length hair and a thick curling moustache that made him look, according to the girls, like Omar Sharif.

'Are you Ciarán?' the bearded one asked as he waded through the throng, 'We're the ones that Criostóir [my father] sent up. I'm Eugene and that's Tony back there, being ate alive.'

'Great to see you!' I said and meant it. I then explained that anyone who came to work on community ventures linked to Ballymurphy were 'students' whether they were seventeen or seventy.

'We'll be anything you want, boy,' Eugene said.

We went indoors and were shortly joined by Tony who looked as if he'd been trampled by wild horses.

'Well boy,' he said, 'You've got your hands full here. These kids are mad. Must be all that trouble up in Ballymurphy?'

'Jaysus boys,' Eugene said, 'We need a plan. What's the plan?'

\* \* \*

Although there was no plan, that afternoon looked after itself. We grabbed the fishing rods, collected some worms and went down to the lake. There, some of the young people fished, others took out the box punts, and others went for a swim, some of the girls opting to go in fully clothed rather than change into swimsuits! After a couple of hours at the lake, we headed back to base and made dinner. It was Spam, instant mashed potato and peas, followed by tea, after which wood was gathered for the evening campfire. There then settled over us, in the grooms' quarters, an enchanted period of calm. We had a few rounds of pool. Some of the boys played darts. Some of the girls read. Mixed groups played board-games. It was then time to head out into the night with a couple of storm-lanterns to light the fire.

Pulling chairs from the coach-houses, we formed a big circle around the flames. Eugene and Tony led the sing-song while the

## Chapter 8

young people alternately joined in or led with their own songs or lay back on the grass and enjoyed the stars and the silence and the bats that flitted every now and then into the firelight.

Some time around eleven, a flashlight shone out of the darkness and we were joined at the fire by a grey-haired man in his late fifties. Dressed in Wellington boots, battered sports jacket and trousers, and cloth cap, he introduced himself as Jack, the Leslies' gamekeeper, who lived alone in the old game-keeper's lodge at one of the entrances to the estate. Immediately, Jack was mobbed and made to feel so fully at home that he became an almost permanent fixture over the coming weeks, calling periodically throughout the day and opening his home in turn to each group of young people. With hindsight, he was probably a lonely man in his own life, and there was nothing more certain to dispel loneliness than a busload of Ballymurphy's young.

'How would you all like to go for a walk in the woods tomorrow?' he asked, 'I was thinking we could go and see what animals and birds we could find, and maybe set a snare for rabbits.'

This offer generated great enthusiasm and I must admit that the possibility of a rabbit or two to augment the food supply was not altogether unappealing.

'Yeah! Brilliant!' Eugene enthused. There was a cheer for Jack.

'I heard the singing on the way down,' Jack continued, 'Is anyone going to sing me another song?'

'Absolutely!' Tony said. He jumped up and went off to the coachhouse to get Jack a chair, while the young people gave a rousing rendition of *The Boys of the Old Brigade*, the Long Kesh anthem. Jack then filled us in on some of Desmond Leslie's background.

'Desmond's grandfather was the $2^{nd}$ baronet of the Castle. He was a man called John Leslie, who was educated at Eton and Cambridge. And, if you believe the stories, he didn't take too kindly to those places. He used to say that Eton was a terrible place - 'gruesome' was the word he used - especially around St. Patrick's Day when the Irish lads were bullied and beaten for being Irish. But, at the same time, he disagreed with the Home Rule movement. He used to lead the Monaghan Militia in the 1890s and had the Ulster Volunteer Force drilling here on the estate in 1914.

'On the other hand, Desmond's father, Shane Leslie, the $3^{rd}$ baronet - and a first cousin of Winston Churchill – became a Catholic when he was at Cambridge and became an Irish nationalist. Same as his father, he hated Eton, with all the beatings and bullying of the Irish students. He wouldn't send Desmond or his brother, John, to study there. Instead they got educated at Benedictine schools in England...'

'Was that where the flying saucers came from?' I asked.

'Ah,' Jack smiled benignly, 'The flying saucers...'

This set off an animated discussion about where exactly flying saucers had been seen in Belfast.

Some time after midnight, we called it a day. Or so we thought. Everybody went to bed, and, apart from the occasional squeak of a bat, there wasn't a sound. However, what Eugene, Tony and I had failed to factor into the equation was that this was the first night outdoors for most of the young people and their first night without electricity. Nor had we considered all the liberties, and configurations of the imagination, allowed by that combination. We hadn't counted, for example, on the presence of woodland 'banshees', or the fact that the boys would sneak into the girls' tent and that everyone would eventually run riot into the night. The only spoilsports would be the three of us. It was a bit like the BTA centre at eviction time, except in the dark and without the benefit of a steel door beyond which the problem could be confined.

In the morning, over the corn flakes, a new plan was formulated.

'Right boy,' Eugene said, 'What we need to do is exhaust the little buggers before tonight.'

'We could take it in turns,' Tony suggested, 'While one of us is running the legs off them, the other two could be catching up on last night's sleep.'

'And we have Jack on our side,' Eugene reminded us, 'We can ask him to go up lots of hills.'

Apart from food breaks that day, we never stopped. We followed Jack through the woods, checking out on foxes, rabbits and badgers. We swam in the lake, raced the box-punts, and had a wood-collecting marathon. We organised football and tree-climbing and a run to the village. And we got Shaun to conduct his tour of the castle, during which some of the girls took great glee in bouncing on the bed of Napoleon's Josephine – allegedly 'to see if it worked'. And at the end of the day we were wiped. The teenagers, meanwhile, were ready for another night on the razzle.

After those first two nights, no further attempts were made to regulate sleep. Instead, we relied on seeing the night through to

## Chapter 8

the bitter end until we were the last persons standing. By then, the woman who had introduced this tactic was standing beside us.

Eileen Costigan arrived from Dublin on the afternoon of the third day. It was like a sparkle had fallen from the sky. One minute she wasn't there. The next, she was framed in the doorway of the groom's quarters, late twenties, smiling, with long fair hair cascading in waves across her shoulders. Although I was expecting her, she still surprised us. It was the suddenness of her appearance (we hadn't heard the car) and the laughter that bubbled up as soon as she had one look at what lay beyond the door.

'Now,' she said, 'There's primitive, there's very primitive, and then there's this.'

'You can only be Eileen!' I said, hugging her like you would a log if you were drifting on the ocean, 'You have no idea how glad we are to see you!'

'Oh God!' she said, 'That sounds ominous.'

At that, there was a great squeal from the direction of the tents. It was followed by an avalanche of bodies, come to see the new 'student'. Like everyone else who met the teenagers, Eileen was immediately overwhelmed by the cheeky friendliness that greeted her. *Miss, you talk funny. Are you married? Is one of these yer boyfriend?* No question was too personal. Soon they all knew that the 'student' was a teacher in Dublin, and that she came originally from a small, Gaelic-speaking community in County Meath.

'Well,' Eileen said when the questions had been exhausted, 'There's plenty of energy to be harnessed. I can see the value in having vast acres of space into which it can be dissipated.'

'We've tried that for the past two days,' Eugene choked, 'And the only thing dissipated is *us*!'

'I see,' Eileen laughed, 'Well, there's always the escape route back to Dublin.'

'Whatever you do, girl,' Tony pleaded, 'Don't abandon us, or all hope will be lost.'

'We'll steal your tyres,' I threatened.

Maybe it was the presence of a strong humorous woman, or maybe it was the change in tactics, but from day three everything seemed to calm down, although it was all relative.

'I have a flat in Rathmines,' Eileen said a couple of days later as we both walked to the village for groceries, 'If you feel like bringing small groups to Dublin, you're welcome to crash out on the living-room floor.'

I have a lingering feeling that it was an offer Eileen lived to regret.

\* \* \*

Week two in Glaslough brought us a group of older teenagers. It also brought Jean, Donal, Donal's brother, Kieran, who arrived on his motorbike, and Jude and Viv, the New Zealand teachers.

'De Baróid!' Kieran said after he'd inspected the site, 'You're an eedjit! How on Earth are we gonna survive five weeks of this? It's like something you'd get for *penance* – instead of four thousand Hail Marys a day! It's the *pits!*'

'Kieran,' Donal said, 'Don't be so ungrateful. This place has had a lot of effort put into it. Just look at all the lovely posters.'

'The posters are about the only things not *rotten!*' Kieran said, but he got over it.

Jude and Viv wandered about the accommodation, peering into rooms as if they expected them to collapse.

'Em, where does one find the ablutions block?' Viv asked. The rest of us roared with laughter. Nowadays you'd probably get carted away in a strait-jacket for laughing like that at such a perfectly sensible question.

Two days later, Jean came galloping through the camp on one of the Leslies' horses and we were all mightily impressed by her equestrian skills. Only later did we learn that the horse was out of control and had already near garrotted her on the low-hanging branch of an oak.

However, despite all, that second week went relatively well. Having had the experience of the first week under our belt was a great plus. We had an activities plan of sorts, weather permitting, and we had more bodies on the ground. Kieran's motorbike provided added entertainment as he taught the teenagers to drive. The arrival of music in the form of Donal's guitar and Kieran's tin whistle seemed to somehow stabilise the evenings. We now concluded each day with a campfire sing-song, often down by the lake, where we had a few tins of beer and ran around in the smoke to ward off the midges.

The beers were a youth-work compromise. After two nights of dealing with the effects of smuggled spirits, and delights such as *Buckfast* fortified wine and *Scotchmac*, we held a council of war. We acknowledged that we couldn't beat the drink-smuggling. The teenagers acknowledged that throwing up was bad fun. Hence the compromise. On condition that there was no more smuggling and

## Chapter 8

no more hard stuff, we'd paddle across the lake each night and bring back a small sack of beers for each of the sing-songs. From then on, honour prevailed and the drink-related problems ceased. Maybe not everyone's ideal solution, but a solution none the less.

After that, the camp ran fairly smoothly and we had a steady flow of excellent volunteers who enriched the experience for everyone. Jean stayed for several weeks. Donal and Kieran stayed for the duration. Cora came up from Cork for a fortnight. Stasia Crickley, who would go on to be a community work lecturer in Maynooth, came from Dublin. Mícheál Mac Cába, an old friend and an excellent musician, arrived from Connemara and stayed the whole of August. And, of course, we had our contingent from Ballymurphy, who included BTA treasurer, Mark Duffy - and Big Ellen Cosgrove, her son, Harry, and Ann Stone who spun into camp like a three-pronged whirlwind.

'To look after our wee childer,' Ellen said. Ellen's daughters, Ann and Evelyn were on the camp.

'A boat!' Ann shouted on her first visit down to the lake, 'Come on Ellen. We'll go for a wee jaunt!'

They both jumped into the back of one of the box punts and tipped it upside down!

Looking back at the photos of Glaslough - one of which is entitled 'dormitory', and shows two iron beds with teenagers sleeping one up, one down, while another huddle lie in sleeping-bags on a wooden floor - it's a wonder we weren't arrested. For six weeks we lived in the woods on Spam, corned beef, tinned ham and instant mash. We washed in the lake, used oil-lamps for light, and sang the nights away, hail, rain or wind.

Yet, a generation on, there's not a single person who was a teenager at those campfires who doesn't rave about the enjoyment of those days. Not a one has ever muttered a complaint. They remember the fun, the relationships, the camaraderie, and a world that brought real respite from a community being ripped apart by war. They remember the 'pirate battles' in the box-punts; the day Ben Sheriden, out on the lake, clobbered a large carp with an oar; the day Mícheál Mac Cába caught the pike and we ate it for dinner. Those nominally in control also remember the days when, for other forms of entertainment, the young people were not found wanting, as outlined by some of the Leslies' visits.

'A group of the lads have mounted an impromptu checkpoint out on the Caledon Road,' an appalled Desmond told us one afternoon. 'It's extremely embarrassing. They formed up ouside the Pillar House and marched through the village in military formation – some in combat jackets and scarves - and they're causing consternation among the passing motorists. They all think it's the IRA.'

'Are you sure it's our lads?' I asked, realising immediately the stupidity of that particular question.

'Do you think it could be anybody else?' Desmond's 56-year-old brother, Sir John, asked. The tall angular Sir John, eccentric papal knight, was home from Rome for the summer.

'It could actually *be* the IRA,' Kieran Fagan laughed, but neither of the Leslies saw the joke. Sir John was positively aghast.

'If it *is* the IRA,' he said, 'Glaslough knew nothing about them until half an hour ago. And besides, where are all the young boys gone?'

'Fishing,' I said, but I knew that if we looked we'd find the rods behind a tree somewhere.

'We'll all be lucky if the Gardaí haven't got them by now,' John said.

With that, Donal and I agreed to go immediately and reclaim our charges. Sir John expressed his profound gratitude. (Sir John, 4th Baronet of Castle Leslie, made headlines in 2002 when he inadvertently tipped off the media that the ill-fated marriage of ex-Beatle, Paul McCartney, to Heather Mills was to be celebrated in the family church on the estate. Greeting them at the gate in his own version of a tam o'shanter, the 86-year-old former POW famously declared on live television 'It's on Tuesday. But it's a secret.')

Further consternation was caused up in the big house a few days later. Desmond and Shaun arrived down at the camp looking glum.

'They've chopped down a young oak tree,' Desmond said.

'Strategically-placed on the avenue from the castle to the coach-houses,' Shaun added, 'It was planted twelve years ago.'

They both waited for an answer. I apologised, supposing that it would be pointless standing the tree back up again.

'I must say,' I acknowledged, 'I feel far worse about that than the checkpoint episode.'

'One sometimes wishes that neither of two options had occurred,' Desmond said sadly.

Then he and Shaun left. But the Leslies were either very forgiving or very crazy: that afternoon Shaun loaned us the family catamaran

## Chapter 8

which, for the next few weeks could be seen hurtling up and down the lake at breakneck speed until Donal and a couple of others managed to become airborne in it!

The very next day after the oak mishap, Mícheál and I were sitting at the campfire when we heard the awful sound of chopping.

'Oh no!' I said to Mícheál, 'Not another strategic oak!'

We both took off in the direction of the chopping sound – which became a sickening tree-collapsing sound as we ran. However, if consolation were to be found, it was the fact that this was not an oak, but a mature ash, a little off the track.

'Right!' I said to the four culprits, 'I don't want to see any trace of tree! Gimme that axe.'

Fifteen-year-old Liam Stone who was recovering from a recent gunshot wound to the thigh, handed me the axe.

'Youse are makin' an awful fuss over an oul' bit of a tree,' he said.

'No,' I said, 'The point of the fuss is that it *wasn't* an oul' bit of a tree half an hour ago.'

'This is the second one in two days,' Mícheál added, 'And you know how Jack told us the ash trees are used for hurleys. Maybe they're counted.'

'Mícheál!' Liam's friend, Seán Adams, said, 'Yer head's a marley. Who's gonna go around countin' fuckin' trees!'

Micky Vallelly helpfully suggested setting fire to the forest to cover our tracks.

Micheál and I then took turns chopping the tree into manageable lumps, and hacking away at the stump, and rearranging the soil, until not a sign remained that a tree had ever stood there.

'Take every last chip back to the coach-houses,' I told the four loggers, 'I want only ashes.'

'Right lads!' Seán Adams snapped, 'Let's get rid of this tree.'

'By the lordin', lovin', livin', lightin' Jaysus!' Mícheál said, admiring my problem-solving skills, 'You're like some top general, make no mistake about it!'

Later that evening, Sir John appeared and we thought all was lost. However, he had come to leave us a box of biscuits. He then engaged some of the young people in conversation.

'Do you have a lot of shooting in the streets?' he asked.

'Here,' Bernie Callaghan said, 'See him there? [She pointed at Liam Stone], 'He got shot.'

'Oh my goodness,' John said, 'Was it bad?'

### In The Woods Of Truagh

'Bad enough,' Liam said, 'It was in my leg.'
'Is it possible to see it?' John asked.
'Aye,' Seán Adams piped up, 'If yer a *fruit*!'
Fortunately, the Belfast accent slid over the head of Sir John.

Then two of the lads, who missed the bus one morning hijacked a car and followed us down to Monaghan. (We never mentioned this to Desmond or Sir John.) And some villain caused a minor rip in one of our tents, for which the Irish army later sent us a repair bill for 28 pence! We also had to send a couple of the lads home after they started burning chairs in the fire instead of resorting to the bother of cutting a few logs.

'You're in trouble now,' Teresa Mulvenna jokingly said, 'You just sent home the brother of one of the top Provies!'

Somehow, as we gradually shed the layers of civilisation, our plight came to the attention of the outside world. My parents arrived one afternoon with a carload of roasted chickens and cakes and biscuits and looked sadly at what had become of their eldest son. A week or so later, Stasia Crickley turned up from Dublin and made an enormous pot of stew, upon which young Jim Fegan gave his own inimitable verdict.

'Fuckin' pepper! he roared and hurled his plate at the coach-house wall.

'Imagine what would have happened,' Stasia said, 'if I'd made chilli con carne!'

Jim and Norma Lynch, from Cootehill in County Cavan, turned up with a plan. Jim, a balding, slow-speaking man in his late forties, had been commanding officer of the Cavan-Monaghan brigade of the IRA during Operation Harvest, the border campaign of the late Fifties. He had stayed with the Officials after the Split. Norma, a chatty, exuberant bundle of blonde nervous energy of about the same age, was the proof that opposites attract. Together, they embarked on a campaign to acquire some old disused coach-houses and grooms' quarters at a place called Dartry, not far from Cootehill, as a permanent base for a 'Shankill-Ballymurphy' camp.

'The fact of the matter is,' Norma said, 'that the Protestants of the Shankill are just as down-trodden in their own way as the Catholics of Ballymurphy. This place we're looking at belongs to the Irish Department of Lands. So, no excuse. If the shower in Dublin want to do something for the North, here's their chance. There's a great deal of local enthusiasm for a Shankill-Ballymurphy camp. All we

## Chapter 8

need is a caretaker lease.'

Norma and Jim then organised myself, Cora, Donal and Kieran Fagan, and about 20 Ballymurphy teenagers around to Dartry for a look - to the dismay of the resident hippies. After the inspection tour, they brought us back to Cootehill for the night. There, Norma fed us all a big fry. She then rooted out every spare blanket and cushion in the house and in the neighbours' houses and we somehow managed to scatter ourselves across the chairs and ground floor of the modest house. For bedtime stories, Jim sat back in his armchair like an old seanchaí, produced a .22 pistol, removed the bullets and passed the gun around.

'There's a yarn with that gun,' he told us, 'Last year we were raided here by the Special Branch, looking for guns. A whole posse of them arrived in and searched every inch of the house - up the chimney, in the attic, under the doormat, even in the toilet cistern. And all the time the gun was sitting in plain view, in that child's holster there.'

He nodded towards a toy gun-belt hanging over a chair.

'Too obvious by far for the Gardaí. Every one of them who saw it probably thought he'd look really stupid if he starting pulling a child's toy from its holster!'

Having taken on a whole new persona, the gun was passed around again for a second viewing before we all went to sleep.

Over the coming year, the Lynchs made gallant attempts to secure a tenancy in Dartry for the envisioned Shankill-Ballymurphy camp. From a government whose rhetoric on reconciliation had been loud, that would surely be forthcoming. In fairness, the Department of Lands didn't refuse, it just ignored the request. The only sign of Dublin having ever received any correspondence was a token visit to the Shankill Road by Dr. Garret FitzGerald, Dublin's Minister for Foreign Affairs. Nevertheless, the Lynchs stayed attached, Jim always hoping that eventually the Provisionals would all morph into Officials.

When Jim died in 1996, his graveside oration was given by UVF leader, Gusty Spence, who turned up unannounced. By sheer coincidence, Norma and I had formed part of a small delegation who attended a UVF prisoners' support function on the Shankill Road in April 1995, shortly after the loyalist ceasefires of 1994. We had been invited along in recognition of the work carried out by *Between* (the renamed Association for Human Rights in the North) since 1970 on behalf of prisoners' families from both sides of the divide. Jim, who'd been with us in Belfast city centre for an earlier *Between* rededication event, had gone elsewhere to visit friends.

'Jim would love this,' Norma said, just before four armed UVF men staged a show of strength, bringing about all sorts of subsequent hullaballoos about the breakdown of ceasefires.

While we were driving up and down to Glaslough and sleeping on floors in Cootehill, the political and military landscapes in the North were changing under our feet. With the renewed IRA offensive, and the upsurge in sectarian assassinations, everywhere, for everyone, became increasingly dangerous.

On one occasion, I was hitchhiking back down to Glaslough after a short visit to Belfast when I made the mistake of standing too close to the perimeters of Corcrain estate on the outskirts of Portadown. Engrossed in the hitchhiking, I failed to notice the very pertinent detail of the two masked men in khakis who had climbed over a fence at the top of an incline on the far side of the road. It was only when one of them slipped and lost hold of his baseball bat...

*Oh dear!* came the thought, *I could be very dead!* In a panic I grabbed my bag and took off down the Armagh Road on two stems of wobble with the UDA men in full and hot pursuit. That could have ended very badly if it wasn't for the timely intervention of a Lurgan man who screeched to a stop and shouted, *Get in for fuck's sake! Are ya mad or what!*

\* \* \*

On July 18th British Secretary of State, William Whitelaw, announced a traffic ban in central Belfast. The city, the British army declared, was now bomb-proof. On Friday, 21st July, the IRA set out to prove the army wrong. Between 2.15pm and 3.30pm they set off 21 bombs, each preceded by a warning to the Public Protection Agency, considered by the IRA to be a reliable means of relaying bomb warnings to the British army and RUC. In nineteen cases the warnings were acted on and there were no casualties. In two, they were not. At Oxford Street Bus Station and Cavehill Road shopping centre, a total of seven civilians and two soldiers were killed while many others were injured. Ten days later, at four o'clock on the morning of July 31st 1972 the British launched Operation Motorman. 21,000 troops, supported by Centurion tanks and hundreds of armoured cars, swept into the no-go areas of Belfast and Derry and imposed virtual martial law. The second battalion of the Parachute Regiment was sent in to take Ballymurphy. A number of young IRA

## Chapter 8

Volunteers missed the assault: they were singing songs over a tin of beer at a campfire in the ancient woods of Truagh. Across the lake in the big house, ghosts were trailing through the corridors and Desmond Leslie was watching the night skies for the next coming.

Eleven days later, as the IRA regrouped, word filtered down to Glaslough that 22-year-old Micky Clarke and 18-year-old Anne Parker from Ballymurphy had been killed. A car-bomb they were driving had detonated prematurely. That night, those of us who were a little older tried to console the teenage girls in the camp. They were distraught: Anne Parker, their friend, had planned to be with them in Glaslough.

'I can't cry any more,' Rosaline McBride said, 'I've no more tears left from all the friends that were killed in the last year.'

Jack, the old game-keeper, turned up that night with bars of chocolate. The weather-beaten woodland philosopher who had earlier brought the group on a woodland adventure, looked set to cry. Sitting by the fire in his Wellington boots and battered sports jacket and trousers, he peered out from beneath his cap and listened to the resurfaced stories of Internment Week and the horrors that fifteen and sixteen-year-olds had lived through. Jack did his best to find a way in which he could sympathise without adding to the pain.

'The devil will gather his own,' he said in the end.

'Not if we get there first,' one of the young lads said. A year later the same lad ran past me in the street with an Armalite rifle in his hands.

Jack passed around the chocolate and we made some tea and sandwiches.

'Bate that down yer neck!' Micky Vallelly said. The French say, *Bon appétit*.

\* \* \*

When the Glaslough camp finished, Micheál and I stayed behind to clear up and were invited to dinner up at the castle by Desmond and his second wife, Helen. Around a great table, the two of us sat, unshaven, in our battered jeans and wrinkled shirts, to plates of artichoke starters - something neither of us had ever seen before - and felt decidedly out of place. The next day, Micheál went off to Conemara and I went back to Ballymurphy where the Paras had settled in, bringing to the streets a naked, all-pervasive violence like nothing that had been before.

'They're after taking over all the schools and all the green spaces,' old Billy said when I arrived in Glenalina Park, 'Nothing now except Wild-West forts and corrugated iron.'

For the first time in my life, I was under full military occupation. 'They're battering people right, left and centre,' Billy said, 'Things have got awful bad.'

Over in north Belfast, the home of Frank Gogarty had been attacked again by a loyalist mob and the family had been forced to flee. This time the attack had been fiercer than usual and Frank had called the RUC and the military. They arrived, but stood by for several hours while the attack continued. Finally, a senior RUC officer demanded of Frank that the local masked commander of the UDA be allowed to search the house for arms. Although outraged, Frank could do nothing to prevent the search. Later, after the attack ended, a gun, dropped by one of the attackers, was discovered in the garden.

Shortly afterwards, the Gogarty family fled the house; and while I was down in Glaslough, oblivious to all this, Fintan Gogarty and our Niall, who was a friend of Fintan's, drove a truck from Cork to rescue what they could of the family's possessions. It was an operation that involved several retreats in the face of further Mount Vernon attacks. The furniture was then driven to Cork where it was stored until the Gogarty family could find a new home.

Later, the IRA did Frank Gogarty the only favour they could have done him under the circumstances: they blew up his house. That way, IRA thinking went, he couldn't go back and get himself killed, and he could claim compensation from the state.

# Chapter 9
Resistance

Brigadier Frant Kitson, British counter-insurgency guru, had taken Mao Zedong's analogy that likened the guerrilla fighter to a fish in water, and concluded that if you can't catch the fish, you pollute the water. In Ballymurphy the Paras were the storm-troopers of Kitson's ideology which had rolled into town with Operation Motorman. Polluting the water translated into destroying the community's ability to function, and instilling such terror that personal survival became every individual's sole purpose. The expectation was that this would isolate and expose the IRA.

Ballymurphy was placed under 24-hour military assault, with patrols of fifteen to twenty soldiers racing through back-gardens and bouncing suddenly out of entries to search, interrogate, batter and arrest passers-by. In support of the patrols, the streets were cruised by Saracen armoured cars with Browning machine-guns trained on any available chest. These in turn were supported by smaller ferrets and heavy Saladins - small six-wheeled tanks sporting machine-guns and 76mm cannon. The slightest pretence was used to shoot up the locality or gun down individuals, while lines of men and boys, and sometimes women, were frog-marched off under a barrage of boots and rifle-butts to be taken away for brutal interrogation which included what later became known as water-boarding. The beatings in the streets became so arbitrary and violent that men took to going abroad only if accompanied by a woman, whose presence might temper the level of abuse.

In the dead of night families were subjected to repeated raids: children were dragged from their beds; parents and older kids were beaten; floors, ceilings and stud walls were ripped apart; valuables were stolen and furniture and fittings were wantonly destroyed. Outside, parked cars were rammed; fences were ripped down; clothes lines were snipped and the clothes trampled; windows were broken by marbles fired from catapults; and airguns were used as a matter of form against children.

Porch lights were installed by some families as a comfort measure for their children and an attempt to provide some street lighting, but these were smashed by the military and people were warned that they would be shot if the lights were replaced.

Closer to home, Donal and Kieran Fagan were pushed from Kieran's moving motorbike by soldiers on the Springfield Road. They were then dragged off for interrogation to Black Mountain school, occupied by the military since Motorman began.

It was about this time that the relationship between myself and the Paras weakened when I took to standing out in front of Saracens to write down their number-plates whenever the soldiers sang sectarian songs, and gripping my chest and falling about like the dying baddie in old Westerns whenever the Brownings turned my way. With the 20:20 of hindsight, the latter was a bit silly and often ended in sudden and heavy arrests, but it gave a sense of personal satisfaction: it was a small statement of sorts. In mid September I talked to Donal about doing something more constructive.

'We need to take on the Paras,' I said.

Donal looked at me and laughed.

'And have you got any ideas?' he asked.

'They're handing us a campaign,' I said, 'All *we* need do is document what *they're* doing and expose it on the wider stage.'

'We...?' Donal said, 'Like, all two of us...?'

'We'll find a few others,' I said, 'And we can start to gather statements straight away.'

'If you're game,' Donal said, 'I'm game. But I wouldn't mention it to the Paras.'

In the coming weeks two fronts were opened up. One was relatively sensible and organised, and took the form of a political counter-offensive. Fronted by myself, Donal and a small group of local people, and supported by the Belfast-based Association of Legal Justice and the Cork-based Association for Human Rights in the North, this was designed to expose the Para atrocities in the face of a wall of silence from church, state and most of the media. In pursuit of this, I collected statements from a wide range of people who had suffered Para abuse. The testimony of people like 18-year-old Vera Stone demonstrated the sheer random nature of the military violence:

'After the social every week the military wait outside the community centre to arrest the men and abuse the women. They spit at the women and use abusive language. Last night, Saturday, November 4th, we were leaving the centre at 12.30am.

## Chapter 9

*The soldiers were there as usual. They waited outside until the bulk of the crowd were gone. We were last out. About 35 of us left together. As we were heading home they stopped us and told the boys to get spreadeagled against the wall. They then started to kick them. They then let the fellows go; but as they left they grabbed two of them by the hair. The girls turned around to protest at this. The soldiers then just took a charge at us, like a riot squad. They swung the butts of their rifles and kicked us and trailed us by the hair. They laughed as they did this, and called us 'Irish whores' and 'Fenian bastards' and said we were 'the type who took 30 bob a turn'. I was kicked to the ground and beaten by a rifle butt. I was then dragged by the hair along the street and my clothes were ruined. My boyfriend shielded me from one blow and he himself received a broken arm and eight stitches in his head. Later on, while walking down Ballymurphy Crescent, a mobile patrol followed us, calling us names. They then stopped us and pulled the fellows into the Saracen and beat them up.'*

The statements were used as the basis of a dossier which was widely disseminated, and published by Amnesty International. All statements were signed by those who made them but the originals were held in Cork to protect the signatories from army reprisals. All were, however, counter-signed by me, and that signature stayed. This led to a further deterioration in the relationship between the Paras and myself when they raided Billy's house and found a copy of the dossier in my room. I arrived in to find a red-faced Para holding the document at arm's length.

'This is about US!' he barked.

'It is.' I answered.

'Be under no fucking illusion mate,' he said, 'We don't take kindly to people writing bad stuff about us.'

'Unfortunately, I don't know anything good,' I said.

'Fuck you, Irish bastard,' he said and stormed out of the room. The following Sunday, I was on my way down Glenalina Crescent to buy a pint of milk at a local house-shop when the Paras drove a six-wheeled Saracen armoured car onto the footpath behind me in a determined effort to end our worsening relationship. I managed to throw myself over a garden wall but it was close. Ten minutes later, as I spoke to Ann Stone's young son, Séamus, who was also there to buy milk, a foot-patrol came out of an entry and the officer, when he

saw me, aimed his rifle straight between my eyes.
'He's going to shoot,' eight-year-old Séamus said, and I must say I believed him.
To this day I'm not sure if I don't owe my life to the four additional potential witnesses who arrived around the corner in the nick of time.
There were other occasions when people warned of soldiers waiting late at night in Billy's garden, and I was given an alternative bed for the night. Meanwhile, the letter-writing campaign continued from the community centre, and earned me an unexpected visit.
It was about eleven o'clock on a Tuesday morning. I was alone in the centre and seated at the typewriter when the office door opened. A man in his mid twenties, with long hair and a wispy beard, walked in.
'My name's Tommy,' he said with a forced smile, 'What about ya?'
'Not too bad,' I replied.
'People are sayin' you're sendin' out letters about the Paras...'
'That's right,' I said, starting to feel a bit wary, 'What about it?'
'We do that kinda thing,' he said, 'And we like to keep it that way.'
'Who's *we*?' I asked.
'*We*,' he said, 'That's all you need to know.'
'I'll tell you what,' I said, 'I'll probably go on writing letters.'
He looked at me with frustration building up in his face. Then he stormed off. The next time I saw Tommy, he bought me a drink in one of the shebeens in the area and we became friends.
'We didn't know who you were,' he said, 'Whether you were a Stickie or a Provie or some looper in between. We still don't know, but you're probably OK.'
'Who's *we*?' I said and we laughed and shook hands on that.
Not wanting to fully monopolise the Paras' attentions, our little committee made an attempt to get the Catholic hierarchy to also raise its voice in defence of the communities being battered under Motorman: we sent a delegation to see Cardinal William Conway, Archbishop of Armagh and Primate of All Ireland. It consisted of Seán McCann, Chair of the Association of Legal Justice and a teacher at St. Thomas' School in Ballymurphy; Jenny Quigley's husband, Seán, who was also a teacher; Lily Quinn of Divismore Park who had chased the kids who were battering the Taggart and who'd recently been shot in the wrist while lying in her own bed, and later hospitalised after a separate Para attack on her home;

## Chapter 9

Anna Andrews, a quiet woman who gave much of her time to the charitable works of the St. Vincent de Paul Society; and me.

But the Cardinal was too smart for us by far. By the time we arrived, he'd summoned to his aid Canon Pádraig Murphy, Parish Priest of Ballymurphy, who had already, despite having never met me, taken to describing me in clerical circles as 'that Communist up in Ballymurphy'. (I had been warned by Noelle down in Des Wilson's house.) Each member of the delegation made a presentation, describing personal experiences and the general trauma being experienced by the community while the Canon did his utmost to deflect whatever we said and he and the Cardinal chucked eyes at one another across the table. When we'd finished, the Cardinal pronounced, but it was clear that the decision had been made long before we arrived.

'I'm afraid I can't speak out against what you've documented,' he said, 'Otherwise I might appear sectarian.'

'Sectarian!' Seán McCann croaked, 'How would condemning the brutality being meted out by British paratroopers to your flock appear sectarian!'

'Besides,' the Cardinal said in an attempt to make us feel better, 'I know of far worse cases in other places.'

We were supposed to feel great now, having been brought into his confidence. We got up and walked out.

'And,' Seán Quigley said as we left, 'I wish to register my personal disgust at having to come all the way to Armagh before I can meet with my own parish priest, despite my many requests.'

We left the great halls of Armagh in disgust and disbelief, with both of the women in tears.

'You know,' the gentle Anna Andrews said afterwards, 'For the first time in my life I felt like saying "f..." to another human being.'

In the coming decades, with the exception of Cardinal Tomás Ó Fiaich and a handful of radical priests, all of whom were themselves pilloried, Conway's church didn't do any more madly well when it came to taking sides in the struggles that wracked the nationalist communities of the North. In fact, back through history, they were generally on the wrong side.

Despite the obstructions we encountered along the way, however, our campaign against the Paras was a sufficient thorn in their side to warrant a mention in David Barzilay's *The British Army In Ulster*, and it's generally believed that their tour of duty in Ballymurphy was terminated prematurely as a result of the stink we, and our Cork supporters, managed to raise.

The second anti-paratrooper front was a personal one, premised on an intentional passive-resistance strategy of several strands.

The first was to ignore them. When the armoured car whined up behind in low gear or an English voice shouted 'Hey you! Come fucking 'ere!' from someone's garden, you just walked on. At one o'clock in the morning in a dark street, this was down to pretty fine tuning. It required an accurate assessment of the level of murderous intent in the unseen enemy's voice as he repeated his demand with increasing belligerence. When the bullet went up the spout, and the shout changed to, 'You either stop now, or I fucking-well shoot!', it was normally time to quit. Although not without the indignant consideration that *If I was deaf, that bugger would've shot me.*

A second strand had to do with pockets. This happened once on Glenalina Road. I was on my way to the community centre along with 16-year-old Ben Sheridan, and the ubiquitous two Saracens pulled up ahead, on the far side of the street. The back doors of the second Saracen opened and the soldier seated on the rear right-hand-side called to us.

'Hey you, come fucking 'ere!'

'Keep walking,' I said to Ben.

'Are you right in the head?' Ben said, but he also kept walking.

'You!' the same soldier yelled again, 'You fucking deaf? Come fucking 'ere!'

'Oh,' I called back as if we'd only just noticed them, 'You talking to us?'

We then diagonally crossed the street in the direction of the armoured car which was about thirty yards away. The critical thing now was that it was a cold afternoon and I had a file under one arm and both hands in the pockets of a three-quarter-length jacket, which prompted a new order from the boyo in the rear left of the Saracen.

'Get your 'ands out of your fucking pockets!' he yelled.

I ignored this unreasonable request and Ben and I kept on walking towards the back of the Saracen. This excited the man very much.

'You completely fucking deaf mate?' he yelled, 'Get them 'ands out of them fucking pockets!'

'My friend,' Ben said, 'I think you should maybe get your hands out of your pockets.' But, as this was now a stand-off between me and Great Britain, hands-out-of-pockets was out of the question.

'We're winning Ben,' I whispered, 'We're winning.'

'Winning like fuck,' Ben said.

We were now closing in on the Saracen and the soldier on the left was sort of hysterical.

'YOU STUPID DEAF IRISH FUCKING BASTARD! GET THEM FUCKING 'ANDS OUT OF THEM FUCKING POCKETS - NOW!'

Whereupon we walked up to the back of the vehicle.

'And what can we do for you?' I asked the guy on the right, ignoring our apoplectic friend. During the ten-minute check that followed, the boyo on the left never uttered another word. One for Ireland, I thought.

'You can just imagine the stick he's gonna get,' Ben said when the Saracen moved off, *You couldn't even get him to take his fuckin' hands out of his fuckin' pockets...'*

It was all I could do, not to burst into song.

A third strand was to talk to the Paras in Irish. This often acted as an effective repellent. As few Paras appeared to have a terrific command of English, anything 'foreign' was terrifying.

A fourth was to take their guns right out of their hands.

On the evening of October 9th 1972, as the nights came falling in, two propitious events collided: the drink stash of the Russell Court Hotel on Belfast's Lisburn Road was declared 'bomb-damaged' as the hotel had recently been bombed by the IRA; and Jean Campbell celebrated her 23rd birthday.

As it happened Big Michael Quigg, the boyfriend of Jean's sister, Anne (my atrocious guide back from Viv and Jude's party), had connections in the Russell Court, and arrived in with his massive arms full of the bomb-damaged booze. This included several bottles of spirits and a bottle of Benedictine brandy liqueur, which I shall never forget.

Along with Michael, the guest list at the party included all the Campbells; Viv Holmes and Jude Goldfinch, the two New Zealand teachers who'd been at Glaslough; myself; and Matt from Australia, a social science graduate who was doing some voluntary work in Ballymurphy but was unused to its demanding social mores.

It was an exuberant night, with tumblers of whiskey and vodka being chased by glasses of Benedictine and pints of Guinness and Harp. I remember at one point being out in the hall talking to Viv when she started to levitate up towards the ceiling. I then realized that it was in fact me who was sliding down the wall. At a later stage I heard Jude's voice behind saying, 'My god! He's having another glass of that Benedictine!' I felt like one of those Spartans at Thermopylae, which might explain some of what happened next. As I sat on the settee beside Ellen Campbell, there was a commotion by the living-room door. A diaphanous haze gave shape to dim, red blotches which were gradually determined beyond reasonable doubt to be paratrooper berets. The enemy was in the room! Matt, who had couped early, and was on his rubbery way home through the blacked-out streets, had been nabbed by the Paras and had given away the source of his perdition.

'Murderers!' I bawled as they filed into the living room, 'Bloody Sunday murderers! You wouldn't be so brave if...'

But, before I could finish, Ellen grabbed me around the neck and pulled me across her lap, kissing me full on the mouth to shut me up. Then, Ireland called, and with great difficulty I made the noble choice, pulling myself upright and back into the fray.

'Massacre...!' I accused a soldier who was standing at the living-room door with a Sterling sub-machine gun, 'Murderers!'

At this juncture Viv staged a diversion.

'Have you all been let out of Borstal for the day?' she asked one of the Paras who was trying to get Jude's name.

'My name?' Jude said, 'Why, it's Lady Elizabeth Windsor!' (the British queen)

As Jude further explained this delicacy, I recognised one of the soldiers: he was from somewhere south of Dublin, going by the accent, and called himself Séamus McGarth. Fair-haired and thick-set, it would be fair to say that he and Ballymurphy didn't get on. He'd been part of a patrol that had lifted me a few days earlier.

'Well, look who it is!' I said, 'Paddy the Para!' Séamus wasn't pleased with this: he probably got it all the time. 'Thass a big gun you have Paddy,' I said, 'Gizz a look at yer gun.'

At that I reached for the SLR with both hands and started to pull. A surprised McGrath pulled in the other direction. The Para at the living-room door pointed his Sterling at my chest. Back and forth went the rifle as, despite the Benedictine and whiskey, I got the upper hand. Eventually, McGrath snatched out the magazine and I got the rifle, spinning around and aiming it at the officer's head. That may have been the closest I ever came to getting myself killed. I remember the Para at the door jerking the Sterling upright and

## Chapter 9

to this day I don't know why he or one of the others didn't shoot. By now, we weren't particularly good mates and my prints were all over McGrath's rifle. Later consensus around Ballymurphy was that a madman from Cork had got away with it. Others had died at the hands of this regiment for showing their face in the street. The officer, however, threw a fit.

'Never!' he screeched like a fishwife, 'Never, ever aim a gun at anyone unless you intend to shoot them dead!'

I aimed the rifle at the light. Then McGrath snatched it back, and John Campbell took up the cause.

'Here Paddy,' he said, 'Can I have a look at your bang-bang now...'

Years later I learned that the foolhardiness of youth can have untold outcomes. I was in the home of Anna Andrews – who'd been part of the delegation to see the Cardinal - when she began to reminisce on the Para campaign and the times that were in it.

'Do you know what,' she said in the end, 'During all those terrible times two things gave me hope. One was the awful way in which the officers treated their own men which made me realise that we shared something small in common with the ordinary paratrooper. And the other was that a young person would stand in front of their guns and brazen them down.'

I must say I had never thought of it like that; but I loped out of there like Wyatt Earp leaving the OK Corral.

Then, out in the garden, I encountered Anna's husband, Liam, local artist, informal Irish language teacher and sometimes philosopher, who was probably well into his sixties. He was standing at the gate with a can of petrol and a match, ready to set fire to some nettles, when the Brits showed up.

'Have you seen any terrorists lately?' one of them asked.

'Sure,' Liam said, 'Aren't I looking at seven of them right now...'

They weren't getting it good from any side.

\* \* \*

During that first year in Belfast I went back to Cork a few times to see Cora and my family, but felt curiously disconnected from the city, as if a plug had been pulled somewhere. On three occasions, the other-worldly contrast between life on the two parts of the island was brought into sharp relief on my return to Belfast. On the first, I was making my way up the Falls Road, where full-scale redevelopment was still under way, when a young man, leaning casually against a corner wall, spoke to me.

'Here boss,' he said, 'Go in this way, and don't come back out onto the Falls for at least ten minutes.'

In the derelict street into which I'd been directed, a young couple passed by, looking for all the world like students. The guy was tall, and wearing a long grey overcoat and he had his left arm draped over the woman's shoulders. The woman, slim with a long loose skirt, had her right arm around the man's back. They were chatting casually as they made their way towards the main road. Something, however, seemed wrong and made me look around. It was only then that I noticed the barrel of a rifle hanging from inside the man's coat. Shortly afterwards, in a moment frozen in time, a single shot rang out, followed in that back street by a terrible silence. When I got back to Ballymurphy I heard that a soldier had been shot dead on the Falls Road.

On the second occasion I had just walked out of Great Victoria Street train station into a heavy drizzle when a van pulled up right in front of me in the forecourt of the Europa Hotel, and two men jumped out and ran off. For a second or two I stood there transfixed, watching the wipers swish back and forth, and thinking, *Oh my!*

'I think there might be a bomb in that van,' I mentioned to other people coming out of the station.

'Oh,' they said, and we all moved back with the surreal calm that governed such events in Belfast in 1972. There would most probably be a warning and time to clear the area as killing civilians was not on the IRA wish list. Later, I stood 200 yards away with a crowd of onlookers as the British army fired some kind of blank bazooka shells to try and dislodge the timing mechanism of the bomb. They failed and it exploded, adding to a long list of attacks that would eventually leave the Belfast Europa with the dubious distinction of being the most bombed hotel in the world.

On the third occasion I was again on the Falls Road when an army patrol 150 yards away came under fire. They panicked and started to fire back in any old direction, which included mine. Based on sound Belfast advice, I went up to the nearest door and rapped it.

'Excuse me,' I said to the middle-aged man who answered, 'Do you mind if I come in out of the gun-battle?'

I remembered having once asked somebody in Cork if I could step in out of the rain.

## Chapter 10
### The House That Jack Built

Five months after arriving in Ballymurphy, as the war moved from prolonged gun-battles and nightly sieges of British bases to one of sniping and sudden ambushes, I moved my bed from under the hole in Billy's ceiling to 42 Ballymurphy Road. In September, Cora had come north for a long weekend and had reminded me that, seeing as I was no longer planning to come home within the year, she was coming to Belfast in the spring. We needed a place of our own.

The new house - one of Ballymurphy's curious back-to-front houses - had belonged to Jim Bryson, his wife, Sheila, and their young son, Jim junior, until the British army rendered it uninhabitable. They broke in while Bryson was on the run and his family was out and destroyed everything that could be destroyed. They pulled down ceilings, ripped up floors, smashed the toilet and bath, slashed the settee and carpets, broke all windows and interior doors, ripped out water pipes, punched holes in the stud walls of the bedrooms, fired seven bullets into the TV, took all the family's clothes and poured paint and (nice boys) their own piss on them, and took the very eggs out of the fridge to smash against the living-room walls.

Following the destruction, the Brysons moved to another house further up the street and their former home became another of Ballymurphy's derelict shells - the windows and doors sheeted in corrugated iron to deter vandals. It remained so until October 1972 when I arrived down from Billy's one afternoon, kicked in the front door and declared a republic. In that time of anarchy - nobody paying rent, rates, gas or electricity - I became a squatter in the property of the Northern Ireland Housing Executive.

As I surveyed the wreckage left behind by her majesty's forces, there was a knock on the door. It was Mrs. Maguire, an older neighbour from two doors up.

'I heard you moving in,' she said euphemistically, 'And I thought you might like a bowl of soup.'

She handed me a steaming bowl filled with 'Belfast Soup', the only *vegetable* soup in the world made with the leftover carcass of a roast chicken as a stock-base.

'Thanks very much,' I said and ate my first meal in my new home.

Over the next couple of months I graduated from sleeping on the floor to an old fold-up metal bed, and cooked various types of lobscouse on the coiled elements of a vintage electric heater lying on its side, or ate the food - including steaks - raw (raw spuds are stinking!), while I knocked the house into liveable shape. This entailed several trips on foot to Corry's timber yard to pick up the necessary materials. It also involved a degree of risk as the front gate of Corry's lay directly across from the bottom of Springmartin Road. Going in was generally OK as you were through the gate before the enemy could muster. But coming out, laden down with eight-by-four sheets of chipboard and hardboard, you were a vulnerable target.

Twice, I had to retreat back inside, along with youth-club stalwarts, Stevie Mallon, Brian Fegan and Brendan McCorry, who'd come along to give me a hand. We then had to find us a nice man with a van who'd smuggle us back to the top of Springhill Avenue. On both occasions, as the van made its tell-tale turn to the left, it took the full rain of the rocks and bottles meant for us. However, by and by, the materials were hauled safely back to Ballymurphy Road and the work progressed. I sheeted over the broken floors with chipboard, faced the doors with hardboard, replaced the toilet, papered over the holes in the stud walls, patched up the ceilings, and got local glazier, Pat Devlin, to re-glaze the windows.

'What are you gonna do about the water?' Pat asked, 'You can't live here with no water pipes.'

But we did. For the three years that Cora and I lived at 42 Ballymurphy Road the only water in the house was from the cold tap in the kitchen which was stuck at the full 'on' position and controlled from a stopcock under the sink. To have a bath, we heated water in a vintage washing machine (that had a mangle for squeezing the water from the clothes) and siphoned it into the bath. To flush the loo, we carried buckets of water from the kitchen. During parties, we took the buckets out the back door, up the entry and in the front door as the bathroom was at the front of the house. One Saturday night, during one of those parties, Rory McGuckian from the Springfield Road came in from the kitchen looking grimly through his beard.

'You ain't never gonna flush the loo again,' he said, 'Somebody has turned that tap in the kitchen off, and there ain't nobody, ever, is gonna get it back on again!'

## Chapter 10

'The stopcock!' a dozen voices shouted.

42 was a four-bedroom house, although two were little more than boxes. It had a small unkempt front garden and, being a back-to-front house, the living room faced the larger unkempt back garden. This 'garden' was nothing more than a sloping mire with a doorless coal-shed where kids mitching school came to smoke and deal cards. Cora and I, like everyone else in the area, used it to burn off our bin when it filled with rubbish. It was also a run for the British army who zig-zagged through in perennial avoidance of imagined snipers, whose rifle barrels might appear at any moment from the roof tiles of some nearby house. 'Hey boy,' the kids used to shout at them, 'The IRA will get ya.' There was no point in any gardening attempt as fences were simply ripped down by the military who trampled through a dozen times a day - although our next-door neighbour, Mr. Bennett, persevered. He operated a relentless programme of fence-strengthening, adding barbed wire and improvised booby-traps to thwart the military advances. The strategy included daily soakings of the garden perimeters.

'They hate mud.' he told me.

But, despite appearances, there was a touch of elegance about 42.

In March 1973, shortly before Cora arrived, my great grand-aunt Maggie down in Cavendish Street passed away. Great grand-aunt Josie, who suffered from St. Vitus' Dance, was consequently taken into care and I inherited some of the antique furniture that had filled the house. A glass cabinet, beautifully-carved chairs, a chaise langue, a bed and massive wardrobe, and a drop-leaf table were moved from Cavendish Street to Ballymurphy Road in a truck furnished free of charge by the very Tommy who had objected to my early letter-writing. As it drew up outside Maggie's house, I noted that it looked suspiciously like the truck that had ferried the Ballymurphy men to Lenadoon on the day the ceasefire had broken down, and that a lot of the same faces appeared to be on board. My grandfather, the old Belfast IRA man, who'd come home from California, was on hand to supervise.

'My god Ciarán!' he said as he inspected the removal squad, 'I thought you said you had some *men* coming here, not a load of *boys*!'

'Some of these *boys* may well have moved half the town,' I said.

Gerry Anderson, formerly of the 3rd Northern Division, Irish Republican Army, and photographed with that unit on the top of

Black Mountain in 1921, missed the point.

'Never leave a boy to a man's job,' he muttered.

But, despite his misgivings, he had to admit that the squad did a good job. He didn't notice how they tossed their eyes about with big forgiving smiles behind his back.

'The perfect home,' Tommy said when the last piece of antique furniture was added to the three-piece suite I'd bought in Ross's auction for 60 pence, 'Yer missus will love it.'

Meanwhile, the house had been given several names.

Back in October, Donal and I had been for a drink in the town and were on our way to Castle Street in the dark and the rain to catch a Black Taxi to Ballymurphy, when providence took a turn: we stumbled on a freshly-bombed paint shop in Smithfield.

'Donal,' I said, looking through the protective barriers that had been loosely erected around the pile of rubble, 'Doesn't the lord work in strange ways? Paint for my house.'

'You're not serious!' Donal laughed.

'Donal,' I said, 'That paint will go to waste. There must be tins that survived.'

'You *are* serious,' Donal groaned.

Shortly afterwards, we were rummaging through the unstable rubble, gathering up any large tin that looked undamaged when a military patrol arrived.

'Sarge!' we heard, 'We got *looters* 'ere!' Then the rifles were cocked.

'OK you two!' a second voice barked, 'You're under arrest.'

Now, having never fancied myself as a looter, I was quite affronted.

'Excuse me,' I said, 'We're respectable youth workers and this paint is for a youth club.'

This seemed to have a sobering effect on the Brits.

'Let's see what you've got,' the sergeant said.

We held up two large tins each.

'Ok,' he said, 'But get the fuck out of there now!'

'We're on our way,' Donal said, 'Would you mind holding these while we climb over the barrier.'

Paint dripped on army boots and we were happy. We then continued on to Castle Street where The People's Taxis picked up their passengers. This service had come into play as a response to the disruption of public transport caused by rioting and the regular burning of buses. To fill the gap, some enterprising individuals had gone over to London and bought a few black taxis, and from such

## Chapter 10

acorns a continuous jeepney service had grown up in nationalist areas of the city, and was later emulated in loyalist areas. Great was our shame then when we disembarked on the Whiterock Road and found a puddle of white gloss on the floor of our People's Taxi.

It was now raining heavily, so we made a bolt for the community centre where we stemmed the leak in the paint tin with a plug of toilet tissue. Soaked from the rain and dripping paint, we went into the office to dry off and found it unusually full of BTA members, all gathered around a slightly-built man in a heavy overcoat who was sitting on a table. He was in his late forties, had dark hair sleeked back from his forehead, and was wearing glasses. Although I'd been expecting a giant, I immediately knew who he was. The previous day, I'd been down in Ballymurphy Drive when Tess Cahill, the wife of the interned BTA secretary, had come racing up the street. A gentle, wiry and fearless woman in her mid forties, Tess had been among the Ballymurphy women who had smashed through the British army's curfew of the Lower Falls in July 1970. With her head of dark hair, uplifting sense of humour and wry smile, she seemed incapable of harming a fly, a mistake made by many a British soldier.

I had come to know Tess through her three older sons - Joe, Frank and Philip. Seventeen-year-old Joe had the misfortune of sharing the same name as his uncle, the IRA's Quartermaster General, and therefore suffered much abuse at the hands of the Brits. Young Frank, who was sixteen and pretty much on the run, could occasionally be seen darting around the area with his friend, Paddy McBride, both furtively peering around corners, looking for the British army. The British army could also be seen furtively peering around corners looking for Frank and Paddy. (We used to call them Butch Cassidy and Sundance.) The third son, 15-year-old Philip, helped at the community centre. Despite regular military raids on the house and the pressures of raising a family of nine, the Tess who was charging towards me was generally unflappable. I'd never seen her in such a state. She skidded to a halt and grabbed me by the arm.

'Frank is getting out!' she squealed and threw her arms around me. She then whooped with joy and charged off in the direction of home to break the news to her family.

When Donal and I arrived into the BTA office, the small man took one look at us, soaked from the rain and holding the dripping paint tins, and his face split into a huge grin.

'Ciarán, Donal,' Mrs. Mac said, 'This is Frank Cahill.'

Frank slipped down from the table. One of the first of Ballymurphy's internees, his release had come about as a result of tribunals that had been set up in September by the British to give a legal gloss to internment without trial. In the lottery that followed, Frank had been lucky.

'Pleased to meet you both,' he said, 'I hear you're getting this place into shape.'

'Where in the name o' Jaysus did youse get all that paint on yer shoes!' Big Alice Franklin howled as the paint dripped onto the office floor.

'His fault,' Donal said, 'He nearly got us shot down in Smithfield - climbing around in a bombed-out paint shop when the Brits came and threatened to arrest us as looters!'

'Two head-the-balls,' Alice said.

'Balloons!' Frank grinned. 'By the way,' he added, 'Tess and I are having a few drinks in the house on Friday night. You're both welcome to call in and join us.'

It was the beginning of a friendship and working relationship that would span the next nineteen years – until Frank's death in 1991.

On the Friday night, Donal and I called around to Frank's house, along with Jean, Jenny Quigley and Jan McCarthy. The house and garden were packed with friends, neighbours, relatives and members of the BTA, all come to celebrate Frank's release from Long Kesh. Some time towards midnight, in the midst of a mighty sing-song, I couldn't help but notice that the entire group of young lads, with whom I'd had the brush at the community centre, was also present and in great form. There was no animosity: by now most had been to Glaslough, and they knew about my war with the Paras and had either figured that I was OK or wouldn't be around for very long. Towards the end of the night, next-door-neighbour, 52-year-old Rossie, was called for a song. Rossie, like Billy Scribbons, was one of the last Protestants in the area.

'Quiet now!' Frank called, 'A bit of shush for Rossie who's going to give us *The Ould Orange Flute.*'

Rossie, a small, smiling, round-faced woman with curly hair and glasses, began the satirical Orange song:

## Chapter 10

> *'In the county Tyrone, in the town of Dungannon*
> *Where many a ruckus meself had a hand in...'*

'Imagine the reverse up the Shankill,' Jean said.

'A respectful silence now,' Frank junior whispered in Jean's ear, 'A respectful silence.'

The odd whoop of support followed Rossie through the song until she reached the end of the last stanza.

'All together now!' Frank senior called, and everyone chimed in to Rossie's party piece:

> *'...as the flames soared around it they heard a strange noise*
> *'Twas the old flute still whistling "The Protestant Boys"*
> *Toora-loo, toora-lay*
> *Oh, it's six miles from Bangor to Donaghadee...'*

(Many years later, two of Rossie's grandchildren – Ihab and Andre Shoukri - would become notorious UDA chiefs in North Belfast! Poor Rossie would've turned in her grave.)

A few days later, while Donal and I were painting the stairs and landing of 42 a bright orange with the Smithfield paint, Frank called in to inspect the work. After checking out the hidden holes, the water system and the electric fire on which I was still cooking, he chuckled a kind of no-hope chuckle.

'The House That Jack Built,' he called my revered new home, and found no reason over the coming years to change his mind. Everyone else just called it '42' or *The Students' House* - based on that common local belief that anyone who came to work in the community was a student. Mark Duffy, the BTA treasurer, who fell through a sheet of newspaper into the water tank on his first visit, called it *The Asylum*.

\* \* \*

Over the coming months, Frank Cahill revived a number of projects that had lain dormant since his arrest. These included the resumption of the BTA's building programme, and the return to the area of Tony Spencer, an academic from Queen's University who had been invited by the BTA to coordinate an extensive survey into the area's needs, and had been doing so until the Internment derailment. He also attempted to salvage the remnants of an industrial development experiment that had been all but destroyed when the military commandeered the people-controlled industrial estate on the Springfield Road. As part of Operation Motorman it had become one of three massive 'Wild West'-style forts that now surrounded Ballymurphy. Meanwhile, Felicity had left the area; Donal had become a full-time worker at the community centre; and we'd been joined by Phylis McCullough, a stylish chatty woman in her early twenties who, when she wasn't at the BTA, worked as a singer in the clubs of the city. Occasionally, her laid-back husband, Tommy, would also show up. Mark Duffy, who had fallen into my water-tank, became a part-time worker. All was calm, all was bright as we rolled on towards the last Christmas I would ever spend in Cork.

I travelled down on the afternoon before Christmas Eve, crossing again the Irish border - that surreal boundary between worlds - just after dark. Arriving too late in Dublin for the regular service to Cork, I took the late-night mail-train. On board, I shared one of two, mostly empty passenger carriages with four women and 'The King of the Hippies', a long-haired, wild-eyed, bearded Englishman accompanied by a dog and a fox. When the conductor challenged him some time during the journey about his menagerie, the King argued that these were his children. They were travelling with him, he explained, as part of the current family deal being offered on the railways of *Córas Iompair Éireann*.

On my return to Belfast, someone gave Des Wilson a set of tickets to see a play in Dublin, entitled *Blood on the Diamond Stone*. Des, Noelle, Frank and Tess Cahill, Jean Campbell, Donal and I drove down for the night to find that the play was all about the close-up horrors of the North. When the curtain came down, we sat there, shell-shocked. We had similar feelings a year or two later when Cora, Donal and I went over to Queen's Film Theatre in South Belfast to see *The Battle of Algiers* and walked seamlessly out into gunfire and a patrol of zig-zagging British soldiers.

# Chapter 11
## The Umbrella

Cora and I were married in Cork in March 1973. The wedding was a moderate affair, restricted to immediate families and partners, a few special guests, and my grandfather who was visiting Cork from Belfast after great grand-aunt Maggie's funeral. But nothing was lost in style. Cora turned out in a flowing white dress made by my mother who, using her considerable dress-making skills, also produced my suit. This was a double-breasted, blue-black affair with the bell-bottoms of the time, complemented on the day by platform boots which were the height of fashion. We spent the following week in Kerry, hitchhiked back to Cork, and spent a couple of days with our families before heading back north.

On the morning we were leaving Cork, my mother reached in under the stairs and pulled out a large black umbrella.

'I picked this up the other day,' she said, opening it up to reveal its heavy, double spokes, 'I thought it might come in handy - ideal for blustery Belfast downpours.'

'God, that'll be great,' I said, 'An umbrella that doesn't disintegrate in the next big wind.'

Cora and I took the umbrella back to Belfast, but it never saw that big wind. It died a death on our first night out in the city centre, and would be forever synonymous with the little-known Battle of Castle Street, the opening salvo to Cora's life in Belfast.

\* \* \*

April 1973 was no better a time to go to Belfast than May 1972. It was still a place that took a terrible toll on the nerves. When you walked about, you were conscious that every parked vehicle could explode without warning. At night, in the blacked-out streets, every approaching car could harbour assassins. When you sat in a pub, you knew that it could be bombed or machine gunned without notice. When you knocked on someone's door at night, you caused the house to fill with silence. If you persisted, you might get a distant and reluctant 'Who is it?' If a knock came to your own door, you applied the same caution. Lots of dead people told you why. Thousands of people were fleeing, and those who were arriving, unconnected to the war, were an odd mix - people with a mission, head cases, and people who swore they'd be home soon.

We were only in the house a few hours when there was a knock at the door. I answered to find 17-year-old Stevie Mallon outside. Stevie had by now become one of the lynchpins of the BTA youth club. Calm, solidy-built, with a deathly droll sense of humour and a poker face, he was also prone to impulse. During one of the early refugee crises, when he'd been evacuated to England, this impulse had gotten the better of him. The cops had arrived in a street in Bolton one day to find the tarmac daubed in huge letters. 'Sons of Britain, beware!' the letters read. Which would have been OK except for the paint drips that led down the street and back to a tin in the shed to the rear of Stevie's adoptive home. Stevie had met Cora during her September visit. He knew we were back and the impulse struck again.

'Hiya mucker,' he said, 'I'm here to invite yourself and your gorgeous new wife out for a drink on Saturday night. I was thinking of that pub off High Street where they have the folk nights.'

'Come on in,' I said, 'And we'll see how Cora feels.'

'That would be lovely,' Cora said, 'But would it be safe.'

'Safe as the Titanic,' Stevie said.

'And we all know what happened to that...' Cora said.

'I'll have you know,' Stevie said, 'It was in good shape when it left Belfast...'

On the Friday night, I threw on the wedding suit and the platform boots and the three of us took one of the People's Taxis into Castle Street - me sporting my brand-new umbrella. As usual, the city centre was a ghost town. Earlier in the day, however, there had been frantic activity in Wellington Place when the RUC had tied a rope to a young man's leg and forced him to walk back to the car he'd been driving and remove explosives while they stood at a distance. There had also been a gun-battle at the South Armagh border, and a 76-year-old woman had been shot in the thigh during an ambush on the Falls Road. However, despite the emptiness of the streets, a great night was had in the pub, with a full house oblivious to the mayhem happening around them. One of the barmen enjoyed himself so much that he could hardly stand by the end of the night. Eventually, the last rousing medley was played and it was time to go.

As soon as we stepped out into the street, we heard that there had been a bombing at a bar in the nationalist Short Strand area.

## Chapter 11

This was when you became conscious of the fact that night time was when unwary drunks were dragged off and murdered. That night, however, there were no cars on the street to signal possible assassins as we quickly made our way to Castle Street. There, we joined a handful of older people at the unofficial taxi stand and waited for a People's Taxi that would take us to Ballymurphy. As we huddled in a doorway from driving sheets of drizzle, listening to sporadic bursts of distant gunfire, a 14-strong loyalist gang arrived from the direction of Millfield.

'Not good my friends,' Stevie muttered as they began to call us all the *Fenian bastards* of the day. However, things might have passed off peacefully had they not got worse. We ignored the taunts, but the loyalists spotted better prey - a young couple walking up Castle Street towards the taxi stop. They charged down the street and got stuck in.

'OK Stevie,' I said.

I handed Cora my lovely new umbrella.

'Keep that safe,' I said.

Without having thought it through, Stevie and I ran down Castle Street and hurled ourselves into the thick of things. I grabbed at the shoulders of the nearest guy, pulled him around and hit him on the nose, causing him to cup his face in both hands and fall backwards. Stevie grabbed a second and threw him against the wall with such force that he bounced back and landed on his arse. The diversion caused the gang to momentarily scatter, which gave the couple a chance to get up and run off. However, it also left myself and Stevie with the full calamity, which included two injured lads who were now very mad.

'Not good again my friend,' Stevie intoned as the gang re-formed around us.

Despite the odds we did OK for a while, but my attire wasn't geared to unarmed combat. The double-breasted coat, flaired trousers and two-inch platform boots didn't greatly lend themselves to high kicks. In fact, I lost my balance, slipped in the wet street and went down, copping a boot in the mouth and a busted lip. From street level, things were now looking very bad. But the night was saved: half a dozen young nationalist heroes came out of a chipper in Castle Street.

'Orangies!' one of them shouted and they charged to the rescue. The downside was that one of them grabbed my brand-new umbrella from Cora as he passed.

'That's my brolly!' I howled as he ignominiously used it to batter the guy who had landed me the kick. 'You'll wreck it!' I shouted, but he motored on. By the time he was finished, there was little left that resembled an umbrella.

'Sorry boss,' he said, as he tossed aside the tattered, spoke-twisted remains, 'But you know how it is with Orangies.'

Everything now got out of control, with more loyalists and more nationalists joining the brawl until it was impossible to tell friend from foe and you just hit anyone who looked like they might hit you. Eventually, it took seven Land Rovers of armed troops to break it up.

'Stevie,' I said at this stage, as Castle Street resembled El Alamein, 'Straighten your tie and let's get the hell outta here.'

'My friend,' Stevie concurred, 'You might have a point.'

'I should've known better,' Cora said as we hurried off up Castle Street, 'A quiet night out my arse.'

The following day, Frank Cahill called.

'Balloons!' he said, 'Keep that up and you'll end up tatie-bread.' (Belfast rhyming-slang for *dead*.)

By now almost 700 people had been killed in the Troubles and over 10,000 wounded. Since the outbreak of the war, Ballymurphy had seen 31 civilian deaths (18 killed by the British army, three by the IRA and 10 by loyalists). There had been a further 14 British army deaths. Thirty-one of those fatalities had occurred since my own arrival. Dozens of others had been wounded in gun-battles, army shootings and sectarian attacks. Being battered to death in Castle Street might've been for a good cause, but the end result would've been the same.

'You were bloody lucky,' Frank said.

A week after the Castle Street fracas, 27-year-old Eddie O'Rawe, also from Ballymurphy, wasn't so lucky. April 12$^{th}$ was a day of rockets, grenades and sniping. Eddie, an IRA Volunteer, was in Cape Street in the Falls area with a companion named Seán Rowntree. Both were unarmed when they were stopped and searched by British troops. They were then gunned down in cold blood. Eddie O'Rawe was killed and Seán Rowntree was badly wounded.

Eight days after the killing of Eddie O'Rawe, on April 20$^{th}$ 1973, Frank, Donal, Cora and I were having a cup of tea in 42 when a double explosion came from the direction of the Taggart.

## Chapter 11

'What was that!' Cora said.

'Not grenades. Not blast bombs,' I said.

By now, everyone in Ballymurpy, including myself, was an expert on the aural nuances of low intensity warfare. An hour later, we learned that the double bang had come from the first of many Russian-made rocket-propelled grenades to be fired by the IRA in Ballymurphy. The British army had a new headache: the IRA had taken charge of a consignment of RPG-7s from Libya a few weeks earlier.

'That'll sicken 'em,' Frank said, 'They'll be out of here before Christmas.'

'Is that not a bit optimistic Frank?' Donal laughed.

'Not a bit of it,' Frank said.

\* \* \*

I don't know when the British army came to seek my help in preventing its obliteration, but I believe it to have been some time in early 1973, whenever the Welsh Guards had taken over the Ballymurphy posting.

I remember for some reason that it was a cloudy morning, threatening rain, when there was a knock on the front door of 42. I answered to find an officer of the regiment standing there, looking a bit sheepish.

'Hello,' he said in a strong Welsh accent, which sounded not unlike a Cork accent.

I expected a raiding party to swoop past but it never happened. Instead, the man before me made the most astonishing offer.

'Is Bryson about?' he asked.

'I have no idea where Bryson is,' I said, 'But he doesn't live *here* any more.'

'Well, if you see him can you pass on a message from us. Tell him we don't want any bother while we're here. We're Celts too, the same as you.'

'I have no idea where Bryson is,' I repeated.

'Well, tell him anyway,' he said, 'We just want to do this tour of duty and get home again. He and his boys don't bother us, we don't bother them.'

He then backed off deferentially and left me standing at the door with an unhinged jaw.

In time, I might have considered that I'd imagined the incident. However, when I mentioned it to one of the alleged local IRA

Volunteers, he described how the Coldstream Guards had also attempted to buy their way safely through their tour of duty.

'They found an Armalite under a bed in one house,' he told me, 'Then they called all the people in the house together and told them they'd leave the rifle where it was provided no attacks were made on them. Another day, a four-man patrol ran into a house after a woman who had a rifle up her coat. When they caught her, they told her they knew she'd come in with the rifle, gave her the date they were leaving, and asked that word go out that they didn't want any attacks mounted against them before then...'

All is fair in love and war.

And, going back to the Welsh Guards, the Celts consideration may have been working both ways: in 25 years of the IRA's war against the British state, not a single bomb was ever planted in Scotland or Wales.

\* \* \*

After the close shave in Castle Street, we tended to restrict ourselves to the clubs and bars of West Belfast. This did not mean any greater safety. Clubs and pubs in nationalist areas were just as likely as any others to be hit, and people on their way home were often murdered. But, there was a *sense* of greater protection. Vigilant doormen, grilles and 'air-locks', and a heightened awareness of strangers, led to what was really a false sense of security, but it was better than none.

However, since the pubs closed at midnight, and *nobody* in their right mind was ever ready to go to bed at that ridiculous hour, Cora and I began to throw post-pub parties at 42. Beginning the week after Cora arrived, they became firmly-ensconced cultural extravaganzas that became legend. Simultaneously, Cora, Donal, Kieran and I established the West Belfast Hedonist Society. Driven by the motto *Pleasure for pleasure's sake!*, we concluded that just because there was a war didn't mean that life had to be all bad. In no time at all everyone who mattered knew that every Friday and Saturday night (unless we were away) was party time at 42. On nights punctuated by riots, shooting and bombings, people would spill from all sorts of establishments, near and far, and with the homing instinct of the converging zombies in *The Night of the Living Dead* they would close in on Ballymurphy Road. On occasions, they came from as far away as Dublin, Cork, Derry and Galway. There would also be guest appearances by those younger chaps, allegedly from 'B' Company.

## Chapter 11

Before leaving for the pub, we'd replace the living-room light with a 60-watt green bulb. This added ambience to the meaningful posters plastered across the wall opposite the fireplace, one describing the toxins that made cigarettes so enjoyable. Some time around midnight, under that trademark green bulb, Donal and his guitar would anchor the music, Frank Cahill would take over as Master of Ceremonies, and Kieran Fagan would add the tin whistle if he was about. People of all ages would flood in with their carry-outs, other musicians would arrive, and the loo-bucket would start doing the rounds. Out the back door, up the entry, and in the front door to the back-to-front bathroom. And, every Friday and Saturday night, without fail, the British army would turn up.

The first indication would be the static of their radios outside in the yard, followed by the English, Scottish or Welsh accents. This would be the cue for the big living-room curtains to fly back and communications to begin.

Jan McCarthy who always arrived in a long, black evening gown would then fill the window with her bubbly frame. Pirouetting up and down and blowing kisses at the face-blackened troops, she would, in her loudest English accent, burst into a rendition of *The Army, the Navy and the Air Force*. This was all about ladies of the night and the boys in the Queen's service. Meanwhile, the crowd behind would provide the background dancers and an excellent assortment of exotic faces. As soon as Jan finished, we'd all strike up in a great chorus of that anti-war song *Where Have All The Flowers Gone*, moving quickly to *Where have all the soldiers gone? Gone to graveyards every one*.

But our efforts to produce battalions of conscientious objectors met with no known success.

Yet, despite regular raids of the house at other times, the army kept its distance. In three years of continuous partying, they never once came in, although the distinguished guests were in clear and full view. With hindsight, I suspect they beat one another up in all the bases for the privilege of our back yard on a Friday and Saturday night.

There was ever only one altercation. It was a winter's night and Donal was out in the yard feeling a bit seedy when the Brits appeared in a shower of static.

'What's your name?' one of them asked.

'Bugger off,' Donal said.

At this, the soldier punched him in the stomach. If he did, Donal justifiably threw up all over him. The crowd, drawn by the commotion, spilled towards the back door and the patrol took off through the gardens with an outraged Donal in hot pursuit. Our Niall, who was up from Dublin for the weekend, grabbed my arm.

'What's happening?' he asked.

I explained and told him that the loud roars receding into the darkness belonged to Donal.

'Well Jaysus!' Niall said, 'I don't mind coming to a fella's rescue, but there's no way I'm chasing the fuckin' British army through the gardens of Ballymurphy in the dead of fuckin' night.'

Fair point, well made.

Then there were the many one-off events. Like the night Gerry Finnegan, the local Methuselah-bearded Community Relations Officer, arrived in with Max and Shay. Max, an Austrian hippy with long blond hair, wore a maxi-type denim jacket over his jeans and told us that his full name was Blue Max. He sang and played the guitar and had what we presumed was a wooden leg that jutted out in front whenever he sat down. Shay, stubble-chinned with dark, curly locks, was from Dublin and played the wash-board. Story was that they'd discovered they were sharing the one girlfriend, so they ditched her and went on the road together, busking for a living.

'Are you going to play us a song on that guitar or what,' Frank asked.

'Sure man,' Max said and opened up with Bob Dylan's *Blowing in the Wind* just as the IRA opened up with a burst of gunfire somewhere close by.

'Here big lad,' a rather tipsy Joe McMullan (Mrs. Mac's husband) said in the middle of *Blowing In The Wind*, 'Have y'ever heard of the IRA, the Provisional Irish Republican Army?'

Joe was very patriotic and keen to impart history.

'I'm Blue Max,' Max said, 'I have no interest in this fucking IRA.'

There was a deathly silence.

'You'll be fuckin' black and blue Max if y'ever say that again,' Joe said, squinting his eyes and rearing up fiercely.

'Now,' Frank said, 'We'll have Joe for a song. A big hand for Joe!'

Another night, Peggy Burns came in from the bathroom to make a quick announcement. Our Niall, up from Dublin again, had just turned out a row of hot poteens (with hot water and sugar) to avoid the third-degree throat-burns associated with cold poteens, when

## Chapter 11

Peggy shushed everyone.

'There's some guy out in the hall,' she said in a low voice, 'with a gun in his belt. And nobody knows who the fuck he is.'

In another society, this might have prompted concern for the party hosts. But, in Belfast, not a bit of it.

'We're away home,' everybody said, 'See youse all on Monday.'

They all shot out the door, leaving myself, Cora, Donal and Niall with the man with the gun and his pal. Although Niall was for jumping them both, reason prevailed and the actual upshot had the six of us sitting in the living-room drinking the hot poteens, with us four pretending it was perfectly normal for forty-odd people to funnel out the door in twenty seconds flat, and the other two pretending that they didn't know that we knew they had a gun. The man with the gun and his pal eventually left when the drink ran out. Some time later, somebody told us they were Provisional IRA from the Falls.

And there was the night that Donal decided to go home at three in the morning rather than stay over.

'I'll drive you,' Niall offered but he didn't have a car.

'I'll loan you my car,' Eileen Costigan said. In Eileen's later opinion, this was a bad move.

'I'd better come to show you the way home,' Cora said.

As the night raged on, the four of them set off for Andersonstown.

On the Andersonstown Road, as Niall turned into St. Agnes Drive, they were hit broadside by an armour-plated jeep, driving through the blacked-out streets without lights as was their wont at the time. All four were hurled into the street, and were lucky not to have been killed. It cost £5 to have the demolished remains of Eileen's car towed to the scrap-yard, and Niall ended up on crutches. And I had to find £500 cash on St. Patrick's Day to bail him out of Townhall Street RUC station.

On many of those Friday and Saturday nights, just when it seemed that the party was beginning to flag, Gerry O'Donnell from Divismore Park would turn up. Gerry, who had a huge curling moustache and long thick hair like Jesus, would be coming home from some gig. He would have with him various permutations of his folk group who, with banjos, guitars, bodhráns, flutes, fiddles and whistles, would instill in us all a new lease of life.

Cora lovingly called them 'Gerry O'Donnell's brass fucking band'.

# Chapter 12
## The Bike

Not long after Cora arrived in Belfast I bought a second-hand motorbike. Kieran Fagan, who'd recently had a lucky escape as he slid along an English motorway when the chain of his own bike snapped, drove me over to some street off the Knock dual carriageway to look at it. It was a gold Honda 250 that gleamed in the sunlight like a polished penny.

'What do you think?' I asked Kieran.

'It looks OK,' he said, 'But you can never be sure with second-hand.'

'I'll take it,' I told the seller.

'Well' that's a snap decision if ever I saw one,' Kieran said.

I paid the seller his asking price, mounted the bike and drove it back to Ballymurphy, where I found a parking spot in the hallway beside the bottom of the stairs. Cora thought I'd been a bit impetuous.

'How do you know it's not a crock?' she asked as we ate the dinner.

'Only one way to find out,' I said, 'Grab your coat and we'll take a run down to Lisburn.'

'Can we have a cup of tea first? To finish our dinner?'

'We can have tea when we get back,' I said.

We left the plates on the table and I pushed the bike out into Ballymurphy Road.

'You take the helmet,' I said, 'From the back it'll look better.'

I kick-started the bike and we set off - down the Whiterock Road, down the Donegall Road and onto the M1. Eight minutes later we reached the turn-off for the A1 where we'd have to leave the motorway and circle about to get back onto the Belfast-bound carriageway. The bike was going a dinger.

'How much money have you got in your pockets?' I asked Cora.

'About one pound twenty,' she said with caution in the voice.

'Great!' I said, 'We're going to Cork.'

'What about your work?' she yelled.

'I'll ring Donal. We'll swap nights.'

'Oh God, no...!' she said and clung on tight.

In line with the general state of lawlessness that governed the

## Chapter 12

North, I had no tax, no licence, no insurance and no helmet, but nobody cared. Whenever we were stopped at a military or RUC road-block they checked for ID - my employment permit did the trick - and they checked for guns and bombs. Everything else was immaterial (and so it would remain until I sold the bike almost three years later).

To my parents' great surprise, we arrived at their door, eyes bloodshot from 264 miles of wind, just after midnight. Two days later, after saying hello to everyone in Cork and borrowing the cost of the journey home, we drove back to Belfast, fully comfortable with the bike's roadworthiness. I could now move freely and confidently around Belfast and avoid the dangers of walking. However, there were things I had yet to learn.

In September 1972 I'd embarked on the Youth & Community Work course mentioned during my interview for the Ballymurphy job. It was an in-service course that allowed work and study at the same time. Though based in Jordanstown Polytechnic, it involved many outside residentials and workshops, some of which took place, from May 1973 onwards, on Tuesday mornings at Corrymeela House in Upper Crescent. This meant travelling from Ballymurphy down the Donegall Road through the loyalist Village and Sandy Row areas. Every Tuesday morning at roughly quarter to ten, my big, shiny gold Honda would come down the republican end of the Donegall Road, pass the rows of abandoned, bullet-scarred houses that formed the interface, and continue on into town. Anyone who remembers Belfast in the spring of 1973 will know how that would go nowhere good.

On the morning in question, I was fully relaxed: blue cheesecloth shirt and denim jeans, collar-length hair trailing in the wind, shells from Iran around my neck, sleeveless, embroidered sheepskin from Afghanistan on my back. At the interface of empty streets I stopped at a red light, watchful for any sign of trouble. Everything was nice and peaceful. Leaning forward on the handlebars, I wondered what it would be like to travel across Asia on a motorbike. I was, I believe, somewhere about the Khyber Pass when I felt something whiz past my right ear. It was followed by the loud sharp crack of a high-velocity rifle. A couple of blank seconds later I realised that I'd just been shot at! It came as a terrible shock. I was, as far as I was concerned, a nice guy who didn't deserve this. And it had been close. I'm told that you only feel the wind of the bullet that has most

# The Bike

of your name on it.

Lying flat to the tank, I did a screeching wheelie through the red light and, like a man with cross-hairs on his back, gunned it down the Donegall Road, waiting for the next awful shot. Although there was no sign of pursuit I was sure the gunman was following. Or had maybe taken a faster route and was waiting up ahead. If anyone had stood out in front of me that morning, even a centenarian on a zimmer frame, they were goners.

By the time I reached the junction with Sandy Row, I'd completely revised my relationship with the demography of Belfast. Any attempt to kill you helps focus the mind that way. Despite my harmless Southern origins, someone had been waiting to shoot me. I felt traumatised. My shiny gold bike had fingered me.

'What the hell happened to you?' fellow student, Alf Midgley from the Shankill, asked when I got to Corrymeela House, 'You look like you've seen a bloody ghost!'

'I did,' I said, 'Mine! I've just been shot at!'

Alf was a man of about forty, a trade-unionist from a Labour background who'd been warning me to stay clear of loyalist areas.

'The difference is,' he'd explained, throwing his eyes back in his head as he did when he was being serious, '*You* might be able to guarantee *my* safety in Ballymurphy, but *I* couldn't guarantee *yours* on the Shankill. If you're a 'Fenian', you're fair game. Nobody's gonna ask who you are. And, if they did, you'd be a goner anyway...'

If you want to live, his advice ended, don't make patterns.

\* \* \*

The bike also changed my relationship with the dogs of Ballymurphy. To put this in perspective, you'll need to understand that those dogs had been involved in a protracted war against the British army ever since the first military invasion of Easter 1970. They had faced armoured cars, CS gas, batons, rubber bullets and live rounds, and now they were after me.

Although the bike bore no resemblance to a Saladin, Saracen, Whippet or Pig, or any other military vehicle to have ever sullied the streets of Ballymurphy, I became an object of hate to be savaged on sight. Having perfected their strategies over the years, large packs would rise to the first sound of the bike and rush to the corner of the street. There they would wait, heads down, sinews taut, teeth bared. As soon as I slowed down to take the bend, they would pounce as one and tear at ankles and calves. Even with sturdy walking boots, I

## Chapter 12

took hits. But as they say in Irish, a person without a plan is no more value than a pig. I thought, *If they can have a strategy, so can I.* It took some time to perfect, but in the end I could be seen slowing down well before each bend. This would dupe the dogs into thinking the corner had moved and prompt a premature attack. Whereupon I would accelerate, shout *Geronimo!* and lash out with both boots. Dogs would land in shrieking heaps.

'The sane people of Ballymurphy are beginning to sound me out to see if your mind has left your head,' Frank Cahill confided, but I didn't care.

'I can't be outsmarted by dogs,' I told him.

In later times the bike developed an appalling affliction, akin to some kind of mechanical flatulence. It would start with a dragging effect, and would gradually build up into a gaseous swell until release came in one atrocious fart that you couldn't possibly separate from a gunshot. In a city full of jumpy, trigger-happy troops, a backfire like that was a terrible liability. It didn't help the civilian nerves either and had a particularly debilitating effect on the lads who worked around at the Lazy Acre, due to the sedentary lifestyle that had evolved in that quarter.

The Lazy Acre was around in Springhill. It had begun life as the Riverbed Landscaping Scheme, initiated by the Borough of Belfast Urban and Rural Improvement Campaign, but nobody called it that any more. The idea was that local labour would pipe the Clowney stream that ran between Springhill and Ballymurphy so that the waste ground between the two estates could be converted into playing fields and a children's playground. It was a fine idea, and so it would remain. It could've been the war, or the roughness of the terrain, or the continuous arrests of the workers, or the loaning of the JCB for community ventures (including the demolition by the IRA of an army sangar at Corry's), or the easy conversion of gable walls into handball alleys; but whatever it was, it worked, and the scheme didn't. And so grew the legend of the Lazy Acre. Years later, when the scheme finally folded, it was widely rumoured that the greatest burst of activity to ever afflict the site occurred one Tuesday morning when I was leaving for Corrymeela House and the bike backfired in Ballymurphy Road.

'There was a scatter like you never seen,' Big Barney McGivern of the BTA - who worked on the scheme - told me later, 'Every one of us hit the dirt, dead cert it was a sniper!'

I would've done the same myself. In fact I already had. The morning after Cora and I had driven to Cork, I was standing at my parents' gate on Evergreen Road, talking to my oldest sister, Fionnuala, when a passing car backfired. Like Barney and the boys, I threw myself flat to the ground. The only difference was that I was in Cork where a shot hadn't been fired in anger since 1923.

# Chapter 13
## The Suit

The wedding suit came in dead handy when I was summoned to the Long Kesh tribunals that had freed Frank Cahill.

Mrs. Sloan, the wife of Larry who sold the fish on Fridays, arrived into the community centre one afternoon while we were trying to evict the younger children. A thin, harassed-looking woman, Mrs. Sloan's nerves were shot through. They were shot through from the war. They were shot through from the accidental shooting dead of her 16-year-old son, Michael, at an IRA training camp in January 1972. And they were shot through from the constant military raids on her home. With a half-smile, she nipped in through the steel side door while I was on guard.

'My God!' she said, 'You could get yourself killed out there. Is this what youse have to do to get those childer out?'

She was nodding towards Donal who was racing around the hall, trying his best to grab children so they could be chucked outside where they could call us *de Boink-boink* and *Chisel* and batter the steel door with rocks while demanding we give them back their mothers' bricks.

'The darlings!' Donal shouted as he ran past.

'Could I talk till ya for a minute?' Mrs. Sloan said.

'No problem,' I said and we went off to one side while Philip Cahill and Tony Crooks held the breach.

'Would you go up to the Kesh and talk for our Tony?' Mrs. Sloan asked.

That was not too long after I'd seen Tony racing through the cemetery with the Paras doing their best to stop him with Sterling sub-machine guns.

'Of course,' I said, 'Just say when...'

On the appointed day, I put on the wedding suit and took the Long Kesh bus up to the internment camp along with Mrs. Sloan. It was a depressing place, like something from Hitler's Germany plonked in an old airfield outside Lisburn. Barbed wire cages and Nissan huts held hundreds of men, none of whom had been charged with anything. The tribunals were meant to give an air of due process to the concentration camp image. As we waited our turn, we had a cup of tea in the visitors' hut run by the Quakers - the only facility at the camp.

'He has no chance,' Mrs. Sloan said, 'But we have to try.'

After an hour or so, I left Mrs. Sloan at the Quakers' hut and went through security. I was a witness, I explained, for Tony Sloan. Everything I had in my pockets was taken from me and put into a manilla envelope. I was then led into the camp to the hut in which the tribunal was under way.

When I arrived, Tony was already seated. It was all very informal - the judge without robes, plainclothes cops, a couple of screws and me.

'Can you tell us anything about this young man?' the judge asked.

'I can,' I said, 'He's a respected member of the community who helps me at the youth club. He comes from a good, hard-working family...' All of this was true. As well as selling fish, Larry Sloan was a major player in running the Sloan's Club, a shebeen built on Larry's inspiration in memory of his son, Michael.

The Special Branch, who had a different view, interrupted, but the judge told them to shut up.

'Go on young man,' he said to me.

I told him all the good things I knew about Tony, and went back to the Quakers' hut. We waited for news; and when it came nobody was more surprised than me. Tony was released and came whooping out of the camp gates. Outside in the car-park, Mrs. Sloan charged across to where I was standing and swung out of my neck.

'You're an *angel* from Heaven!' she squealed.

A week or two later a woman from Springhill called around to 42.

'Would you go up to the Kesh and talk for my Tommy?' she asked.

'Tommy Who?' I said.

'Tommy Ramsey,' she said.

'You better tell me about him,' I said after a brief tussle between obligation and doubt.

'Well,' she began, 'Before he got interned he used to work in the community around in Springhill and Westrock...'

On went the suit again and up I went to the tribunal to tell them all the good things I knew about Tommy Ramsey. Tommy, when he saw me take the stand, thought I was Special Branch and couldn't believe his ears. He wasn't released, but we were friends forever.

'Wait till I tell you about the first time I laid eyes on yon,' he'd say to everyone whenever we ran into one another up in the Sloan's Club.

## Chapter 13

    After my failure to have Tommy released, Cora figured that it wouldn't be long now before *I* ended up in Long Kesh.'

* * *

The suit also helped negotiate a truce in Ballymurphy between the Provisional and Official IRAs.

The bad blood remaining from the feud of March 1971 was further exacerbated when the Official IRA declared their unilateral truce in May 1972. By the spring of 1973, hostilities had spilled over into warfare between supporters of both IRAs. As anyone who didn't align themselves with one side or the other was stateless, this meant a community divided into two camps. Discos became major flashpoints, and that meant trouble for the likes of us and the BTA.

It wasn't helped when two young Official IRA members arrived into the office with drawn revolvers during one of our Friday night discos at the community centre.

'Turn on the lights,' one of them said, 'We want to knee-cap so-and-so.'

'I'm sorry,' I said, 'The lights don't go on until half-eleven.'

Looking at their guns to see if they were still there, they repeated the demand. They got the same answer, now backed up by Donal who confirmed that no lights went on until half eleven. Confused, they left. Ten minutes later, the local Provisional IRA commander (who was all of seventeen) turned up with a couple of lieutenants, all armed but too late to sort out the Officials. There were probably people on both sides that night who were very lucky that the lights didn't go on until half-eleven.

The spring of 1973 became increasingly a time of guns about all the local youth centres and discos began to close down: one in St. Thomas's School when two sub-machine guns, eight pistols and a nail bomb were discovered among the clientele; and a second in St. Aidan's when young men from each side turned up with Armalite rifles and Thompsons. Then, on May $7^{th}$, all hell broke loose at the community centre.

At the beginning of the year, we'd convinced the BTA to buy state-of-the-art disco equipment and were now running two very successful discos a week. With DJs, Philip Cahill, Chuck McKinley and Seán Butler (whose uncle had been killed along with Fr. Fitzpatrick during the Westrock massacre), these attracted hundreds of teenagers. But our success was our undoing. On the night of May $7^{th}$, I found myself alongside Cora, Donal and Big

# The Suit

Alice Franklin, trying to quell a riot - successfully at first, then very unsuccessfully. It began with the Gary Glitter song variation: *I'm back. I'm back. Fuck the Sticky-backs*; but this time, a stash of weapons was produced by some of the Officials: hurleys, pokers, pieces of scaffolding. In defence, the young Provisionals grabbed anything that could be broken off anything else in the hall.

If there was anyone you'd have wanted on your side that night, it was Big Alice. In the months that followed internment, she'd been a formidable member of Ballymurphy's hen patrols - groups of women who followed military patrols through the area, blowing whistles and banging bin-lids to warn off IRA Volunteers. A formidable asset, she was renowned for single-handedly terrorising the forces of Perfidious Albion with the scientific use of a very colourful tongue projected from an almighty larynx. She was also, as you'll have gleaned from earlier text, a pillar of the community and a great woman for defending community rights. When trouble broke - no matter where in Ballymurphy - Alice had the knack of being there. Locally, she was held in staggering measures of ardour and awe, but mostly awe. When Todler, second only to Jim Bryson, had once test-fired a rifle and accidentally took out Alice's chimney-pot, sending a shower of soot into the big woman's living-room, he had run for his life rather than face Alice.

Although our numbers were small on the night of the riot, and the hall was left in a shambles, we didn't do badly at the beginning. We managed to separate both factions and agree an orderly exit. This was mainly due to Alice roaring things like: 'Is this how youse are gonna get yer united Ireland!' and 'If ya don't stop that fightin', I'll kick the friggin' arse o' ye!'

The agreement was that the Officials would leave first; and despite the insults being hurled each way this was accomplished without blood-letting. However, as the Provisionals left, the Officials lined up on both sides and some bottles were thrown. And despite Alice's fearsome interventions, the numbers overwhelmed our pacifying efforts and mayhem prevailed. One young lad's life was probably saved when Donal threw himself between him and the iron bars raining down from a dozen pairs of hands. Later that night running gunfights broke out between the two factions and the same lucky lad was grazed in the head by a bullet. As Donal, Cora, Alice and I rushed around Ballymurphy, trying to deflect the protagonists, I came to a sorry conclusion.

## Chapter 13

'We need to close the senior club. Bored teenagers are better than dead teenagers.'

After several more days of firefights, I donned the suit again and headed for the Turf Lodge home of Official IRA leader, Ronnie Bunting, to negotiate a ceasefire. Ronnie was the son of Major Ronald Bunting, a former sidekick of the Reverend Ian Paisley, who had presided over one of the seminal incidents of the Troubles - the ambush of civil rights marchers at Burntollet Bridge in Co. Derry in January 1969. While Ronnie junior spoke for the Officials, the Provisionals were represented by Barney McGivern who had dived for cover from my motorbike and whom I'd previously known only as a member of the BTA.

'Now, now,' Ronnie said, when I described two of the Official disco-rioters as thugs, 'Don't be using any emotive language.' But the negotiations were successful, and calm between the two factions prevailed for a while.

'Keep your head down,' Ronnie called as I was leaving.

In 1974, Ronnie became part of the breakaway Irish National Liberation Army which disagreed with the Official IRA's ceasefire. In 1978, he became its military leader, holding the position during a particularly active period, during which Airey Neave, Colditz escaper and close friend of Margaret Thatcher, was killed by an INLA bomb as he left the House of Commons car park. In 1980, gunmen broke into his home in the Lower Falls and shot him dead. Noel Lyttle, another INLA member was also killed and Ronnie's wife, Susanne, was wounded. The attack was claimed by the UDA but SAS involvement was widely suspected.

We never did discover whether or not it would've been OK to re-open the senior youth club because, shortly after the truce was put in place, Donal and I resigned from the community centre. Phylis McCullough, our other co-worker, had long ago fled.

The situation at the centre had become impossible, partly due to the feuding, and partly to in-fighting plaguing the BTA and embroiling myself and Donal. Eventually, in the middle of a row with Mrs. Mac, I grabbed the typewriter and hammered out a full-page letter of resignation.

'Lemme see that!' Donal said. Two minutes later he had counter-signed it; and we both walked out, jobless. No notice, no holiday pay, nothing. Just jobless and relieved. Cora met us at the door.

'What's happening?' she asked.

# The Suit

'Looks like the end of working in Ballymurphy,' Donal said.
'Not at all!' I said, 'Haven't we got a base in Ballymurphy Road?'

In a jaunty mood, the three of us walked down to Ballymurphy Road and set up the Ballymurphy Detached Project at 42, an enterprise described by the uncharitable Kieran Fagan as the Ballymurphy Deranged Project. The following day I signed on the dole down in Corporation Street where some nice man wanted to give me a train ticket back to Cork!

During the next few weeks, we installed a *Roneo* ink-based duplicator provided by my father's group in Cork, and Donal and I managed to bid against one another down at Ross's auctions for a filing cabinet. Cora and I moved our living room to one of the bedrooms, made an office of one of the smaller bedrooms, and turned the ground floor into a community facility. Meanwhile, despite the nice man in Corporation Street, the dole came through and sustained us for the next seven months.

The project thus established would go on to pioneer the concept of detached youth and community work in the North of Ireland. At its zenith it incorporated 26 separate programmes, involving some 50 local volunteers, the vast majority in their late teens and early-to-mid twenties. Along with other community activists in Greater Ballymurphy, we developed a system of mutual support that brought together all the estates of the district into a single loose unit of community co-ordination and organisation, based on the ideal of a community movement. We also took on board numerous human rights issues, an ethos later carried over into 42's offspring, the Upper Springfield Resource Centre.

From the beginning Cora became a central pillar of 42. As well as taking responsibility for many activities, she held the fort while the rest of us were away and took on several projects of her own. These included helping a young girl who had suffered brain damage undergo a programme of re-training, and developing a homework club in the house for older teenagers. Cora has always been a doer. While others sit in counsel over a problem, Cora quietly attacks it with a clear strategy. She's also a people's person, who can win over most hearts. As the weeks grew into months, she became the rock on which 42 stood firmest.

While the house became a local resource centre, the drum of the Cork *Roneo* never stopped spewing ink over everyone in range and providing the community with a printing press. As the republican

149

## Chapter 13

movement was an integral part of that community, it was only natural that Eugene Trainor would arrive at the door with wide eyes peering from a curtain of black hair, a huge smile on his face and the wax stencils of *The Tattler*, the local republican newssheet, rolled up in his hand and a couple of reams of paper under his arm.

'Is there ink in the machine' Eugene would ask. I always had a feeling that he was just waiting for the day when I said *No*, so that he could yank a big tube out of his back pocket.

One day Eugene brought yellow paper with *The Tattler* stencils. The following day the house was raided by the Brits and there were still some sheets sitting in the *Roneo*.

'Look Sarge,' one of the squaddies said, 'Yellow paper!'

I gave him a funny look as if he was losing his mind. The officer told him to wise up.

And Kieran Fagan had his car taken from the front gate so many times by both IRAs that he wasn't sure in the end who owned it. *The People's Car*, we used to call it.

'Aye,' Kieran used to respond, 'But the friggin' people don't put the friggin' petrol in it, do they?'

Then he'd tell us his recurring cake story - which, I'm convinced was some kind of trauma-reducing therapy - about how he and Donal were away in the Shetland Islands and Donal spent the last of their money on a big cake which Kieran, in protest, wouldn't touch. And how Donal ate most of it before Kieran managed to snatch away the last crumbs in a life-saving swipe.

Eventually, Kieran made a stand one day when two 17-year-old Official IRA members turned up at the door of 42 and demanded his car.

'Lads,' he said, 'No!'

The next thing he knew he had a revolver in his teeth.

'Well lads,' he said, 'if you feel *that* strongly about it...'

# Chapter 14

The Summer Of '73

Despite being jobless, we managed a reasonable programme that summer, although not entirely as planned.

In March, Donal, Viv, Jude and I had gone to Glaslough, all set to begin preparations for a 1973 camp, when Sir John appeared at the coach-houses, looking all flustered.

'What are you doing here?' he asked.

'We're starting to get things in order for this year's holiday scheme,' I said.

'Oh no,' John said, 'There can't be a summer camp this year. We can't accommodate it. We need the buildings for something else.'

It was a bombshell. With a great sinking feeling, I looked at all the equipment spread around the site. It would cost a fortune to move it anywhere else, even if we had somewhere else to move it.

'It would've helped if we'd known before now,' I said to John, 'It's a bit late to look for anywhere else.' *Slippery,* I thought, *are the tiles of the big house.*

At the same time, felled oaks, masked road-blockers, airborne catamarans, and images of Josephine's bed being trampled, flooded my brain.

'I'm terribly sorry,' John said, 'It was only meant for last year.'

Despondent, we headed back to Ballymurphy to break the news. However, once back in the city, we rallied. As 42 was without a phone, I phoned Cork from the Maguires' house, two doors up. I explained the predicament to my father who promised that the Association would step in. This was great news: all my life I'd known that, if you asked my father to do something and he said yes, you could wipe it off your to-do list. Immediately, work got under way in organising a camp in Ballyandreen in east Cork, close to the seaside town of Ballycotton. The site was provided by the students of University College Cork, who had refurbished a large house as a residential centre. Buttressed by a group of selfless voluntary workers, my father set about organising separate weeks for young people from the Shankill and young people from Ballymurphy. Businessmen, Richard Woods and Johnny Hornibrook, provided transport and other resources while Willie O'Brien, who had revolutionalised

## Chapter 14

the Irish building trade by pioneering the importation of heavy machinery into Ireland, ran functions in his house and gave the use of his much-appreciated swimming pool. Denis Long, an experienced caver, organised expeditions to the caves at Ovens.

From our end Cora, helped by three young women from Springhill took charge of the actual camp. In Dublin, they were met by volunteers who ferried them across the city from Connolly Station to Houston Station. In Cork they were joined by the Association volunteers, with our Niall arranging to stay with them at the residential centre. By all standards, the Ballyandreen camp went well. The only casualty was Niall who woke up one morning with a necklace of mackerel-heads wrapped around his neck.

Meanwhile, Tomás Walsh and Dave McAuliffe, two young men from the Ballyphehane area of Cork organised for another group of Ballymurphy's young people to stay with families in their neighbourhood. When I arrived down a couple of days later, the Ballymurphy boys were in the local park, about to play a game of football against a team of local lads. However, all was not well: the Ballymurphy kids were complaining that the Ballyphehane kids of the same age were a 'shower of Free-state giants'.

By the time Cora came back from Cork, we'd managed to secure other holiday places on someone else's scheme in the prestigious Petoria boys' boarding school in Enniskillen, and had organised a two-week camp for Glencolmcille in Co. Donegal. Cora agreed to accompany the group to Enniskillen. Donal agreed to run the Glencolmcille camp, assisted by Debbie Pickvance from Bristol, one of fifteen British and Dutch students who'd come in on Felicity's and Fred Bass's summer play-scheme. A child of the Sixties with black rippling hair to her waist, Debbie could've stepped straight from Max Yasgur's field in Woodstock and was a big hit with the boys. Donal was also joined by Gerry O'Donnell with the hair like Jesus, and Gerry's friend, John Carey from Andersonstown. John, slightly built, with Lennon glasses and collar-length hair sliced off at the forehead, was a student-teacher, fluent in French, who was learning to play the fiddle and found the 42 parties greatly to his artistic tastes.

The accommodation in Glencolmcille would consist of a small marquee and three ridge tents. All but one of the tents were provided by our Cork supporters who had borrowed them from the Irish army. The other came from the stores of the N.I. Association of

Youth Clubs in East Belfast. When I went off by bus to collect this last tent, I brought two 14-year-old lads from Ballymurphy along.

'Hey Speedy!' one of them said to the other as we crossed the Lagan, 'What friggin' river is this?'

'Haven't a baldy,' Speedy said.

That, to my mind, was beyond amazing: the River Lagan flows pretty much through the centre of Belfast.

The last piece of equipment to be collected was a rubber raft from Glaslough. Debbie and I drove down on the motorbike to get it. The job needed two as the bike had no carrier and we had to lay the deflated raft along the tank and saddle, and sit on it. This considerably raised the bike's centre of gravity and caused the odd wobble on sharp bends. (I would soon have cause to remember this.) Back in Belfast, Donal told me he'd had an offer from one of the other English volunteers to also go to Donegal.

'It's Nathan,' he said, 'The last person on Earth I want to see in Donegal. He'll cause a friggin' riot!'

A few days earlier, around in Jan McCarthy's house, Nathan (stone-cold sober) had been telling us why the English had occupied Ireland.

'They came over to teach the Irish how to govern themselves,' he'd explained.

On the second Saturday in July, Donal and Debbie loaded up, collected Gerry O'Donnell and John Carey, picked up their charges and left for Glencolmcille. An hour later, Nathan left in his Saab to catch them up. To this day, I think Donal must have made some kind of Faustian pact: Nathan never made it; he ran his Saab into a narrow bridge somewhere west of Killybegs and, though unhurt, was left with far more pressing fish to fry.

Coincidentally, Jean and her family were also in Glencolmcille that summer. Jean had booked a holiday cottage for the whole family and their quaint, pious Aunt Biddy, a large countrywoman from Newry who spoke English as a foreign language. The availability of such a house also attracted havers-of-a-good-time. Our Niall turned up from Dublin with Fermanagh man, John Molloy, recently shot in the arse by a ricochet while spectating over a pint of Guinness at a gun battle in Crossmaglen.

At the beginning of the camp, I drove up to Donegal on the motorbike. It was a gloriously sunny day so I took the narrow clifftop road from Killybegs to Carrick - which was unfortunate for a flock of

## Chapter 14

chickens that lived along that road. Normally, a bike would kill one chicken. Mine killed four and the rooster in a plume of scattering feathers. When I went back to apologise at the small roadside farm from which the chickens had sprung, I was met by a quite chilling attitude.

'Sure, you couldn't help it,' a woman in a blue, speckled dress said, 'We'll just have to eat the stupid bastards now.'

*Jesus!* I thought, *Good job it wasn't me that got killed!*

In Glencolmcille, I found Donal, Debbie, Gerry O'Donnell and John Carey pitched on the dunes behind the beach. They had so far managed to prevent any major fallout from the camp, and rabbit was on the menu. Young Stephen Fegan had, after waiting patiently for hours outside a burrow with an upraised tent mallet, come up trumps. Then, unexpectedly, my parents turned up with 8-year-old Cathal and 7-year-old Neasa in the car. My father had with him several gallons of tent water-proofing liquid as the army tents leaked like sieves. And while we all painted furiously to beat the next shower of rain, Neasa fell in love with Jean's young brother, Willie.

Meanwhile, up in the Campbells' cottage, there was chaos as a dozen people tried to fit into a house made for six. When I arrived in, there was a big stew on the boil.

'Yer just in time,' Jean's Aunt Biddy said to me after meeting me at the gate, 'ta tek me down till the shap.' She then got up on the back of the bike and nearly threw us both on the first bend.

'Will ya straighten *up!*' she screamed as she tried to force me back upright as we curved into the bend.

'Jesus Christ Biddy!' I shouted back, 'Don't do that again! You'll kill us!'

'Then, will ye fer god's sake slow *down!*' she said.

'Biddy,' I said, 'I'm only doing 20 miles an hour.'

'Then, fer fuck's sake,' pious Aunt Biddy squeaked, 'Will ya slow down till ten!'

'De Baróid!' John Molloy said back in the house, 'Don't tell me you're still inflicting those Ballymurphy childer on the wider, unsuspecting world. And, if so, my next question to you is *What do you call a woodpecker with no bake?*'

'Down here, we say *beak*,' I corrected.

'Aye,' John said, 'And the answer is a fuckin' head-banger.'

Later, after the pub, Rob Waygood and I came off the bike while

# The Summer Of '73

chasing rabbits across the football pitch behind the beach at one in the morning. Rob, a long-haired Englishman with large-framed, wire-rimmed glasses, was over to organize the details with Jean of a plannedf trip to India. The rabbits, had we caught any, were to further augment the food supply down at the camp.

'Fuck me!' Rob said as we lay on the ground after hurtling between the goal-posts and ploughing into a sand dune, 'We nearly got that bugger!' Rob had a sense of fun I wouldn't have associated with the English at all.

When the camp was over, Niall came back with me to Belfast and, for some reason, I had the raft on the bike again, spread along the tank and saddle. In Mountcharles, we stopped for a pint - only one, which was legal at the time - and took off again down the twisting road at 60 mph. We then came around a sharp corner to discover we were in an S-bend and going too fast. I went down to take the second curve, but the raft had pushed the centre of gravity too high. The bike took off from under us, sailing along the road on the crash-bars like it was on a pair of skis. Niall and I sailed along behind, bouncing off the tarmac in a trajectory that would've been fatal had anything been coming the other way. I remember seeing him at one point, suspended behind me in foetal position about two feet off the ground, eyes closed and teeth gritted. Then he hit the ground and bounced again. With not a helmet between us, we were lucky. We were bruised and torn - I still have an odd-shaped bone in my left knee - but we were walking.

'The only thing about accidents,' Niall said after testing that no limbs were broken, 'is that they're all different.'

\* \* \*

That same summer, Cora became a voluntary helper with the 123 Mountaineering Club, run by ruddy-jowled ex-Brit, Norman Patterson. Norman had a big heart but managed to get just about everything wrong.

'Norman is thinking of opening a mixed youth club up on the Springfield Road, at the Springhill/Springmartin interface,' Cora said after a couple of meetings, 'He's out of his head!' Thankfully, that idea came to nothing: the building was wrecked before anyone had a chance to be killed. The club then brought a mixed group of Ballymurphy and Shankill kids off to the Mourne Mountains for an adventure weekend. One of Norman's other helpers brought along a load of chocolate to coax the young people up the mountains.

## Chapter 14

'Guess what!' Cora said on her return, 'Norman is working on a plan to bring disabled children over the mountains in sedan chairs! And, when we were down in the Mournes, a helicopter suddenly appeared in the sky and we found that he was after organizing for the British army to join us as part of the weekend! With no consultation with anyone else! We'll all get done for fraternising with the enemy.'

Shortly afterwards, *Between* in Cork (formerly the Association for Human Rights in the North) sent a small truck full of furniture and other necessities to the club's newly-rented weekend cottage in Annalong on the Down coast. I went to Dundalk to meet the truck and guide my father and the driver, Corkman Martin Thompson, to Annalong. We arrived to find that the club had met its end. Some Shankill Road members had burned the cottage to the ground. Martin took one look and spun the truck around.

'Just in case the people who did this are anywhere about,' he said, 'I'm outta here!'

Back in the Murph, community leaders mourned not the passing.

A week later, a group of us left Ballymurphy to expand our social territory to the Shamrock Club in Ardoyne, a small republican enclave in North Belfast. At the end of the night, when we asked the barman, who'd never seen any of us in his life, if we could get a carry-out, he handed us a litre-and-a-half of vodka.

'Youse can replace it in the morning,' he said. Marlies Thesalaar, one of several Dutch students in the company, was flabbergasted at such trust. We were too but pretended it was a normal streak of Irish character. We were then invited back to someone's house where we stayed until morning.

'It's far too dangerous to leave Ardoyne this time o' night!' the woman of the house said, 'The Huns (Loyalists) have the place surrounded. Youse don't want to get yerselves shot by the Huns now, do youse?'

# Chapter 15
## A Scary Joint

A couple of days after the riot at the community centre, I met Frank Cahill up at the Bullring and he floated the idea of a community festival.

'The people are battered after Motorman,' he said, 'They need a lift, a morale boost, something to raise the spirits. I'm thinking a community festival for Ballymurphy would do the trick. That would get people thinking positively again, especially running alongside the developments that are happening around the Survey and the work units.'

'What about a festival for the whole area?' I suggested, 'It would be a great chance to get everyone working together at the same time.'

'You know what?' Frank said, 'I couldn't agree more.'

Three days later we organized the first meeting at 42, which drew in people from all the estates and both republican traditions. The festival dates were set for August 12$^{th}$ to 19$^{th}$ and a magnificent organisational feat got underway.

In those days there were no grants for events like this. We were on our own. Yet, the idea captured the imagination of everyone across the eight housing estates. Every community group and facility in the area became energized. Events were planned centrally by the committee and they were planned at the local level – down to the very streets. Even Fred Bass's summer play-scheme was absorbed into the whole. A huge billboard, we decided, would be erected above the Bullring shops. Using a pegboard and large moveable letters, the events of each day could then be advertised for all to see. (Admittedly, there were a few unexpected messages up there some mornings, but generally, the board was spared abuse.) Money was raised locally and from a small number of outside sponsors, and prizes were bought. And, without any prompting, the women began to make bunting from old clothes, first one street, then another, until the whole area was festooned in an ocean of fluttering colour. Then came the question of military activity.

'We can't have children playing in the streets and bullets flying everywhere,' 18-year-old Kate McManus said, 'There needs to be a

## Chapter 15

ceasefire.'

'Is everyone in agreement with that?' Charlie Heath from Westrock asked. Charlie was Chair of the committee.

'Agreed,' Jenny Quigley said and everyone nodded.

'Well, that's simple,' Steve Pittam laughed as he came from the kitchen with a pot of tea, 'Charlie can get both sides by the scruff of the neck and just bang their heads together.' Steve accompanied his infectious laugh with a curious trademark hopping motion that denoted something particularly funny.

'The IRA won't be a problem,' Frank Cahill said, 'We can talk to some people about the place here and they'll sort that end out. That just leaves the Brits.'

'*Just!*' Steve howled and his head shook until I thought it would fall off.

'We need to send someone up to the Taggart,' Frank continued undaunted, 'to talk to the Major.'

'I wonder who we could send?' Charlie Heath asked.

'You!' Frank said without hesitation, 'The best person to send is always the chair.'

Whether that was true or not, we all agreed, and Charlie was dispatched off to the Taggart the very next day. An hour later he came back to 42.

'That place is very bad for the bangers' (nerves),' he declared. 'I'm never goin' back near it again.'

'What happened?' Cora asked.

'Well, whenever I arrived, they wouldn't open the gate. Then, in the end, when they let me in, I was brought into the Major's office at gunpoint. "NAME!" the Major bawls as soon as I walk through the door. "My name is Charlie Heath," I tell him, "I'm here to see if there could be a wee ceasefire during our festival..." "ADDRESS!" your man bawls and that's how the whole thing goes – him bawlin' his head off and me tryin' to explain all about the ceasefire... I don't think it went very well.'

But, in the end, we got the ceasefire, unspoken but effective, with no hostilities from either side from August 12th to 19th 1973. Sometimes humanity broke through the crust of war like that. It happened the same when a young child was knocked down and killed outside 42. The little boy had called to Bennetts' house-shop and ran out between two parked cars straight into the path of a third. The one who tried to safe his life was a young British paramedic who

## A Scary Joint

risked his own safety as he tried to give the kiss of life. On another occasion, a soldier was shot in Whitecliff Crescent, not far from Ellen Cosgrove's house. Big Ellen, whose bottle would hammer the tables as hard as any for the chorus of *The Provo Lullaby*, ran from her house with a cushion and put it under the dying soldier's head. 'We hate the Brits for what they do to us,' she explained later, 'But we don't have to sink to their level. He was somebody's son...'

\* \* \*

On August 12$^{th}$ the festival got under way with a big parade. Well, it wasn't really a big parade. The Liam McParland Accordion Band (two of whose members had been shot the previous May) came marching up the Whiterock Road, followed by a couple of hundred people. Tess Cahill and Jan McCarthy were there. Jenny Quigley and her new daughter were there, accompanied by Donal who was pushing Jenny's pram. Kieran Fagan was there with a camera. Gerry Finnegan, the previously-Methuselah-bearded local Community Development Officer (nicknamed *Funnygun* by some in Ballymurphy) was there, stripped to the waist and white as a ghost, with his great beard shorn away, leaving nought but massive sideburns. Steve Pittam was there with a small crowd from Moyard, carrying banners, flags and a couple of whistles and balloons. It didn't look like much, but it was the beginning of one of the most participative events the district would ever see. Since then, there have been many festivals - indeed, the Upper Springfield festival was the forerunner that inspired *Féile an Phobail*, the West Belfast Community Festival which has become one of the biggest annual events in Belfast's social and cultural calendar – but, apart from Upper Springfield mark two, the level of community participation has never, in my opinion, been equalled or surpassed.

For the next seven days, every street was full of people enjoying themselves. There were no great props and there was no fancy equipment. People clapped their hands or blew a whistle to start the sack race. At the other end, two people held a piece of string. To accommodate the kids' parties, families brought the chairs and tables from their homes, made cakes and biscuits, and sealed off the streets with bins so the kids could have them to themselves. In the clubs there were old time waltzes and discos and pensioners' nights and bingo. There were guider (boxcar) races and tugs-of-war and fancy-dress. The street theatre put on by Fred Bass's students was led through the district by a painted clown in a bowler hat. In

## Chapter 15

the women's netball tournament, Big Alice Franklin turned out a scary team dressed in white shirts, knee-length woollen socks, and short, red pleated skirts, who beat the crap out of all opposition to take the coveted cup. At the Bonny Babies competition, the judges fled once their decision had been made. There were music nights and debates and painting competitions and 16-milimetre movies, including the historical classic, *Mise Éire*. And some enterprising young people cracked open the fire hydrants in several streets to provide fountains in which overheating kids could dance.

Unfortunately, there lingers no great photographic record; but the photos that do exist show a community determined to give it the best, while the massive notice-board announces the offerings as the days progress. And while people in their thousands spilled from their homes to pack the streets, they also became part of the new unified social movement that eventually had more than eighty voluntary community groups looking after the needs of a single square mile.

The festival also attracted some of the people who had worked on the Glaslough camp, along with Joe Dennehy from Cork who now lived in Dublin and who, with his shoulder-length black hair, black beard and black beret, bore an uncanny resemblance to Che Guevara. Given that one of Che's grandmothers came from Galway, we all suspected some distant dalliance up Joe's family tree, but we never mentioned that.

'I'll be there for the festival,' Joe said when he got the whisper. To this day, he swears it almost cost him his life at the céilí in St. Bernadette's school.

Joe always had a great sense of humour. But humour sometimes eludes the eye of the beholder. And so it was at the céilí.

'You're not getting past,' Joe joked in his gravelly voice to one of the young barmen who was collecting glasses. Simultaneously, he pretended to block his way from our table, where he and I were the only people not out dancing - mostly because standing up had become a challenge. Joe's banter, however, was construed as an affront to Ballymurphy by a group of lads who were making their merry way through a sea of booze at the next table. An exchange of insults passed both ways.

'Free State bawstards!' somebody called us. Joe and I rose unsteadily to the challenge.

'Right...' I said to Joe, 'How many of zhem... are zhere?' It took a

# A Scary Joint

while to work this out. 'Two... Four... Six... Eight!' I counted, 'Thaz four each... Joe, grab two bottles.' What we would have done with the bottles has never been defined. Nevertheless, we moved on the enemy, but I was deflected by a dazzling impairment of motor skills. As I veered inadvertently off to the left, the next person to appear in my line of combative vision was Cora.

'Ciarán love,' she reasoned, 'There's no point in getting annoyed with people. We're all here to have a good time.' But I was having none of that!

'They started it...' I said.

'Look at you!' she said, 'You can't even stand! And you're gonna take on eight Provies, are you?'

'Provies?' Joe said, 'What shaggin' Provies!' In my next image of Joe, he had forsaken me and was tripping off across the dance floor, dainty as a pixie, in his very own take on what would later become known as *Riverdance*. Beyond my range of vision he danced off into a corner and melted in amongst a bunch of older women who were having a sing-song. Within minutes he was lashing out all the choruses, while Frank Cahill tried to persuade the lads at the next table that Joe and I were friendly forces. However, I was having none of that either.

'Lettum up!' I said to Frank.

But a punch to the jaw sent me tumbling down some steps in the hall. Cora was polishing up on her negotiation skills.

'Now!' She said, 'Do you still think you're capable!' I have, in my life, encountered few arguments more convincing. Later Joe and I made up with the other table through Paddy Tolan, the brother of my elusive lookalike, Tommy. When I mentioned our alleged similarities, Paddy told me he'd introduce us, first chance.

In the end, I never did meet Tommy Tolan. He'd already been recaptured by the British in November 1972 and interned until 1975. He was shot dead by the Official IRA during a feud in July 1977, shortly after returning from his honeymoon with his young wife, Maureen McGuinness.

By then, Todler's friend, Jim Bryson, whom I'd also never met, was also dead.

\* \* \*

Jim Bryson's brother, Bobby, used to sometimes call at our door if he was passing late at night with a skinful of drink.

'Our Jim might be lookin' this house back,' Bobby would say. But

## Chapter 15

Jim was far too busy a man.

Built like a bull, Jim Bryson first hit the headlines in January 1972 when he and Tommy Tolan, and five other internees, escaped from the *Maidstone* prison ship in Belfast Lough. Caked in grease and butter, the 'Magnificent Seven' swam through the icy water to shore and hijacked a bus. They then drove to the Markets where residents were astounded to see a group of men disembark into the freezing cold in their underpants and varying stages of nakedness. (Todler's underpants had been left behind on the sharp edge of a *Maidstone* porthole so that all that remained was the rubber band. Bryson was wrapped in a seat cover from the bus. Tommy Gorman was wearing the bus driver's jacket.) It is even rumoured that, while waiting for a change of clothes, they sat in a bar and one or two grabbed a pint in this ungodly state. After a brief sojourn down South, Bryson and Tolan went back to Ballymurphy and quickly earned a place on the British army's shoot-to-kill list, as the unit they led took a heavy toll on army numbers during ambushes and sniping attacks, and ferried massive bombs down the Falls Road to the city centre.

In September 1972 Bryson was arrested and charged with possession of a handgun. The following February his trial took place at Crumlin Road courthouse but he declined the invitation to attend. As he was being escorted through the dank tunnel that led from the prison to the court, he pulled a gun and he and another prisoner overpowered their guards and stripped them of their uniforms. Bold as brass, they walked through the courthouse towards freedom, but only Bryson made it. Outside the prison he dumped the uniform and hitched a lift to the Falls Road from two off-duty members of the Ulster Defence Regiment who thought they were running a mercy errand to the Royal Victoria Hospital. That night, I had just arrived at the bottom of Glenalina Park when an enraged patrol of the Coldstream Guards fired on a group of kids celebrating the escape around a bonfire in Ballymurphy's blacked-out Bullring.

'Houdini is gone again,' one of the kids shouted as he ran past me a minute later. Then more shots rang out and everyone went home to watch TV while Bryson went on down south for a spot of rest and recuperation. But, events were conspiring against his run of luck.

In August 1973, as inter-IRA tensions simmered again, he came back to warn off the Ballymurphy Officials. In Maggie's Tavern, a swashbuckling shebeen in Maggie Smith's back garden down in Divismore Park, he pistol-whipped a number of Officials. The Officials responded with a death sentence, to be carried out on August 31st. From late that afternoon there wasn't a child to be seen anywhere in the lower end of Ballymurphy where Officials and Provisionals were openly carrying guns. Cora had the library open at 42 but nobody came. You just knew that something bad was in the air. At seven o'clock, as we finished our dinner, heavy shooting broke out somewhere to the back of our house.

We learned later that, earlier in the day, Bryson and three others had been having a meal in a safe house in New Barnsley when word arrived that the Officials were combing Ballymurphy for him. Simultaneously, another Provisional (the same one who'd been grazed on the head the night of the disco riot), was on his way to Bryson's home in Ballymurphy Road with a similar warning when he was shot at by the Officials. Lucky again, the bullet literally parted his hair.

When Bryson heard what was happening, he sent for a car and he and the other Provisionals drove down to Ballymurphy where they bumped into a leading member of the Officials. Bryson advised him to go and tell the Officials to think again. Seconds later the four in the car came under fire from the derelict flats above the Bullring.

Convinced they were being shot at by the Officials, they moved into Whitecliff Parade and fired back at the flats for the next 20 minutes. But the gunmen in the flats were a patrol of the Royal Greenjackets who radioed the Taggart for help.

Eventually Bryson decided to flush out the 'Officials'. At the same time, neighbours spotted military reinforcements climbing over the railings of St. Bernadette's school and taking up positions in entries adjacent to Whitecliff Parade. They shouted a warning but whether or not it was understood is unclear.

Either way, the four men got back in the car and reversed out into Ballymurphy Road - in clear view of the flats and the incoming reinforcements. We heard the sustained gunfire as the car took off down Ballymurphy Road and was riddled with high-velocity bullets. Nineteen-year-old Paddy Mulvenna (one of those who'd marched into the community centre on my first day) was shot dead and 25-year-old Bryson was mortally wounded. James O'Rawe was wounded while trying to escape and the fourth man got away. The car ended up in a garden two doors away from Bryson's own home. Then the firing died down and there was a deathly hush, followed by

## Chapter 15

people screaming. Cora and I went outside to see Mrs. Moan, who lived up the street and was seventy if she was a day, come tearing towards us at a gallop. Her thin legs seemed to be spinning two feet off the ground.

'Bryson's shot!' she screamed, 'Get an ambulance! Quick, for God's sake, somebody get an ambulance!' Then the ice-cream van came up the street playing *Three Blind Mice*.

Jim Bryson died on September 22$^{nd}$. I was one of the thousands who walked at his funeral, escorted through Ballymurphy by an IRA colour-party. At Milltown cemetery, we heard Máire Drum, Vice-president of Sinn Féin, tell the mourners that 'Generations as yet unborn will live to hear the name of Captain James Bryson'. Thirty-seven years later, his image, along with Paddy Mulvenna's, emblazons a gable wall in Ballymurphy close to his and our former homes. In it he stands upright, holding the old Lewis gun from Cork.

* * *

Towards the end of the summer, John Carey and I had a close encounter. We'd been at a party over in the university area when Sammy Willis, a community worker from Springmartin, offered us a lift home.

'No problem,' Sammy said, 'Sure I'll be going right up your way.'

Sammy and his wife had an old banger that, as John and I were about to discover, exuded an unhealthy roar every time it saw a hill. In it, we left the university area, drove into the city centre, and headed off up the Shankill Road, cocooned in the bonhomie of drink. The plan was to first drop a Canadian student in Highfield, the loyalist estate next to Springmartin, and then continue on to the top of Springhill. There John and I would make a bolt for it and Sammy and his wife would double back. At about half two in the morning, as we turned off the West Circular Road up a sharp hill to deliver the Canadian, Sammy's car stalled like a cart in a boghole. Sammy tried again and the car roared but went nowhere. A second later we were surrounded by seven agitated UDA vigilantes who appeared from nowhere. The fact that one of them was carrying a gun was potentially not good for me and John. Sammy's wife took a mild panic attack and swung around.

'Whatever happens here,' she squeaked at me, 'don't you say a word! And don't either of youse even think of getting out of this car!' She needn't have worried: John and I were stuck solid.

Recognising Sammy, the UDA men calmed down, but still checked out the car. 'Students,' Sammy said and the Canadian spoke up to give a modicum of cover. At the time I had a damaged blood vessel in my nose which usually bled at all the wrong times, but for once it went against the grain. Just before we'd stalled, it had started again and I had a tissue pressed to the bleeding. This distracted the UDA men, one of whom was leaning in Sammy's window.

'Somebody welt ya one son?' he asked.

'Wa-a-agh,' I said, stuffing the tissue further into my Southern gob. The five of us then sat tight in the roaring car while the seven UDA men pushed us up the hill.

Such was the fright of the occasion, that the Willises decided that we should stay the night with them and go on to Ballymurphy in the morning. Shortly after daylight the next day I woke up on the floor of Sammy's living-room to the sound of John's voice, virtually falsetto.

'Jesus Christ!' he was saying, 'Where the fuck is this!' He was looking out the window at the blocks of Springmartin flats covered in loyalist graffiti. He then flopped back on the settee on which he'd slept. 'Oh gawd!' he said, 'Every time something like this happens to me, why do I find *you* lurking in the background?' Gradually, as the brush with the UDA took form, he began to groan horribly. 'It's all coming back to me now,' he said, 'You know what? There are times when this town is one scary fuckin' joint!' I tried to think of times when it wasn't.

After breakfast, Sammy walked us down the Springmartin Road past the empty, bullet-scarred interface houses to the barrier at the Springfield Road. It was the longest walk of my life, with an awful heat in the middle of my back.

'Run for it!' I said to John as we reached the Springfield Road. We sprinted up to the top of Springhill Avenue, vaulted a makeshift barricade and made our way back to 42. In the house, Cora was a bit worried that we might've been shot.

'It was bad enough that there was no sign of you, but when I was standing at the gate, some woman I've never seen before in my life came along to cheer me up. "That's a terrible sad house you're living in. The second last person who lived there took her own life, and the last one was shot dead by the Brits. A terrible sad house." "Well," I told her, "It's a happy one now." Then I was having visions of her coming back tomorrow, saying "I told you so." And, by the way, we

## Chapter 15

have company – a Frenchman with nowhere to stay.'

The Frenchman was no great surprise as 42 doubled up as the unofficial Ballymurphy hostel. Sometimes we'd come back from a weekend away to find the house full of perfect strangers. Up to twelve at a time, sleeping three to a bed and all over the floors, and sharing excitement that occasionally caught them off guard.

Fortunately, none of them were there on the day of the ambush.

# Chapter 16
## The Gloves

Among the many roles fulfilled by Cora at 42 was that of librarian to the small children's library we ran from the living-room. This complemented similar libraries run by Jenny Quigley in Glenalina Park and Des Wilson around in Springhill, and mostly involved preventing the children from climbing up the shelves and jumping up and down on the motorbike parked between the living-room door and the stairs. Once those activities had been completed, each child would go off with *armfuls* of books to be read by next week. In time, Cora's efforts would attract the attention of the assistant chief librarian in Belfast Central Library who began to donate boxes of books. Many years later, when Ballymurphy finally got its own proper library, the same man would cite 42 as the first step along the road to that library.

On one of the weekends when I was away on my Youth & Community Work course, Cora was alone in the house, about to open the library, when the IRA turned up. When I got home on Sunday she told me what had happened.

'I was getting mentally ready to open up for the kids. Then there was a knock on the front door. When I opened it three guys came in, and one of them had a rolled-up blanket under his arm. Then they closed the curtains and said not to worry, they were from the IRA, and they sat down. Next thing, they took a rifle out of the blanket. They were all friendly and were probably doing their best to make me relax - they even made me a cup of tea - but I don't have to say, I was shaking in my shoes. At the same time one of them kept going out into the entry. Then after what seemed like hours, he came in and called the others and they all went out the back door. Just after that, I heard shooting from the entry. They were after firing at the army, but they missed. Then they went running up through the backs. And they took your motorbike gloves...'

'What!' I said, 'They took my *gloves*! You're not serious! Those gloves cost three pounds!'

That was it! The last straw. My gloves gone! Frank Cahill thought I should calm down: they were, after all, only a pair of gloves.

'Far more important to look after the nerves of the wee woman after an experience like that,' Frank advised.

'The wee woman's nerves are fine,' I assured him, 'But those gloves cost three pounds...!' That, I should mention, made them expensive gloves in their time.

Despite Frank's opinion, news of the outrage was broadcast on the bush telegraph and I can only assume that the IRA panicked. Word must've gone down to the Army Council in Dublin that they had a problem. Because, two days later a smiling, well-dressed, neatly-groomed stranger in his early twenties turned up at the front door.

'Irish Republican Army,' he said when I answered the knock, 'Sorry about the gloves.'

He handed me a small white envelope in which were three crisp pound notes.

About a year or so later I organised the first of several locally-based training courses in Youth & Community Work which were accepted under its aegis by Rupert Stanley College in East Belfast. The purpose of the training was twofold: to bring some basic accreditation to the people engaged in the area's community organisations and to further cement the concept and unity of purpose of a 'Greater Ballymurphy' - a defining goal of our work at 42. Based on a belief that the community itself had a vast reservoir of knowledge and skills that could be mutually developed, we began each course with a session designed to find the group equilibrium and demonstrate the process. (You have knowledge. I have knowledge. When we sit down together and share it, it becomes learning.) We then used this as the basis for the next session and so on. Outside support and skills were brought in only when deemed desirable by each group. (We were leaning heavily on Brazilian educationalist, Paulo Freire.) Each course ran in the house over a four-month period, one evening a week, and was facilitated by Donal, Jean, Frank Cahill and myself. The initial course drew in twenty participants, one of whom was Cora.

At about nine o'clock on the first evening we broke for tea and she discreetly called me into the kitchen.

'Two of the guys who came that day are on the course,' she said.

'What day?' I asked.

'The day of the ambush,' she said.

'Good job I got back my gloves,' I said.

'Stuff you and your gloves!' she said.

# The Gloves

We went back outside with the tea and a couple of loaves of toast and neither we nor the two lads let on. Many years later one of them was among 38 IRA men who staged a daring breakout from the H-Blocks of Long Kesh.

# Chapter 17
## Dublin

---

Given the awful stress of life in Belfast, it was only natural that we should seek occasional refuge elsewhere. That elsewhere became Dublin.

Ever since the Glaslough camp, we'd been availing of Eileen Costigan's offer of opening up her Rathmines flat to visiting groups of young people from Ballymurphy and to parties of ourselves. Consequently, many a night was had on Eileen's floor and Eileen herself became embroiled in the social life of 42 and our other Dublin bases. One of the Dublin bases was a house in Waterloo Road with a most chequered history, past and future. The other was wherever our Niall lived, which moved from Palmerston Road to Terenure to Leinster Road in Rathmines.

Over the years, many of our Cork and Dublin friends and relatives lived at the Waterloo Road address, but chief among its inhabitants were John Minahane and Denis Hurley, both from Co. Cork. John, a slim sage with dark curly hair, who read voluminously, was a bit of a philosopher. He appreciated the outlandish and would break into a quiet, beaming grin at its regular presentations. Denis, who lived down in the basement and whose straight black hair constantly covered his eyes, was the eccentric of the house, always contemplating schemes that would better the lot of his fellow human beings.

In later times, while John and Denis minded their own business in the kitchen, Colm O'Shea, who used to go to school with me and seemed a nice quiet lad, lived upstairs and planned bank robberies. The robberies apparently went well for a while. Then one day in July 1980 in Ballaghaderreen, Co. Roscommon, Colm and two pals robbed the local bank and found a Garda roadblock waiting for them at a place called Loughglynn. They rammed the Garda car and in the ensuing firefight, Colm was shot in the chest by a Special Branchman, armed with an Uzi sub-machine gun. The Branchman and another Garda were shot dead. Patrick McCann was later caught at the scene. A third man, Peter Pringle, was arrested after a two-week manhunt and spent 16 years in jail before his sentence was quashed and he was released. Colm and McCann were each sentenced to death, commuted to 40 years in jail without remission.

My cousin, Seán, also lived at the Waterloo Road address after abandoning university and leaving Cork in the early Seventies. Seán, who became an accomplished rock-climber, used to demonstrate the skills by climbing up the living-room walls, while he and John and Denis were building up the base of the British & Irish Communist Organisation, which ultimately had a world membership of not too many.

Joe Dennehy lived there at a time when he spent much of the day in bed reading the *Irish Times*. Then one day he and Niall and fellow Corkman, Martin McGrath, were inspired to embark on a fishing venture off the coast of Cork. It was a disaster. Joe couldn't swim and dreaded the sea. Martin got seasick every time he saw a wave. And Niall took along a crate of Guinness to make the fish surrender. By the time they finally sank the boat, they were infamous for running aground on sandbars, smashing into piers and terrorising the fishing communities perched along the whole of Ireland's Atlantic rim.

In the summer of '73, Niall would crash at Waterloo Road while living nearby in Palmerston Road, where he had teamed up with a doomed Matchless 500, a bike that achieved much fame as it took him around Ireland on a career that eventually ended up embedded in a stone wall in the north of County Kildare. Joe had been with him on the Dublin-bound leg of that journey but fortunately hadn't joined him on the south-bound leg.

'I'm reasonably sure we clocked 100 mph on the up-leg,' he recalled, 'So my "Che" beret wouldn't have provided much protection against a wall at speeds like that. We also did a runner from a restaurant in Kildare - funnily enough, *by accident*. And I remember having to do a sharp U-turn on Nassau Street in Dublin to turn a headlong attack on a wide row of cars into something akin to a victory parade as we led them proudly up that stately boulevard past Trinity College.'

In Cork, the bike made a particular mark when it nearly did for Dave, the lodger who lived in Joe's mother's terraced house in Blackpool. 'That guy is stone mad,' Dave used to tell Joe, 'He's gonna get you killed!' Then one night, when Dave was in the living room, Niall and Joe arrived on the bike with plans to go for a drink.

'Leave the bike in the hall,' Joe told him, 'so it doesn't get vandalised.' Joe held open the front door while Niall lined up the bike. In front lay the hall, the living room opening off to the

## Chapter 17

right, and the stairs. Dave, who heard all the commotion, came to investigate - just as the motorbike shot past the living-room door on one wheel, bowling him over and ploughing up the stairs until bike and rider lost momentum and came tumbling back down.

'What did I tell you!' Dave screamed at Joe, 'I told you that shaggin' lunatic will get you killed stone dead!'

And, for a while, Harry Bellingham from Derry, who helped with the Cork camps and of whom more will later be heard, lived at Waterloo Road.

The other base in Dublin was wherever Niall lived.

There would be many parties in Niall's abodes, but the most memorable was held in 1975 in a Leinster Road bedsit he shared with cousin, Seán. Up to the point of the party, that weekend would've been best remembered for a most enduring noxious smell from which there was no escape. Most smells you get used to, especially if you go to sleep with them in your nose. But this was different: you went to sleep on the floor and it was in your nose; and you woke up on the floor and it was in your nose again.

'It's been there for weeks,' Seán said on Saturday morning, 'Niall thinks it's coming out of the walls - like something from *The Exorcist*.'

'*The Exorcist* my arse,' Donal said, 'Nothing as bad as that was ever in *The Exorcist*.'

So bad was the smell that we couldn't stick it any longer and a full search was organized.

'Oh Jesus!' Seán said after about ten minutes, 'Take a look at this. I think I've found it.' It was a mackerel head that had fallen down behind the sideboard.

'Shit!' Niall said, 'The last time we had mackerel was three weeks ago!'

At the time, both Niall and Seán were on the dole, but they had an arrangement with the women who ran the stalls down in Moore's Street: at the end of the day, they had first choice of anything that was to be dumped. As a result they lived pretty well, and occasionally scored a mackerel.

'Wouldn't it be a terrible scandal?' Niall said as we feasted on the remains of Moore Street that night, 'Two men on dole die of gout!'

Niall had also managed to buy himself another bike, a big BSA which he stabled in the garden, not far from the window of an allegedly cantankerous woman named Mrs. Dixon, tenant of a neighbouring bedsit.

'Mrs. Dixon's nerves are bad,' Niall explained, 'She thinks the place is haunted.' This was a couple of nights after he'd arrived back at the house past closing time, aimed the bike at the front gate, and tore through the hedge instead. A terrified Mrs. Dixon, looking out the window of her ground-floor flat, thought her end had come as a riderless bike came hurtling through the dark like the fourth Horseman of the Apocalypse.

'Imagine!' Seán said, 'The woman's a mental case!'

Then came the party, when, on the Saturday night, after the bedsit had been fumigated, we went to the pub and a crowd followed us back to Leinster Road. Once inside, Niall pulled me to one side.

'We have a load of gatecrashers here,' he said, 'and they haven't a drop of drink between them. We need to get rid of them.' The bearded, long-haired, six-foot Niall then reached up and grabbed two antique cavalry swords he had hanging on his wall. He pulled one from its scabbard and threw the second at my feet.

'Come on!' he roared, swinging the sword above his head, 'Get up and fight!' On cue, I jumped up and we began to slash with the swords. Sparks flew from the steel and people around us dived for cover. This was so convincing that, not alone did the gatecrashers flee, but so did most of our friends. Then, mission accomplished, the sword fight took on a life of its own, until Niall took off out into the common stairwell, slamming the bedsit door behind him. I followed but he'd vanished. *Where could he be?* I thought, *other than the toilet?* I charged up the stairs to the bathroom which sat on a split level between floors. Sure enough, it was locked.

'Come out ya pig!' I yelled, banging on the door with the sword. I then stepped back and hit the door a big boot which caused it to burst open.

'Zorro!' I roared, swinging the cavalry sword above my head before stopping myself dead. Perched on the bowl, with her jaw on her lap, sat a horrified, bug-eyed woman from one of the other bedsits! I could only hope that it wasn't Mrs. Dixon.

'You didn't see my brother?' I asked meekly, trying to salvage something of the situation, 'He has a beard.' She never answered.

As part of all this carousing up and down the country, I was sharing a room for a few days on one occasion with an untidy member of the *Fórsa Cosainte Áitiúla* – the Irish local defence force - when a tidy streak got the better of me and I set about brushing the floor. When

## Chapter 17

I poked the brush in under an old wooden wardrobe, something caught and I gave a sharp tug. I kind of wished I hadn't when a sleek little hand grenade rolled out across the bedroom floor! Seems everyone was running gear to the North, and it didn't much matter who owned it.

\* \* \*

In the late autumn of '73, my Youth & Community Work course went to England to avail of short work-placements in Manchester. There being no cheap flights in those times, we travelled on the night ferry from Belfast to Liverpool. Unfortunately, it was a journey that coincided with the going home on leave of a large contingent of British soldiers who got progressively more drunk and loutish in the ship's bar as we crossed the Irish Sea, one stripping naked to impress any passing children with a table-top 'dance'. To avoid any misunderstandings, I took my rucksack outside, spread my sleeping-bag under a set of metal stairs on one of the decks, and went to sleep. An hour later I woke up with a jolt to find two soldiers hammering the shit out of one another on top of me!

'Hey! Hey! Hey!' I shouted but neither took any notice. Helpless, with my arms pinned to my sides under the sleeping-bag, I could only watch as the heavier one pulverised the other one until he stopped moving. *Oh Jesus*, I thought, *he's killed him, and now he'll kill me because I'm a witness*. However, the blood-spattered killer went off, leaving the dead weight of his victim slumped across my chest. I had one hell of a job getting my arms free of the sleeping-bag so I could heave him off.

'Excuse me,' I had to say to the officer when I found him, 'I think one of your soldiers might be dead.'

'What!' he roared and was all set to arrest me until I explained that it wasn't me who'd killed him. He then raised the alarm and officer and ship's crew all raced in my wake to the murder scene. But, when we got there, it was all very embarrassing: a jug of water and the corpse came back to life.

Shortly afterwards, in September, Jean and Rob left for India but the relationship didn't last the trip. After she and Rob parted, Jean went on alone and lived for a while on a Hindu ashram. When she came back after a year, she brought me a picture of Ganesh, the elephant god. Ganesh, as you should know, is the Hindu Lord of Success, the Destroyer of Evils and Obstacles, and the deva of intellect and wisdom. Need I say more?

'For the People's Friend,' she said and you just knew it came from the heart.

In November 1973, Frank Cahill resigned from the BTA and threw his lot in with 42. He figured we had a plan and liked it. He also provided the project with crucial moral support and added some notable ideas of his own. Donal, meanwhile, had gone off to study Youth & Community Work at the Polytechnic, but continued to work on a voluntary basis, and live part-time, at 42.

By year's end, the death toll for 1973 had come to 250. Sixteen had died in Ballymurphy.

# Chapter 18
## The Year Of Collapse

At the beginning of the New Year, after seven months on the dole, the Belfast education authorities created a post in support of our expanding project. I was employed again. The renewed financial security meant that Cora and I could head off to the Lake District of Cumbria for Easter weekend.

There could hardly have been a greater contrast between the streets of Ballymurphy and that English Spring of 1974. While the war went on at home and attempts were made to prop up a partial power-sharing deal in Stormont, and children as young as thirteen were being battered in British bases across west Belfast, Cumbria was basking in Easter sunshine. After life in the war zone, it almost felt unfair to be able to wander at will without the fear of a bomb or an assassin's bullet. It was like being back on the road again: we were carefree, hitchhiking from place to place, sleeping in the woods outside Keswick, swimming in the lakes, walking in the mountains. We then returned to Belfast where the blacked-out streets and barbed wire and military checkpoints brought us down to Earth with their customary bang. Passing the red-bricked houses of Whiterock, the most recent killing in the area was etched on our minds. In February, Vincie Clarke had died in a hail of bullets at the hands of the UVF and Jimmy McKenna.

On that long-ago first afternoon, over the Ulster Fry in Crooks's house, the BTA had mentioned McKenna as one of many good reasons one might not survive Ballymurphy. I'd subsequently forgotten all about him until his name had been spoken darkly in mid 1973. Vincie Clarke's brother, Robert, had been shot dead by loyalists outside a builder's yard in the city centre and the word on the street was that McKenna was responsible. Now he had turned up in the flesh in Whiterock. After the shooting of Vincie Clarke neighbours had rushed out to find a car speeding away from the scene with a clearly visible McKenna inside. The sighting had generated a sense of fear completely disproportionate to the capabilities of one man. It was the fear of the enemy within.

Jimmy McKenna had Ballymurphy connections and had come back to fulfil a long-standing promise of revenge. Vincie Clarke had been murdered because McKenna suspected him of being party to his brother's death.

At the beginning of the Troubles, both IRAs had responded to criminal activity in Ballymurphy in a number of ways: several people had been tarred-and-feathered; others were forced to carry out community service; while those suspected of being informers were ordered to leave the country. The Provisional IRA even had its own 'jail' in a small electricity sub-station in Springhill. Then, on November 16th 1970, Jimmy McKenna's brother, Arthur, and Alexander McVicker, two petty criminals, were shot dead on Ballymurphy Road by the Provisional IRA. At the time, they had stopped to talk to Vincie Clarke whose coal lorry had broken down.

As well as sending shock waves through the area, the killings had brought Jimmy McKenna back from Australia. Jimmy was said to have been torpedoed while in the merchant navy during the war, resulting in a steel plate being fitted in his head. Years later, an old acquaintance of his described him as 'a header who was built like a bull and would've gone right through you'. At one time, while dating a woman who lived with her mother down in Bow Street, he'd renovated the mother's house and put furniture in. He was then jilted by the woman who'd clearly seen sense. But Jimmy wouldn't lightly brook such a slight. Arriving down in Bow Street with an axe, he demolished the front door of his lost mother-in-law's home, chopped up all the furniture, and decapitated the family's Alsatian dog.

Undeterred by the fact that the IRA had carried out the Ballymurphy Road killings, Jimmy McKenna got himself a gun and publicly threatened to get even with those who'd shot his brother. His original vengeance mission, however, had come to an abrupt halt after five months when he was lifted on the Springfield Road with a gun in his pocket. At his trial in June 1971 he claimed that he'd found the gun, and had been gathering information on behalf of the RUC, a role confirmed in court by Chief Superintendant Patrick McAndrew. He was none the less convicted of possession, and served a year in protective custody before going back to Australia.

However, there was a strong belief in Ballymurphy that he'd come back again in 1973, and had been behind the killing of Robert Clarke so that Vincie Clarke 'would know how it felt'. It later transpired that he'd also been responsible for the UVF murder in January 1974 of John Crawford in Andersonstown (believed by McKenna to have

## Chapter 18

shot his brother).

Ever since the February killing, Ballymurphy had been in jitters waiting for McKenna's next attack. Was he planning to target other republicans? Or others he simply didn't like? Sightings were happening in all sorts of places and doors were locked hard at night. It was a situation that would prevail to some degree until word came through in 1986 that McKenna had died in Australia.

\* \* \*

Shortly after our return from Cumbria, friendships came to test us. Brian Fegan who'd helped me carry many a sheet of chipboard from Corry's to 42, wanted to marry his girlfriend, Alice. Both were eighteen and perfectly entitled to marry, but there was a snag. A large part of that snag was the opposition of Brian's da, a small wiry man with red hair and chiselled features who looked like he might make a hole through you for a short-cut. The family lived a few doors up from Billy Scribbons and I'd come to know them all well. Therein lay the dilemma when Brian turned up at the door and asked if Cora and I would be bridesmaid and best man.

He'd arrived with Stevie Mallon, the only other person in on the plan, a position based on absolute trust between himself and Brian. (This sometimes took itself to extremes: when Brian once asked Stevie to put his hand against a dartboard so that he could bury the darts between Stevie's spread fingers, Stevie had obliged – until he got skewered to the board!)

'I can't let anyone else know,' Brian explained, 'in case it gets back to my da and the whole thing is blown.'

'Is there no way you could get the parents to come around?' I asked, 'Because, you see, you'll be gone on the boat and we'll still be here.'

'No chance,' Brian said, 'Ask Stevie.'

'No chance mucker,' Stevie assured us.

'So?' Brian asked, 'Do we have a bridesmaid and best man?'

The wedding took place in St. John's church on the Falls Road on a cold April morning. Just the five of us and the priest, and a couple of old women who'd popped in to add credit to their heavenly accounts. As the voices flaked around in the emptiness, rings were exchanged and we all headed off for a bite to eat. Afterwards I relayed Cora and Stevie home on the back of the motorbike, coming off in the dark with Stevie after skidding on ice on Ballymurphy Road. Picking himself up, the droll Stevie shook himself and stated that 'The Lord works in mysterious ways'. Brian and Alice, the happy couple, then left for the Heysham ferry while Cora and went into hiding, waiting for Armageddon.

A couple of days later a wrathful pounding on the front door sent us scattering for the back of the house and the sanctuary of the kitchen. But there was no escape from the wiry red head and chiselled features that swept down the entry and shortly appeared as flesh pressed to the window pane. However, in fairness to the man, he took it all relatively well: there's no point trying to stop the rain that fell last week.

\* \* \*

May 1974 was one of the most momentous months in recent Irish history.

Back in December, at a four-day conference held at Sunningdale, England, an agreement had been thrashed out between a section of the Unionist Party led by Brian Faulkner, the SDLP led by Gerry Fitt, and the Alliance Party led by Oliver Napier, to share power in a Stormont-based Executive. They would also take part in a new Council of Ireland, linking North and South formally for the first time since Partition. The Executive had taken office on January 1st. However, it had immediately run into trouble, with its first meeting descending into an unholy rumpus from which 18 unionists were ejected by the RUC. Since then it had faced the continuing IRA onslaught, an upsurge in loyalist sectarian murders and a political opposition cemented in the form of the United Ulster Unionist Council (UUUC) that rallied its troops around vehement unionist opposition to the Council of Ireland.

In the Westminser elections of February 28th, the level of unionist opposition to 'Sunningdale' was evident when anti power-sharing candidates took eleven of the twelve Six-County seats. This sent the Stormont Assembly into a tailspin, but it managed to hang on until the beginning of May, while Faulkner's embattled wing of unionism tried desperately to back-peddle on the Council of Ireland. Then, on May 14th, the UUUC's Assembly members at Stormont put forward a motion, recommending that the Council of Ireland be rescinded. The loyalist Ulster Workers' Council (UWC), formed in December, threatened strike action if the motion failed. It was defeated by 44 votes to 28, and the UWC called its strike.

Over the next two weeks, the North descended into chaos. Any initial reluctance to support the strike in unionist or mixed areas was quickly remedied by the Ulster Army Council, a co-ordinating body of the loyalist paramilitary groups, and by the open collusion between state forces and the masked enforcers at the loyalist barricades.

On May 16th, William Craig warned that if Sunningdale wasn't ditched 'there will be further actions taken against the Irish Republic and those who attempt to implement the agreement.' The following day three UVF car-bombs in Dublin, and a fourth in Monaghan town, left 31 dead and over 100 injured. (Former Military Intelligence officer, Captain Fred Holroyd, later blamed British military intelligence for organising the bombings.) On May 21st the UWC declared an embargo on all oil and petrol supplies, and there were twelve-hour power cuts in Belfast and long queues for milk and food. Two days later, Faulkner, Fitt and Napier flew to London to demand that troops be used to break the strike. Fitt threatened an SDLP resignation from the Executive if the military didn't take over essential services by May 27th.

On May 24th I took a group of teenagers onto the slopes of Black Mountain. On May 25th a cow was killed close to the same spot when it stood on a landmine meant for soldiers who were raiding a nearby farmhouse. That evening, another type of explosion was heard in New Barnsley. As the loyalist strike choked the North, the city's gas supply had been run down. The gas service had warned that they were maintaining only minimum pressure in the pipes to prevent air from getting in and causing explosions. But, they warned, people weren't to attempt to cook, otherwise they could expect such explosions. As Cora, Steve Pittam, and I cooked dinner around a fire in the back yard of 42 along with Annemiek Rijckenberg, a student from Utrecht, the exact locations of our local sceptics were being pinpointed by the roar of those very explosions.

At 5.15am on May 27th the BP oil refinery at Sydenham outside Belfast was occupied by troops, and shut down. Soldiers then moved in on oil storage depots and petrol stations, which were sandbagged and put under armed guard while government officials handed out fuel permits to essential services.

The UWC threatened that if the military went near the power stations, they would close them down completely, along with water and sewerage plants, two services already severely threatened by the strike. With the Six Counties on the verge of collapse, the flour mills announced that they were closing down, and hospitals warned that only emergency operations were being carried out. On May 28th the strikers announced the final turn of the screw; at Ballylumford power-station, where one of three generating sets was already closed down, they were now in the process of running the others down.

At the same time, thousands of farmers and their tractors were converging on Stormont for a mass rally. But the battle was already won. Just before 2pm, the Executive collapsed, Faulkner's Unionists having resigned. The following day, the British prorogued the power-sharing Assembly.

# Chapter 19
The Dutchies

Annemiek Rijckenberg, tall, fair and very Dutch, had joined us on April 30$^{th}$, the result of a chance encounter at a Youth & Community Workers' conference in Portstewart three days earlier. She'd been staying with Gerry Finnegan over in Ashley Avenue for a learning-in-practice period, linked to her Sociology course back in the Netherlands, and Gerry had suggested the conference. In the course of conversation in Portstewart, Annemiek happened to mention that she was looking for something useful to do while she worked on a dissertation on 'The theory and practice of community work in relation to capitalism-driven urban planning'. She would be in Belfast for two months. I mentioned that we had a spare room. Annemiek took up the offer. Coincidentally, she had taken part in a two-week voluntary camp the previous year in Springhill. Her impression at that time had been of a 'concrete jungle', depressing and constrained, with an atmosphere of fear and despondency. Over the coming months, this would all change as Annemiek immersed herself in the life of 42. Meanwhile, the six-foot tall Annemiek would enthrall the young men of Ballymurphy with the length of her legs and the skimpiness of her skirts.

The opportunities provided to Annemiek by 42 included the development of the Divismore Park Community House. This centred around Lily Quinn (who had chased the kids battering the Taggart tins) and was based in one of two derelict houses, granted to us at a peppercorn rent by the N.I. Housing Executive. The idea was that we would renovate the houses and run them as community facilities, staffed by volunteers. Duly, meetings were organized at the Divismore Park house and Annemiek and I went along.

Now, meetings in Ballymurphy had an eccentricity all of their own which involved everyone turning up half an hour late and discussing everything under the sun except the agenda. This was normal. Everyone expected it. Lily even brought tea and biscuits to make it more pleasant. At the first meeting, Annemiek thought that she was experiencing an aberration. At the second meeting, she suggested that we should plan the meetings for a half hour later as the time didn't appear to suit. 'But,' I explained, 'if we do, everyone will just turn up another half hour later.' Back in Utrecht, Annemiek explained, she wasn't used to this. As for straying away at every possible angle from the agenda?

'The meetings take hours,' she pointed out, 'If we stuck to the agenda, we'd get through in half the time.'

'Yes,' I had to agree, 'But nobody would bother coming any more.'

\* \* \*

On May 31st, less than five weeks after Annemiek moved in, her boyfriend turned up and let the Dutch side down.

Along with a culturally-specific view of time-keeping and agendas, Annemiek couldn't understand how we managed to sleep through gun-battles or, especially, why people consumed so much alcohol in the Rock Bar.

'This would never happen in the Netherlands,' she explained, 'People in the Netherlands drink socially and moderately.' Then Chrit arrived.

Frank, Cora and I were in the house when the door knocked. I answered to find, standing there with an army kit-bag over his shoulder, the hairiest, beardiest guy to ever cross our threshold. Hidden in the mass of long, shiny black curls that blended into the beard was a smile and a pair of eyes from the far side of the Caucuses. My first impression was that he had to be some kind of mountain man.

'You must be ...' I started. I never got any further.

'Chrit!' he said, 'Is Annemiek here?'

'She's upstairs...' I said.

Without further ado, Chrit threw down his bag and shot past me, taking the stairs three at a time. Scratching my head, I went back inside to Frank and Cora.

'Who was *that*?' Cora asked.

Two hours later a sheepish Chrit and a dishevelled Annemiek resurfaced. Cigarettes were smoked and a cup of tea was had. Frank then left to spread the immortal word of Chrit's arrival, and Chrit offered to cook dinner to make up for his abrupt taking of the stairs. It was a good swap. Chrit was, and still is, one of the most creative cooks you'll ever meet.

'He always cooks at home,' Annemiek said as we planned the night's visit to the Rock Bar where we would be joined by Frank, Tess, Donal and Jimmy Burns.

We do the round system in Ireland. Some foreigners think this is

## Chapter 19

some kind of Irish fetish that prevents them from buying a drink. They don't realize that at some point, *Would you like another drink?* means *It's your friggin' round mate*. This misperception earns them a reputation that will follow them and their children to the grave. The round system also carries with it an unquenchable sense of equality. The first of these two considerations did not afflict Chrit or Annemiek: they honoured their rounds. But the second was Chrit's undoing. It so happened that, on the ferry from the Netherlands, he had tasted Carlsberg Special and enjoyed it.

'What would you like?' someone would ask Chrit.

'Carlsberg Special,' Chrit would reply.

As we were all drinking pints, equality deemed that everyone who went to the bar bought Chrit two bottles of this ferocious tipple until he had downed enough to float the Titanic. The horizontal position he'd adopted by the end of the night meant that we had to carry him back to 42. Nobody mentioned the abstemious Netherlands to Annemiek as we made our way up the Whiterock.

Fittingly, Chrit's first night included being stopped by a patrol of flashlight-shining Brits close to Fort Pegasus (MacRory Park Gaelic pitch prior to Motorman).

'What's your name?' one of the soldiers asked him.

'Chrit Ver-stappen,' he managed. The soldier tried to write it down.

'Address?' he asked. The Dutch address made even less sense to English ears.

'What's your name?' another asked Annemiek.

'Annemiek Rijckenberg,' Annemiek said. Another attempt was made at writing as consternation rose in the ranks.

'What's your name?' I was asked.

'*Tá brón orm,*' I said, '*Ach ní thuigim cad tá á rá agat.*' [I'm sorry, but I don't know what you're saying.]

'Sarge!' the Brit bawled, 'We got a bunch of foreigners here.' The sergeant, who was providing cover from the other side of the blacked-out street, headed our way.

Meanwhile, Frank was engaged in a conversation with another soldier while Tess, Jimmy and Cora deliberately chatted away as if the Brits didn't exist.

'Excuse me sir,' the Brit was saying to Frank, 'Can you please take your hands out of your pockets?'

'No, I won't,' Frank said.

'I'll have to ask you again sir,' the Brit said, getting stroppy, 'Take your hands out of your pockets.'

'You want my hands out of my pockets,' Frank said, '*You* take my hands out of my pockets. Go ahead!'

There followed the absurd spectacle of the soldier, with his rifle tucked under his arm, trying to dislodge Frank's hands from his pockets.

'Here! That there constitutes assault!' Jimmy told the soldier.

'And what's the problem here?' the sergeant was asking in relation to me.

'*Ní thuigim cad tá á rá agat,*' I said again.

'What country is this guy from?' the sergeant asked.

'As a matter of fact,' Frank said, somewhat spoiling my stance, 'This man is a Gaelic-speaker...'

'For fuck's sake,' the sergeant said, squeezing his temples, 'Gimme a fuckin' break!'

Further up the road, we stopped below the watch-towers of Fort Pegasus to offer our usual advice to the occupying forces.

When Chrit woke up on his bed later that night to the music and uproar of the regular Friday night party, he thought he was hallucinating. He described it years later to some of his friends at a party in Utrecht.

'There was a green light in the ceiling and the whole place was thick with smoke and people. All kinds of people! Old people. Young people. Straight people. Hippies. There was even a priest! [Des and Noelle had briefly called.] And there was Frank, this old man in a suit and tie, directing the proceedings. And the British army was outside the window. And the people inside were *provoking* them...!'

In a very short space of time, and without the benefit of Annemiek's community involvement, Chrit was wholeheartedly drawn into the life of Ballymurphy. His boundless sense of humour and commitment to the hedonistic enjoyment of all aspects of the local social life endeared him to all. His extraordinary cullinary skills, that allowed him to produce gourmet meals from scraps, added a new angle to mealtimes at 42.

Chrit was also, I believe, responsible for the Bavarian party. It was his ancestry, the fact that his mother came from Russia. On the night in question, everyone else had gone home, Cora and Annemiek were in bed, and Donal, Chrit and I were downstairs serenading one another over a litre of whiskey.

'We could have a Bavarian party,' I said.

'What's a Bavarian party?' Donal asked.

'This,' I said. I poured a dram of the *uisce beatha* into a glass, tossed it back and hurled the glass into the fireplace, where it shattered to sparkling smithereens.

'Yahoo!' Chrit said and he and Donal followed suit. Another shot each and another three glasses went. And another three until the ordinary glasses were gone and the crystal came out. Six shots later, the crystal was gone, and we moved on to the cups. And then the mugs until all we had left was the top of the whiskey bottle. Cora, upstairs, had assumed that there was a riot in the next street. It was only when we headed up the stairs, Donal playing the whistle, myself on the guitar, and Chrit doing well on the biscuit tin... Whereupon she appeared at the bedroom door like some kind of lunatic.

'WHAT THE HELL IS GOING ON HERE!' she roared. Donal turned and fled down the stairs, bent on Andersonstown. Better to face the assassins...

'Chri-i-i-it...' came the voice of Annemiek from the other bedroom.

At the end of Annemiek's two months, she and Chrit spent a further three weeks holidaying in Ireland before returning to the Netherlands on July 24th, but they would be back again and again. In the years to come 'the Dutchies', and many of their friends, would become such familiar figures around Ballymurphy that some people thought they lived at 42.

Indeed, as I write (May 2010), Cora and I are expecting Annemiek for the weekend.

# Chapter 20

All in a Month

By the summer of 1974, the 42 project had grown in leaps and bounds. With Cora a full-time volunteer, and the Fagan brothers virtually living at 42, we were running a broad programme that included several initiatives based on the the recently-published Ballymurphy survey, along with street work with young people, an advice facility, the children's library, a local newssheet entitled *Spotlight*, the homework club, informal education for adults, a second community festival and a multi-faceted holiday scheme. We also maintained our ongoing opposition to military brutality against the civilian population.

While all of this found a great home in Ballymurphy, it caused some consternation to the officers of Belfast Education & Library Board who were, so to speak, paying the Piper. To the powers-that-be what was happening at 42 did not fit neatly within the constraints of the youth service. The youth service had an age-range and a raft of recognised activities that were considered 'normal'. We argued that the issues facing young people were the issues facing communities and could only be dealt with in a holistic programme of community-led development. To support our arguments we quoted Paulo Freire, Mao Zedong, Franz Fannon and Ivan Illich which added further and awfully to the consternation of the men at the BELB. In fairness, however, they made no attempt to pull the plug. Instead, they deployed one of their District Officers to regulate what they clearly considered to be a vortex of chaos with their name written all over it.

His name was Seán Neeson and he was a nice man of about forty with black hair who always arrived with a list of things he wanted to know. But it was to be Seán's misfortune that, no sooner would he be seated to a cup of tea than the likes of young Paddy McGuinness or Danny Courtney - both part of the 42 team - would rush in through the front door, shouting, 'They're hijacking cars all over the place!' There was nothing more guaranteed to put the skids under poor Seán. I have no idea what he wrote in his reports for the BELB, but as time went by his visits became less frequent.

Meanwhile, the shootings and ambushes continued, with several people wounded in June, and three determined attempts to burn down Corry's. On June 29$^{th}$ a soldier was fatallly injured in an ambush at the Whiterock/Springfield junction. Five days later there was a prolonged gun-battle at the same spot.

At the beginning of August, just in time for the opening of the second community festival, Joe Dennehy turned up again. Planning to stay the weekend, he stayed the month, enjoying again the weekend parties where the summer nights brought the crowds in droves and Steve Pittam turned up with his girlfriend, Jane, who had joined him in Moyard as a volunteer. As in 1973, Joe again threw himself wholeheartedly into the festive activities that transformed the streets, but he avoided any céilís. By the end of festival week the area was again uplifted. But the cheer was cut short on August 12$^{th}$ when 12-year-old Cathy McGartland from Moyard, niece of Tommy Tolan, climbed up on the roof of Vere Foster school to rub out an embarrassing 'Catherine loves Tony', and fell to her death through a skylight. A member of *Cumann na gCailíní*, she was given a military funeral which passed down Ballymurphy Road as Cora, Joe and I sat in the upstairs office, sorting out bills linked to the joys of the festival.

Cora, meanwhile, organized a number of educational trips for younger children that summer. Greg Dormani, a New York student who would eventually spend a year in Ballymurphy, accompanied one of the first - to Bellevue Zoo. He came back gog-eyed. 'Shit man,' he said, 'I ain't never seen anything like that. Those kids were climbing up the bars of the tiger's cage!' Anyone who ever saw the kids of Ballymurphy attack British armour might well have questioned who in this case posed most danger to whom.

Our summer camps that year were many – to Cork, Dublin, Wicklow, Donegal, Ballycastle, Scotland and Kent. Every Saturday, queues of young people and their mothers could be found outside 42, bags in hand, waiting for the buses that would take the young people away. This greatly pleased the Bennetts next door who did a roaring trade from their house-shop. It also helped redress the goodwill balance as the Bennetts - and the Hunters on the other side - had by now (unknown to us) moved their bedrooms to the far end of their houses in deference to our weekend parties.

Outside in the garden, we were joined every Saturday by Peggy Burns's brother, Pat, a flamboyant extrovert with a black curly mop, bandit moustache and high-heeled boots, who had returned to Ballymurphy from his travels abroad. According to Peggy, Pat was a dab hand at cooking hedgehogs in open fires, using a coating of mud as a pot. He was also learning to play the banjo. This latter skill, however, would in the long term elude Pat. But it didn't stop him from cruising the town in search of parties, with his banjo in train. Welcomed in as an itinerant musician, he would pick at the strings, then set the banjo in a corner and that would be the end of that.

In the main, that year's holiday schemes were small affairs, running for a week at a time; but the Cork and Donegal camps each ran for several weeks. In Cork, the scheme was again sponsored by the Association for Human Rights in the North, relying on the rattling of collection boxes, the goodwill of ordinary citizens and the inimitable organisational skills of my father. Supervised by Cora, it went very well, as did everything that was ever supervised by Cora.

On the way to Cork, the group was transported across Dublin by Donal Donnelly, a republican who'd escaped from Crumlin Road prison back in 1960 and Pádraid Ó Hairtnéide who led a support group of Dublin busmen. On the train south from Dublin, Philip Bolton and Brendan McQuillen from Ballymurphy, and Jim Carlin from Whiterock, Cora's assistants, convinced all the kids that the cows in the fields were sheep and the sheep were cows. 'They've never been outside the city,' Brendan said, explaining the educational angle to Cora, 'They don't know any better.' In Cork, the group was met off the train by my father and Isobel O'Shea from the Association of Human Rights in the North, and by Claire Dunlea, an old friend of Cora's whose fortune it was to have volunteered for the camp.

After an initial stand-off when the young people ran riot, then packed their bags and said they were going home; and Cora and Claire offered them the bus money, locked the door and waved them off with an 'Ok, cheerio, safe journey, tell your mas we were asking for them. Send us a card'; and the whole group had returned, contrite, half an hour later, just as Cora wondered how she would ever be able to go back to Ballymurphy, there had been no more problems. In fact there had been a small miracle.

A few months after Cora had left Cork, Claire had lost several fingers to burns when a car in which she was a passenger crashed and burst into flames. Ever since, she had covered her hands in bandages. But therapy was at hand. 'Let us see Claire!' the young

## Chapter 20

girls yelled, 'Let us see yer hands!' Reluctantly, Claire removed the bandages. 'Oh, gawd love ya!' the kids yelled. They then ran off, engrossed in some other distraction. The openness of the encounter and the complete acceptance by the young people of her damaged hands chased away Claire's demons. She put the bandages in the bin and never wore them again.

Another group of young people, brought to Kent by Cora, displayed similar charm when travelling through London. Cora recounted how:

'We got on this bus and they were all singing, *The wheels of the bus go round and round*... Then one of the girls climbed over this black guy to get to the window seat. Then she turned around and shouted "Hey mister! Are ya alright? D'ya want a bit o' chewing-gum?" The poor black guy didn't know what to do: he clearly wasn't used to white kids like that. Then they were shouting and yelling on the tube, "Here Cora! Remember the *bombs* in Belfast!" People were looking at them in horror. But, they were a hoot.'

In Donegal, where we had the use of Derrybeg Primary School for a Ballymurphy-Shankill camp, all was not such a hoot. Despite Kieran Fagan's best efforts, the camp went belly-up. When it was over, Joe Dennehy and I hitchhiked to Donegal to help Kieran, Philip Bolton and Jim Carlin prop up what remained of Derrybeg Primary School. In the course of a week, we had to replace 47 panes of glass and two doors, and repaint the entire school to get rid of the graffiti.

The Donegal camp was problematic from day one. The organisation on the Shankill wasn't what it might have been so that Donal and I had to fill the gap - not easy in the summer of 1974. A week before the first group was to leave, we went to an address in the Glencairn area, a long way upriver for us, to find a particular man. When he opened the door, I asked if he was James.

'Oh Jesus son.' he said, 'Get in here fast with that accent!' Glancing up and down the dark street, he hauled us in and slammed the door.

'The man you really want,' he told us, 'is down in the UDA club. But, whatever you do son, let your buddy here do the talking.' Half an hour later, Donal and I found ourselves standing at the door of the UDA club, trying to ensure adequate leadership on a mixed childrens' camp, the very concept of which might well have been anathema to any would-be assassins drinking at the tables.

The following day, we were collecting blankets from Jackie Brown, a co-student of mine at the Polytechnic who ran a youth club in a back street off the Shankill, when it all went wrong again. This time, Síle O'Neill, the teacher from Monaghan, was along. Síle, long hair and fine features, was deeply committed to helping the effort and had accompanied myself and Donal to the Shankill. Síle also had the wonderful ability to fell forests while wondering who was knocking down all the trees. Síle had a strong and loud Southern accent, not easily lost on a narrow street off the Shankill Road.

'Left, right!' we heard, 'Left, right!' as we brought the blankets down from the loft of the youth club. Then, in through the open door marched half a dozen big bruisers who curled around us in a semi-circle before coming to a halt.

'Attention!' the front man said as we counted the seconds left in our lives. They all stood like pokers. 'At ease!' They all at-eased. They then stood there, saying nothing, while we loaded up the Andersonstown Handicapped Association's minibus and did a screech out of there.

'*Síle...!*' I said as we barrelled down the Shankill Road.

Two nights before the camp left, Donal and I were back on the Shankill. This time, we'd driven on my motorbike to the home of Alf Midgley, my other Shankill Polytechnic student, to see if he could organise a couple of helpers for the following week. As we sat in the living-room of the two-up, two-down house, several of the neighbours called in to say hello. Minnie Midgley made tea and small talk ensued. Half an hour had passed when loud voices out in the street proclaimed that trouble had broken out further down the Shankill between the Shankill people and the British army. The loud voices were calling for guns. Hearing this, Donal and I began to sip our tea a little more quickly as all sorts of intemperate yelling built up outside. Then a woman ran into the living-room of Alf's house.

'All UDA personnel report to stations!' she shouted. Half the people in the room got up and left!

'Thanks for the tea!' Donal shouted and we jumped on the motorbike and took off.

'Donal,' I said as we sped down the Shankill, 'Anybody stops us, and I'm a deaf mute person from Bangor in Wales!'

The end of it all was a serious shortcoming in the Shankill volunteer base and the consequent wrecking of Derrybeg Primary School.

## Chapter 20

The Donegal camp also demonstrated the short-livedness of some reconciliation. Every week, when the camp came back to Belfast, the Ballymurphy group was dropped off first and the bus went on to the Shankill Road. This decision was taken on the basis that we could guarantee the safety of the Shankill people in Ballymurphy but they couldn't do the same for us. On one occasion, however, the bus arrived at the bottom of the Whiterock Road to the sound of heavy gunfire and was stopped by the Official IRA who were kindly providing the most up-to-date travel information.

'Big problem boss,' one of them said as I got off the bus to get the lie of the land, 'The Provies and the Brits are at it hot and heavy. It's not safe to go up. You'll need to go around to the Springfield Road end.'

'OK,' I said to the driver, 'We'll go and drop the Shankill kids off first.' Fifteen minutes later we arrived on the Shankill Road and reconciliation went out the window.

'Fenians!' the Shankill kids screamed as soon as they got off the bus. They then chased us down the road with a hail of bricks and bottles. It was this fragile spirit of reconciliation that had left such a mess in Derrybeg.

We eventually repaired the school and made our way back to Belfast, Joe explaining to all on board our minibus how his visit the previous year had brought a near-death experience at the céilí in St. Bernadette's. Poor Joe! It was all about to happen again. Arriving back in the city on a Saturday night, we were on our way to Ballymurphy after dropping two Shankill Road men home, when our minibus broke down - right across the main Shankill artery, just as the pubs were spilling out their clientele! On the bus, along with myself and Joe, were Philip Bolton who was driving, and Jim Carlin who'd recently survived a loyalist assassination attempt. This made Jim not as rational as he might otherwise have been.

'They'll shoot us!' he screamed. His next reaction was to arm. He grabbed a hurley (Irish sporting symbol) from the floor of the bus and, with the power of ten Hiroshimas, made for the side door.

'For fuck's sake Jim,' Philip shouted, diving into the back from the driver's seat, 'Will ya stop bein' a buck-eedjit and put that fuckin' thing down!'

'Grab him Joe!' I shouted. And as the bus rocked to and fro in the middle of the Shankill Road with nobody at the wheel and traffic trying to get around us, Philip, Joe and I wrestled Jim to the floor.

'Jim,' Joe pleaded, not unreasonably, 'Please give us the hurley.

We're attracting an awful lot of attention.'

It took a minute or two, but we finally managed to disarm and immobilise Jim. We then had a hell of a job convincing him to sit at the wheel and steer, so the other three of us could get out and 'casually' push the bus down darkened, hostile side-streets, where one bad move could've had us killed. On the final leg to the Peace Line that separated the Shankill from the Springfield Road, we were watched silently by people who stood in doorways in pools of light and knew that we weren't of them. It was with the greatest of relief that we heaved the bus over the final interface ramp.

'Men of shteel,' Joe said, giving the 's' the west Kerry treatment, 'Hewn out of the solid rock. I was so casual back there, I thought I'd fall asleep.'

We then pushed our bus straight into a conveniently-timed gunfight between the British army and the IRA.

\* \* \*

In the August edition of *Spotlight*, we were praised by the military in the commandeered section of Vere Foster School. Our admirer was the local Major who had recently offered to sort out the area's dogs following a reader's complaint.

After the Cheshires had stolen two copies of the paper from Seán Butler while he was selling it door to door, we publicly demanded 6p restitution. A few days later, I answered the door to a Brit foot patrol and was handed an envelope with 8p and an accompanying note, dated the same day, July 17th. Immediately, we began to prepare for the August edition so we could print the Major's note and *Spotlight's* response. The note read:

*'I enjoy reading the* Spotlight *as it is the only intelligently written local paper available in this area... It is also refreshingly free from the lies, distortions, hypocrisy and hate published in other street papers.*

*As you publicly asked for 6p, I'll publicly reply with an enclosure of 8p as I notice each copy costs 4p.'*

*Spotlight* responded:

*'Dear Major*
*Since the two issues of Spotlight taken by the Cheshire Regiment cost only 3p each we have returned the extra 2p. We should hate to be in your debt.*

## Chapter 20

We are grateful for the 6p restitution. But, please Major, don't patronize us. In this area, with all its sorrow and experience of horror at the hands of the British army, praise from Vere Foster is cause to examine one's conscience.

Your abhorrence of the 'lies, distortions, hypocrisy' of 'other papers' is commendable and edifying. The criterion of your judgement is, no doubt, the invincible reliability of your own informants and the undoubted moral superiority of the master race to which you are fortunate to belong – Daniels come to judgement – go saoraidh Dia sinn.

As for the hate which shocks you in the 'other street papers' – wasn't it ever thus! From Cromwell to Cecil Rhodes the crusader's lot has never been an easy one. Ungrateful wretches that these Irish are, you do your best to rescue them from their evil ways, and they love you not. You take your manly part in a crusading army which (in a heroic effort to save these miscreant Irish from themselves) persecutes defenceless people; beats their children with batons and gun butts; wrecks their homes; tortures and interns without trial their husbands, fathers and sons; humiliates their people; and you get no thanks. They actually hate you for it.

And worse still, there is a certain feeling among ignorant foreigners (how dare they!) in Strasbourg, Aden, India, Cyprus, Cork, that your army has not given the Irish any reason to love you.

We British shall never understand it, shall we?

Yours in sorrow, Editor.'

'Now, you're really fucked,' Eugene Trainor said when he arrived with *The Tattler*. But the British army stayed its distance. Maybe news had spread about the motorbike gloves. One way or the other the Major never got back to us, although the Cheshires almost got back to me.

Whiterock Industrial Estates Ltd., a community-controlled economic experiment being led by Frank Cahill, Seán Mackle and a number of others, had lost most of its thrust when the industrial estate had been commandeered by the British army during Motorman. However, it was still doing its best and had opened a small block-mounting business - *Whiterock Pictures* - in a ground-floor shop at the Springfield/Whiterock junction in December 1973. Ever since, Frank Cahill, Philip Cahill and Peggy Burns were turning out great lines in *Book of Kells* reprints and converting photographs and posters into indestructible wall-mountings. One of the key components of the business was, needless to say, a phone. As phones in those days were rare as fish-wings and 42 had no budget for one, we had to rely on public phones. However, these didn't exist in Ballymurphy, which threw us back on the resources of the community. The result was that John Maguire, our neighbour of two doors up, became the recipient of our calls. To ease the pressure on John, we alternated our outgoing calls between his phone and those of Des Wilson and *Whiterock Pictures*, storing them up so we could make a bunch of calls in a single go.

Not long after we'd published the Major's letter, I was in the back room of *Whiterock Pictures* in the middle of a bunch of such calls when I heard the front door of the shop open. This was shortly followed by the English accents of a military patrol and the raised voices of Frank and Peggy. It was a close call as to which of them liked the Brits the most.

'Aye, you're big brave men,' Frank - a relatively small man, you'll recall - was saying as I came back into the main part of the shop, having concluded my calls. I noticed that his glasses were bouncing on the bridge of his nose. 'You, you and you,' he went on, pointing at the three biggest brutes in the patrol, 'Put down yer rifles and the three of us [he pointed at himself, Philip and *me rather than Peggy*!] will knock the tripe outta youse!' Recoiling in horror, I'd just been volunteered to die for Ireland. However, before I had time to protest Frank's insanity, the Brits saved me the embarrassment. They turned out to be bigger poltroons than me. 'Come on now,' Frank goaded, 'A fair dig.' But, the three big lads turned on their yellabelly heels and walked out.

'Cowardly bawstards!' the un-volunteered Peggy fired after them as a parting shot.

'We'd've bate the shite out of them,' I assured Frank.

\* \* \*

The final weekend of August 1974 was to be Kieran Fagan's last weekend of freedom. After many years of study, he was finally preparing to brave the world of work, having landed a music-teaching post at the prestigious Mt. Lourdes Grammar School in Enniskillen. Donal, ever supportive, had agreed to drive him in the Andersonstown Handicapped Association minibus to his new digs in the town. This would be on the Sunday. Joe Dennehy (still in

## Chapter 20

Belfast) and I decided to go along so we could all celebrate with a drink in the Southern border village of Blacklion. In those days, pubs in the North didn't open on a Sunday - in fact the N.I. Labour Party had committed political suicide on the suggestion that *parks* should open on a Sunday. Some 36 years later Joe would remember the angst that often befell those Northern Sundays:

'I'm sure you've mentioned a particularly dry and hung-over Sunday when Micheál Mac Cába, quietly as ever, pulled out of his pocket the one and only winning ticket for a bottle of whiskey. He'd won it in a raffle (probably to do with the Festival) in the community centre – one of the happiest days of my life, as I was sitting next to him.

'Another happy Sunday that I've never forgotten was when the Donegal singer, Mícheál Ó Dómhnaill, arrived into 42 with someone else who knew the house. Between them, they were carrying a crate of Guinness – needless to say greatly welcomed. The other lad didn't seem to be overly impressed with the craic – I think we were generally less stimulating on Sundays than Saturday nights – and was for heading off. That was OK, but he wanted to take the drink too! I have forever since had the warmest and fondest memory of Ó Dómhnaill's reply: "I've never taken away a drink that I brought to a house". I've often quoted it as the mark of a decent man and a good citizen. I was extremely sad to see just now when I checked his name that he left the planet in 2006 – a fine singer and musician and a very decent man...'

Despite the shooting and bombing and the danger of roving assassins, a Sunday drinking-exodus across the border was therefore part of Northern nationalist culture.

In Enniskillen, we arrived at Kieran's digs to find the Salvation Army outside, playing their trumpets and singing hymns. After getting over the shock of such a reception, Kieran managed to skirt around them without too much damage and drop his bags in his room. On his way out again, the landlady of the digs shared with him her strong views on how lodgers should behave - which included an abstemious approach to alcohol – and which Kieran passed on to what she described as the 'nice lads on the bus'. Consumed with the Sunday thirst, we continued on towards the border

Now, as anyone who has ever been to Blacklion will know, it's no great shakes. Blink and you're through.

'I'm going to blink now,' Donal said. We shortly thereafter found ourselves in Sligo. Having now crossed Ireland, we felt that it wouldn't be right not to give Sligo its share of the tourist quota.

'This is not a good idea,' Kieran droned as he took his first swig of a creamy pint of Guinness.

'It's a terrible thing,' Joe said looking solemnly at the new teacher, 'To watch a man about to commit voluntary self-destruction.'

'My arse!' Kieran said, 'I need to be back in Enniskillen early tonight. I don't want to look like shite on a shovel in the morning.'

'Of course you'll be back early,' Donal assured him and we settled in. By the time we'd had that pint, and the one that followed, and listened to music, and gone for chips, the evening had slipped to well after midnight. By the time we got back to Enniskillen, it was one in the morning and we were all exhausted.

'Well,' Kieran said, 'Thanks a lot for the send-off. I'll see youse all next week.'

'Like fuck...!' somebody said and there was an ungainly rush for the door of the digs, now thankfully devoid of the Salvation Army who, if they'd seen the cut of us, would surely have considered their earlier intervention an abject failure.

'This is no joke!' Kieran said as he tried in vain to bar the door. But it was three against one. Nobody was leaving. In Kieran's room, however, there was alas only one bed. The long and the short of this was that by the time Donal, Joe and I had scrambled aboard to fall into happy slumber, there wasn't much room for Kieran. This resulted in him landing on the floor with loud thumps many times during the night.

'That,' Joe said later, 'was the only time in real life I can actually remember people's feet sticking out under the blanket – the image sticks with me still.'

In the morning we all got up and Kieran prepared for the first day of his new job. He showered, shaved, dressed, then looked in the mirror and groaned horribly. From the neck down he looked immaculate: pressed suit, new shirt and tie, polished shoes, handkerchief sticking out of his top pocket. From the neck up, he was a disaster: swollen bloodshot eyes, grey skin, and hair and beard that refused to budge from bedraggled.

'Well damn you boys,' he said as we wished him luck down in Mt. Lourdes. He later told us that, as he considered where best in the assembly hall he might vomit, he was called up on stage by the head nun, introduced to the hundreds of waiting pupils and invited to

## Chapter 20

make a speech.

'If I could've got hold of you guys,' he confided, 'there would've been one hell of a bloodbath in the corridors of Mt. Lourdes.'

On August $31^{st}$, Steve Pittam married his girlfriend Jane, who had moved into the Moyard Flats with him. The wedding took place at the Quaker Meeting House in Waterford. A great crowd arrived down from Ballymurphy, including Fr. Des and Noelle, Frank and Tess Cahill, Gerry Finnegan, Eilish and Sean Rooney, Kate McManus, Alistair Herron, Roy and Mary Martin, Ethel Moan, and Peggy Burns and her father Jimmy. Everyone had a great time, after which Steve and Jane went off to live on a farm in County Wexford.

# Chapter 21

Living Off The Land

---

In September, Cora and decided to take a break and headed for the Continent. Although we were a bit short on money, we decided to take a month off and hitchhike down to Morocco. This would coincide with a visit to the Netherlands by the second batch of Youth & Community Work students at the Jordanstown Polytechnic. One of the course tutors - Stanley Rowe - had invited Cora along on the basis of her work in Ballymurphy, which meant that I could catch up with her at Chrit and Annemiek's place. The old farmhouse, being rented by Chrit and Annemiek, lay just outside the village of Neer, close to Roermond in the southern province of Limburg. From there it would be an easy hop over to Belgium and down into France.

'It's autumn,' I explained to Cora who was questioning the wisdom of the whole penniless venture, 'Remember what our Niall says, "You're as free as your ability to do without." We can live off the land.'

'Whose land?' Cora wanted to know.

I left Ireland on 12$^{th}$ September with some rudimentary cooking equipment, a change of clothes, a towel, a toothbrush and a razor, all rolled up in a sleeping-bag and space-blanket. Two days later, I landed in Ostende where Cora and I had started out on our overland journey to Afghanistan three years earlier. I hitchhiked on to Neer, met up with Cora, and spent the next two days cycling through the Dutch countryside with Cora, Chrit and Annemiek, and visiting Chrit's family where we met his Russian mother who had so telepathically caused that Bavarian party back at 42.

From Neer, we hitchhiked south through the forests of the Ardennes where two hunters picked us up. They'd been stalking wild boar but had given up and were now on their way home to northern France.

'Some time you should try it,' the driver said to me. That evening, Cora and I had our first opportunity to live off the land. But, much as I might have loved to go after the razor-tusked wild boar, I was without gun and ended up hunting pumpkin.

It was late in the evening, just before dark, at an isolated farm somewhere in the valley of the Meuse. From the road, I spotted the

## Chapter 21

quarry, crouching large and bulbous behind some rabbit fencing. Despite Cora's efforts to talk me out of it, I set off across a small field towards the unsuspecting pumpkins, Swiss Army knife in hand, muscles taut, nerves steeled. From the direction of the farmhouse, the family dog started to howl like a werewolf. I crept on undaunted. Cora, tut-tutting into the semi-darkness from the vantage point of the roadside ditch, saw me hop the rabbit-fence and go to ground. A few minutes later she saw me reappear, staggering up the field, knees buckled under a pumpkin that must've weighed 100 pounds. But, far from praising this first encounter with the European wild, she threw her hands in the air. 'You bloody eedjit!' she snapped, 'What are we going to do with *that*!'

Affronted, I set the monster down before her, and attacked it with the Swiss Army knife, intending to gut it and chop it into manageable pieces that we could stuff into a plastic bag. I might as well have hacked at Sydney Harbour Bridge. There was a much greater chance that the blade of the knife would snap back and slice off a finger than it would ever dent the skin of that pumpkin.

'Bring it back!' Cora ordered.

'We could take it with us,' I ventured, 'Find a bigger knife.'

'Maybe we could hire a truck?' the ungrateful wretch said, 'Take the shaggin' thing back!' Defeated, I staggered away into the darkness. A short distance down the road we rolled out our sleeping-bags under a tree and went to bed hungry.

'Supermarkets...' Cora muttered in the dark.

The following day we had another chance in a field of whispering maize.

'Corn on the cob!' I said and hopped over a gate to collect a few ears. Cora looked on with her hands on her hips in the posture of Doubting Thomas. We then continued south, taking whatever lifts that came our way, one of which brought us briefly into Switzerland. A woman who picked us up nipped in through one side of Basel and exited out the far side, back into France. That was the only time I ever visited Switzerland: it lasted all of half an hour and it was dark. An hour or so later, she dropped us off in Besançon where we went into a park to cook our corn on the cob. We boiled and boiled and boiled two of the ears, but would they soften or sweeten?

'Do you know what I think?' Cora said, 'I think that's cow food. You could boil them to Kingdom Come and you still couldn't eat them.' We threw them away. Living off the land was looking bad.

For a second night I went to sleep with the word *Supermarkets* on the breeze.

From Besançon, we continued on towards Morocco, travelling down the Rhone Valley with Peter-Jean, a mad French student with long black curls and a hooked nose who drove like a getaway. At one point he hit a flock of farm ducks and wiped out most of them in a great fanfare of guts and feathers. He then cut off the main road and brought us up into a belt of wooded hills to visit some hippy friends who lived in an old stone farmhouse. Big bearded Jacques gave us some figs. His two women, Maria and Lottie, both in their early twenties with identical long dark hair, seemed to share blonde little Thérèse who was about two.

Finally, south of Avignon, that walled city that had once been home to popes of the Great Schism, living off the land seemed possible at last: the vineyards were in full fruit. Endless, endless food. Not alone that, but when I was a child, Heaven was a place full of grapes.

'Don't eat the grapes,' a German hippy warned us, 'They'll make you sick.'

'I've heard that one before,' I told Cora, *'Don't eat all your Easter eggs; they'll make you sick. Don't eat all that cake; it'll make you sick...* A load of codswallop!'

I filled a plastic bag and, all along that road to Perpignan, stuffed myself with grapes. When I couldn't eat another one I squished the juice into my mouth. By the time I reached the Spanish border I couldn't look at another grape. By the time I reached Sitges, the German's warning was looking solid. In one of the wandering, geranium-hung alleys of this pleasant Catalonian town, I found myself doubled over on a *pension* bed with ripping pains in my stomach. I lay like that, twisting on the bed, for the next two days - poisoned. The grapes had been sprayed with copper sulphate!

We never did make it to Morocco. But, when we got home in mid October, we had a surprise waiting for us. Greg, the bearded New York student who'd gone on the zoo trip with Cora and the local tiger-terrorisers, had moved in. Having decided to extend his stay in Ballymurphy for a year, he was being sponsored by a Quaker fund to work voluntarily in the area.

Since summer, Greg had been living with the Hartigans, a few streets away. Seán and Ann-Marie were a gentle, easy-going couple with young children; but the pressure of an additional body had

## Chapter 21

proved too much. Greg had arrived in one day and Ann-Marie had his bags waiting for him in the hall. Then someone gave him the key to 42 and we found him, on our return, bedded down in our upstairs living-room.

'You're welcome to stay,' I said once we'd got over the surprise, 'But this is our living-room. You'll have to move into the back bedroom.'

'Shit man,' Greg said, 'I'm really comfortable here.'

'You're still going to have to move,' Cora said, 'We can't have people sleeping in our living-room. Otherwise we have no living-room.'

'Shit,' Greg said, 'Why do you have to have your living-room upstairs.'

'Greg,' I said, 'If you want to stay, you'll need to move your gear into the back room.'

'Shit man...' Greg said as he lifted his mattress and bedding from the floor.

## Chapter 22

Harry Comes To Town

Oil and water poorly mix. First of all, Greg was a vegetarian and we weren't. In order to make life easy for himself, he'd go to the market, stock up, and cook several days' food at a time in several pots, which would leave us with no pot at all. Secondly, we didn't always like the same music. The radio might be on in the kitchen, often just as background noise, and Greg might arrive in saying, 'Gee man, do we have to listen to this shit!' Greg might then reach up and switch it over. As we had no TV, this could be a point of contention. Greg then took to playing the fiddle. He became a committed fiddler and could often be found practising into the early hours in the upstairs living-room, separated from our bedroom by nothing more than an un-insulated stud wall with papered-over holes.

Anyone who has ever listened to the squealing of a fiddle being played by a novice at two o'clock in the morning will understand how that can stir the listener to irrational emotions. One night I lay in bed as the wailing went on into the night.

'If he plays that once more,' I kept saying to Cora, 'I'll fucking well kill him!' The tune would squeak to an end and there would be a few moments silence. I'd wait in deep denial that it was going to start again, but it would. And again. And again.

Eventually I snapped, jumped out of bed and charged in next door.

'Greg,' I stammered as calmly as I could, wiping away flecks of froth from the corners of my mouth, 'It's two o'clock in the fucking morning and I have a meeting at nine. I can't get to fucking sleep with the screeching of that fucking fiddle!' A surprised Greg looked up at me.

'Gee man,' he suggested, 'Maybe you should sound-proof your walls?' Silly-boy me: why the blazes hadn't I thought of that?

It wasn't a fault thing: we were just different. But, there being no fault didn't help. Over the months the tension grew. As a result, friends stopped calling and the IRA, seeing the community workers wilt, offered to chase the tenant off site. Now, don't get me wrong. He was an OK guy and he played the guitar and enjoyed Irish music and had the right frame of mind when it came to the local political

## Chapter 22

situation. He didn't like the Brits any more than we did. But living in the one space wasn't working. Then Christmas began to loom on the horizon and Cora and I wondered how we'd survive a shortage of pots, and the fiddle, and nobody calling, and the radio being turned over all day long. But that all changed on the morning of Christmas Eve, when Harry Bellingham arrived out of the blue. There was a knock on the door. I was out at the time, and Greg answered. Cora, in the living room, heard the hesitant Derry accent asking 'Is Ciarán home..?'

'No,' Greg said, 'He's not here.'

'Sorry friend,' Harry said, backing off towards the garden gate, 'I didn't mean to disturb you...'

'Harry!' Cora shouted from inside and came running out to welcome him. 'Is it you Harry?'

Harry swarmed in with his huge frame and threw his arms around Cora. He had been two days on the road. And so far, his journey had been a hazardous one.

He had left Cork in an old white Ford Cortina with a black roof that he'd bought for a fiver from a man he'd befriended with a fish supper. Harry had been in Stephen's Green in Dublin when the man asked for a cigarette. Harry, with a heart as big as a house, gave him the cigarette, then hauled him off to the nearest chipper and bought him the feed, whereupon the man asked if he'd like to buy the car for a fiver. Now, on his way north, he'd picked up a hitchhiker outside Fermoy. A little further along, he was involved in a slight accident with a woman driving a Volkswagon Beetle. Having neither tax, licence nor insurance, Harry surveyed the situation for a moment before reaching a verdict. 'Well friend,' he said to his passenger, 'I don't know what you're doin', but I'm gettin' the hell outta here!' He grabbed his jacket and a small bag and took off across the fields. A two-day hitchhike later, he arrived in Belfast on the loyalist Donegall Road, having no idea where he was or how he should proceed to Ballymurphy. Eventually he plucked up the courage to ask an older woman for directions.

'I'm from Derry,' he told her, 'I'm neutral in all this here. Can you tell me how to get to Ballymurphy.'

Harry's luck was in. She didn't shout for the UVF or UDA. Instead she gave him directions and explained that she herself was on her way to the Falls to deliver Christmas presents across the divide.

Following the woman's directions, Harry arrived at the top of the

Whiterock Road and made his way to the Sloan's Club. He went into the club, offered to buy some punters a drink and found himself out the back with a gun to his head. It was only when he told the boys with the gun that he was in the area to visit myself and Cora that he finally convinced them of his bona fides. He had then arrived at our door and, but for the timely intervention of Cora, would have been away again. But now, with a whiskey in his hand and a roof over his head, he was in full floral flight.

Harry was a drifter who'd breezed into Cork a couple of years earlier. Alone in the city, he was passing down the North Mall one night when he heard music coming from *Dún Laoi*, where the Association for Human Rights in the North was hosting a group of Belfast families. Meekly, Harry made his way inside and met my father who invited him to join the party. From then on, he'd been a loyal supporter of the work in Cork and a champion of what we were doing in Ballymurphy. He also became a bit of a legend around his newly adopted home.

One look at Harry and you knew not to mess. A solid block of a man with shoulders out to here and tails of blond hair, he looked every bit the wild 35-year-old block-layer that he was. During the early days of the Troubles, he had lived in Derry's Bogside where he gave his full attention to the street battles against the Brits. At one point, the soldiers had identified him as a particular nuisance and had dispatched a six-man snatch-squad to haul him in. Harry, in turn, single-handedly dispatched the six man snatch-squad, riot shields, clubs and all. On another occasion in Cork, he was attacked one night by three thugs while making his way, 'peacefully' as he put it, home. Harry grabbed one of them by the scruff of the neck and the arse of his jeans and scraped him down a pebble-dash wall. However, considerably under the influence as he was, the other two kicked the daylights out of him and left him in a pool of blood. Enraged by this attack on a defenseless citizen, namely himself, Harry staggered back to the digs where the landlady, an unfortunate Mrs. Cush, was watching television.

'Where's the hatchet?' Harry demanded, bursting through the kitchen door.

'Oh God, boy,' the horrified Mrs. Cush said, 'Don't be doing anything mad now. Take your shirt off now, won't you. You'll need to soak that shirt to get rid of all that blood.' What Mrs. Cush was really thinking was, *Shirt off, Harry grounded.*

## Chapter 22

'You're dead right,' Harry conceded and took off the shirt.

'That's better now, boy,' Mrs. Cush said and went out to the bathroom to soak the shirt. When she came back, the shirtless Harry was gone. As was the hatchet. Down to the North Main Street went Harry in search of his assailants. When they were nowhere to be seen, he began a search of the eating establishments, beginning with the Old Kentucky where he lined up the customers and stalked the line, blood streaming to his waist and hatchet in hand.

'Gimme the culprits and youse can all finish yer dinners!' he shouted as he checked each terrified face. He then worked his way up the North Main Street until he was eventually cornered by the cops in a chipper on Shandon Street. Not to be messed with, was Harry. In a bar, you had to be careful with your words as, after a couple of pints, Harry could easily misunderstand what you said. Emotions could go from zero to infinity in one or two innocent exchanges and one could get a glass in the face.

The other thing about Harry was that he was a great raconteur who loved to recount stories of his colourful life. However, he had one disconcerting habit. In almost all of his stories, there was a villain who had done him some harm but finally and justifiably came to a bad end, perhaps with Harry battering him with a shovel or smashing his nose with half a brick. The problem was that as the story progressed, *you* became *him* - the villain, the enemy, and Harry would have you by the throat, spitting venom in your face.

Such was the awe that Harry inspired that, when I went to live briefly at the famous Waterloo Road house in Dublin, many years after the colourful Derryman had drifted on, Denis Hurley who lived in the basement used to hammer home multiple bolts every night with a heavy lead pipe.

'Denis,' I asked one night, 'Why the hell do you do that?'

'THAT,' Denis said with a stare in his eyes, 'is in case mad Harry ever comes back!'

'Not alone that,' John Minihane, the other permanent resident at Waterloo Road, added 'but the whole back garden is booby-trapped. I came home without a key one night and made the mistake of trying to come in the back way. I had no sooner climbed over the fence than I fell into a man-trap. Then I triggered off a killer log that came crashing down from one of the Sycamores and when I complained to Denis, he gave off to me! "I warned you!" he shouted, "There's nothing out there for you but death and destruction!"'

Greg wasn't used to men who inspired such fortifications.

Within fifteen minutes, Harry was in full swing, lowering whiskies, and giving Greg his take on life. What began in the kitchen as a simple declaration of Harry's view of the world quickly moved to an attack on all things English. Within twenty minutes of saying hello, Harry had Greg by the lapels over a bench in the kitchen. 'What have you got to say to *this*!' he was roaring in Greg's face, 'Do you understand friend! I despise *everything* English! Including this foul *language* I'm speaking!'

At the same time, he was doing his best to spit that foul language down Greg's throat. He then released Greg and began to tell us how he'd been ditched by the nun he'd been in love with, how he used to climb over the convent wall at night and throw coins up at the window and sing to her on the way home from the pub, how the nun's brother-in-law and the convent Mother Superior had poisoned his love's mind, and how he was going to sort them out 'by burning them out of house and home'!

'Man,' Greg said, pulling me aside as soon as he got a chance, 'I'm outta here! That guy is totally off the wall man. I'm getting the hell across town until he's gone back to wherever the fuck he came from!' It was terrible but we didn't see Greg again until Harry had left after Christmas.

On Christmas Eve, Cora, Harry and I called around to Frank and Tess and were later joined by Donal, Kieran and Jimmy Burns at the Rock Bar. There, Harry told us that he thought the IRA were a bunch of cowards.

'Gutless,' he said, bringing us closer and into his confidence.

'Oh,' I said, as it was now dangerous to comment, one way or the other, lest there be a misunderstanding.

'I had a plan last time I was in Derry,' he said, 'I went to the IRA and asked for two Volunteers, but the cowardly men – you know, those *cowardly* men – they turned me down!'

'Plan?' I said, maintaining as anodyne a tone as possible.

'Up in Derry, at the checkpoint in Bishop Street, there's always two Brits and as they search you, they crouch down to pat down yer trousers. So I go to the IRA with this plan. "Give me two men," I tell them "Two men. That's all. And we'll go down to that checkpoint with hatchets. And when the Brits are crouched down like that, pattin' our trousers, smash! Splat! Tatie bloody bread!" But they wouldn't even give it a try. No courage, friend, no courage at all...'

# Chapter 22

'Well,' Frank said, 'What can we say...?'

'Dreadful,' I said.

'Just-what-do-you-mean-by-"dread-ful",' Harry asked, each word deliberately spaced as he squinted his eyes at me with the kind of look that could easily presage a forehead in the face, 'What kind of a word is *that*!'

'We're going to have a song now,' Frank said, rescuing me.

More drink was consumed and Harry began to tell us again how he was still in love with the nun.

'But the Mother Superior ruined everything!' he said, leaning across the kitchen table into Frank's face, 'The Mother Superior *poisoned* her mind! Do you understand that? She *poisoned* her mind my friend. But, make no mistake about it, I'm gonna burn her convent to the ground!'

'Ah sure now Harry,' Frank said, 'There's no need for that. You'll get over it in time.'

'*Time* my friend!' Harry shouted, 'It's been two bloody *years*!'

'Happy Christmas,' Donal said, 'And a merry New Year.'

In another corner, they were telling a story about Big Ellen Cosgrove, and Kitty Glennon who lived in Ballymurphy Parade. The IRA had hit the fort on the Upper Springfield a few nights earlier with a rocket while Ellen and Kitty were making their way through Divismore Crescent en route to the Sloan's Club. The explosion sent the two women into hysterics. 'Oh Jesus!' Ellen was screaming, 'It's the club! They [the loyalists] are after hittin' the club!' Eventually, one of the Volunteers who was still in position nearby put his hand on Ellen's shoulder. 'It's OK,' he said, 'It was us. We hit the fort.' Instantly the two women were becalmed. 'Come on Kitty,' Ellen said with a wiggle of her head, 'It's only that oul' barracks.'

On Boxing Day Harry teamed up with an old pal called Ned. A big Gigantopithecus of a man, he arrived at 42 swaddled in a dark overcoat, and sporting a heavy five o'clock shadow. He had, according to Harry, a steel plate in his head.

'Yon lives down the Falls with his sister,' Harry told us when Ned went to the toilet, 'He's not right in the head, if you know what I mean.' This, in Cora's view, was a case of the pot calling the kettle black-ass.

Harry and Ned were old friends from way back: they had lived together in London. In those days, neither of them was working and it was required that they supplement their 'stingy' dole with some hunting and gathering. The hunting, Ned explained, took place in Trafalgar Square.

'We used to sit on one of the benches and throw a few scraps of bread to the pigeons. Then, when they started to land all over us ... squish!' He slapped his thighs together to indicate the demise of a trusting feathered unfortunate that had landed there. Then squish! Another hapless critter met his Waterloo in the fold of Ned's right armpit.

'We ate well most days we went to the Square,' Ned told us, 'But we had to watch for the Peelers. And make sure that none of them oul' tourists seen what was goin' on...'

An example of the gathering, specific to Harry, had been outlined to my mother a little earlier in the year. My youngest sister, Neasa, had been ill and my mother was despairing of the doctors when Harry called for a visit.

'Máire,' Harry suggested, 'You should do the Novena.'

'Harry,' my exasperated mother said, 'I'm fed up with prayers.' This horrified the deeply religious Harry.

'Oh Máire,' he said, 'You should never give up on the power of prayer.' He then went on to illustrate its miraculous potential. 'One time I was down in Brighton without a penny to my name. No money for food or anything else. I was depressed and down in the dumps. So, I went into the chapel and prayed. And while I was praying there, with my head down on the pew, it came to me: all the rich people in Brighton lived down on the waterfront, and on a Sunday they left their front doors open. And the gas meters, full of money, were just inside the front doors...'

After recounting their hunting exploits in London and having a cup of tea, Harry and Ned went off to the Rock Bar. A couple of hours later, Harry came back, agitated and in a hurry to get out of Belfast. Ned's sister, he explained, was 'a bit of a nutter'. After the two lads had 'got rightly' in the Rock, Ned decided to bring Harry home for dinner. However, when the two big lads arrived, the sister had reared up and told Ned in no uncertain terms that they could sing for their dinner. This prompted Ned to try and strangle the sister and the RUC was called. Ned, a big powerful man, battered the RUC vanguard, and British army reinforcements were summoned. At this point Harry excused himself and fled across the street to observe the unfolding catastrophe from the safety of an entry.

'I'm wanted by the British army,' he explained, 'For going AWOL.'

## Chapter 22

'When were you in the British army?' I asked, surprised that such a stalwart Irish patriot would ever consider such a course of action.

'Away before the Troubles,' Harry said, 'I was broke and thought I could get a few bob by joining the army, but it was murder. Up at five in the morning, eating oul' scraps, and putting up with all sorts of bully boys shouting orders from one end of the day to the other in their dirty English accents. But the last straw came when we had to do the gas-masks. They put us all in this big hut with gas-masks on. Then they filled the hut with smoke and made us run around in a big circle so we got some idea of what it would be like in World War I. Can you imagine that! You couldn't see. You couldn't breathe! All you seen was these spacemen coming out of the smoke. After about five minutes, I couldn't take it any more. I was choking to death. So I dived straight out through one of the windows and never stopped... From that day to now, I've been on their wanted list...'

The following morning, Harry headed south.

A few days later Greg moved into Jan McCarthy's house which was lying vacant as Jan had temporarily gone back to England. There, he figured, he was safe from Harry.

# Chapter 23
## The Year Of The Feuds

1975 began on an optimistic note: the Brits were in retreat. Soon, they'd be on their way home and we'd have a united Ireland. Posters declared the Year of Victory.

The source of this optimism was a meeting that had taken place in Feakle, County Clare, back in December. A group of Northern Protestant ministers, led by Reverend William Arlow, had met secretly with the leadership of the IRA. Although the meeting had to be abandoned when a tip-off came that the Irish Special Branch wanted to join in, Arlow arrived back in Belfast with terms for an IRA Christmas ceasefire and a possible extension to a bilateral truce.

On December 18th the clergymen flew to London to meet with British representatives and the following day Arlow flew to Dublin to meet again with the IRA. On Friday, December 20th, the IRA announced a ceasefire from December 22nd to January 2nd 1975. On New Year's Day it extended the ceasefire until January 16th. But the British failed to respond, and the IRA offensive was resumed. Five days later 22-year-old John Stone of Ballymurphy, who'd been on the run for two years, was transporting a bomb along with Volunteer John Kelly when it exploded prematurely, killing them both. But, the new offensive met with a negative reaction, with people feeling that the British should be given more time, and that perhaps they might end internment. Negotiations were re-established and on February 11th the IRA announced a second 'indefinite' truce in return for a calling off of military repression and a number of political concessions. One was the establishment of Incident Centres that would be staffed by Provisional Sinn Féin with a direct telephone link with NIO officials. These centres would monitor the truce and prevent any repeat of the Lenadoon incident that had collapsed the previous ceasefire.

As with the ceasefire of 1972, the indication that the Brits were surrendering to the IRA prompted the loyalists to intensify their killing rampage against nationalist civilians and we were on red alert again. But we could also be a bit blasé when it certainly wasn't warranted.

## Chapter 23

On February 13th, two days into the truce, seven-year-old Deirdre O'Kane of Whiterock ran upstairs to her mother, Monica. A St. Valentine's Day card had just arrived in the morning post. A few minutes later, as they both opened it, the card exploded in their faces. The bomb was one of five posted to nationalists in Belfast that day. A second in Whiterock failed to explode only because the alarm had been raised before Davie Walsh got to open it.

That night there was a related scare outside 42. Cora, Donal and I had been down at the Rock Bar, entertaining a visiting French photographer named Claude who was staying at the house. Some time around midnight, as we walked up Ballymurphy Road, we could see all the commotion: people were being cleared from their houses by the British army. On closer inspection we discovered that a car, stolen in loyalist Silverstream, had been dumped outside our front door. Ominously, there was a Valentine's Day card on the front passenger seat.

This was a nuisance. The night was cold and we'd bought a bottle of *Paddy* so we could top up with hot whiskies once we got home. Carefully weighing up the situation, we dismissed the military panic and brushed past the soldiers. Once inside the house Cora opened the windows 'to let the blast through', if there was to be one, and I put on the kettle for the hot whiskies. Claude, meanwhile, stood at the front door, drunk but not too drunk. 'But,' he insisted with a kind of squeak, 'Maybe there is a bomb.'

'Where's that friggin' crowbar?' Donal said and began to hoke about under the stairs. A minute later he emerged armed with the crowbar and attacked the metallic threat to Claude's peace of mind. As the Brits dived for cover, and Claude proclaimed the presence of lunatics, Donal ripped open the boot of the car.

'There' he said putting Claude's mind at ease, 'No bomb.'

By the beginning of 1975, Ballymurphy, like every other conflict zone in the North, was a place inured to the horrors of war. The community had lived through the pogroms of '69 and had dealt with the resulting influx of traumatized refugees. It had lived through the British army assault of Easter 1970 when CS gas engulfed every home and two-year-old Francis McGuigan, killed by the effects of the gas, became the area's first Troubles-related victim. There had been the six-month riot and the slide into gun-battles and open warfare on the streets. There had been the savagery and mass murder of Internment Week and the Westrock massacre, and the indiscriminate military violence of Motorman. And there had been the other killings in the streets and the sectarian attacks. But nothing was to tear at the heart of the community like the feuds of 1975, the first of which was to break out in February.

In December the Official IRA had split, with a faction led by veteran republican, Séamus Costello, forming the Irish Republican Socialist Party. The Official IRA, furious at the loss to the new group of some of its weapons, struck the first blow when it assassinated Hugh Ferguson in Whiterock on February 20$^{th}$. Five days later, OIRA Volunteer, Seán Fox was killed in retaliation. Over the coming months, the low-level feud would claim four more lives, leave several people wounded, and bring into being the IRSP-linked People's Liberation Army, which would later become the Irish National Liberation Army. The tally of victims would include Billy McMillen, long-time commander of the Belfast Officials who was shot dead, and Seán Garland, national organiser of Official Sinn Féin who was badly wounded in Dublin. On March 9$^{th}$ the feud returned to our own district. Two men burst into a house in Whiterock Parade with guns blazing, but their intended victim managed to escape.

On the afternoon of March 10$^{th}$, as the area dealt with the trauma of internecine feuding, a bit of cheerful news pierced the gloom. Cora and I had been down in Dublin, along with Frank and Tess Cahill to organise the Dublin end of a sponsored wheelchair push. It was being undertaken on behalf of 42 by Whiterock man, Joe Hughes. After staying overnight with Peadar and Kathleen Timmins, friends of the Cahills who lived in Finglas, we were on our way home when we got the first inkling that something had happened. Passing Newry courthouse, we were stopped in Frank's van at a joint military/RUC road-block. Frantic soldiers on all sides were a sure sign that all in their world was not right.

'Is there anything wrong?' Cora asked an agitated RUC man who was checking our IDs.

'A bunch of prisoners escaped from the courthouse,' he said.

'My gawd' Tess said, 'That's awful.' We drove on through the checkpoint and she turned around, bright-eyed. 'I hope to God it's some of ours!' she said. When we got back to Ballymurphy we heard that the escapers were all IRA men. One of them was Gerald 'Fitzy' Fitzgerald from Ballymurphy Drive, who'd been serving a 20-year sentence for a claymore mine attack on the Paras in Rock Grove in July 1971, and to whom the Houdini title, long the mantle of Jim

## Chapter 23

Bryson, had now been passed.

Fitzy's first escape had taken place shortly after the Rock Grove incident. During the attack he'd been shot and captured by the paratroopers. Three days later, on July 16th 1971, as he lay under armed guard in the Royal Victoria Hospital, the Ballymurphy IRA sprang him.

At 6am a 'doctor' in white coat and surgical mask walked up to the two RUC guards, pulled a sub-machine gun from under his coat, clubbed one of the RUC men and held the other up. He was joined by three more 'doctors', also with sub-machine guns up their coats. Three other Volunteers were holding the night porter prisoner. One of the IRA men then lifted the wounded Fitzy, fireman-style, and carried him from the hospital to a waiting car, whereupon he and his rescuers disappeared, Fitzy going to a hospital over the border. That morning in Ballymurphy, leaflets, prepared in advance, were distributed depicting the rescue!

Once he'd recovered, Fitzy returned to Belfast but was again captured, and jailed for his part in the 1971 ambush. Eighteen months later, on October 13th 1974, after months of tension and several riots at Long Kesh, republican prisoners burned the camp to the ground. During the next few weeks, while the prisoners lived among the rubble, one Cage spent its time digging a tunnel. On November 6th the first of 33 escaping prisoners, including Fitzy, reached the nearby M1 motorway in the darkness of the winter's night - and ran straight into military gunfire. Hugh Coney was shot dead. All the others were arrested.

Three months later, as Frank, Tess, Cora and I were arriving into Newry, twelve of those prisoners were at the courthouse, waiting to be tried for the burning of Long Kesh and the attempted escape when they noticed some corroded bars in a lavatory window. They prized open the bars, scaled a 24-foot fence and legged it. Despite the massive British dragnet into which we'd driven, all but two made it safely across the border. When we arrived back at 42, Ballymurphy was euphoric.

But the euphoria didn't last long. During the first weekend of April, the OIRA/PLA feud was eclipsed by an orgy of sectarian shootings and pub bombings that left eleven dead and 82 injured across both sides of the community. One of the dead was 18-year-old Kevin Kane of Springfield Park, one of two nationalists killed when a cylinder bomb was tossed into McLaughlin's bar on the

Antrim Road by the Protestant Action Force, a pseudonym for the UVF. On the Sunday night, the OIRA/PLA feud came back again when three members of the (Officials') Republican Clubs were shot in the legs at Moyard Social Club by the PLA.

As they were shooting people over in Moyard, Cora, Frank, Tess, Donal and I were in the Sloan's Club along with Joe Hughes, putting the final touches to his planned wheelchair push.

\* \* \*

No account of those early years in Ballymurphy could ignore the presence of Joe Hughes. Joe had come into our lives in February. Cora had answered a knock on the door and from the kitchen I could hear Frank Cahill's voice.

'Cora, I'd like you to meet Joe,' he was saying, 'Joe is interested in the children's holiday scheme and he'd like to help by raising money.'

'Hello Joe,' I heard Cora say.

Still listening from the kitchen, I was wondering why Joe wasn't speaking for himself. I then heard a heavy clattering coming from the hallway and went to investigate. In the living-room I found Frank and Cora reversing away from a wheelchair that was maneuvering its way around the parked motorbike. Like Frank and Cora, the wheelchair too was coming in backwards. After a bit of a struggle, it cleared the doorway and I saw that the occupant, a big thin man of about thirty, with a square bony face and dark hair slapped over to one side, was pushing himself along with one foot. Once inside, he turned the chair around and smiled.

'This is Ciarán,' Frank said. Joe stuck out an unsteady, gnarled hand and his smile intensified. I gripped the hand and was surprised at the strength that curled around my fingers.

'Nice to meet you Joe,' I said.

'Hank u' Joe said, his mouth struggling to form the words. These, I was to learn, were about the only words Joe could master.

Tea was brewed and Joe laboriously pulled from his pocket a plastic straw and a small wooden board that he set on his knees. On the board were the letters of the alphabet and the numbers one to ten. Painstakingly, often missing the letters, Joe picked his way through the key words of what he wanted to say as we all resisted the temptation to speak for him. He was proposing a sponsored wheelchair push from Swords to Dublin.

At first I balked at the idea of anyone pushing a wheelchair

## Chapter 23

backwards for eight miles. But Frank assured us that Joe had done several such pushes and had raised thousands of pounds for a variety of causes. He and Joe then collaborated in telling us a little of Joe's story.

Joe had been born in 1942 with cerebral palsy, and had spent twelve years of his childhood in units for people with learning disabilities. Angry and frustrated, he had vowed to break through the barriers that imprisoned his spirit, and eventually made his way back to his community where he dedicated himself to helping others. Although his sole means of mobility was to push his wheelchair backwards with one foot, he found a means of putting this very disability to the benefit of others - by undertaking marathon wheelchair pushes.

As we got to know Joe, he developed a number of short-cut descriptions for those most associated with 42. For Frank, he ran a finger around his eyes (glasses), I was the moustache (which looked a bit like John Cleese doing Hitler!), Cora was the long hair, and so on. And, now in the Sloan's (although he didn't drink, he enjoyed the ambience) he was putting the finishing touches to the Swords walk.

Two months later, at the end of May, Joe completed the walk, pushing his wheelchair the full eight miles from Swords to Dublin. From then on, he was a constant about the house and its projects, heavily involving himself for the next nine years in the community politics of the Upper Springfield.

(Joe's efforts were officially recognised in 1977 when he was awarded the *Spastic Society Award*. The following year he made history by being the only Ballymurphy person ever to receive an MBE, and what's more, to be fully supported in his acceptance of the imperial title. This was followed in 1981 by the *William McKeown Award*, and a *People of the Year Award* in Dublin in 1982. When Joe died of a massive heart attack in the Royal Victoria Hospital in February 1983, tributes were paid from many quarters. Des Wilson called him 'one of the world's workers', while a piece of mine in the *Andersonstown News* described how Joe had been fighting since the day he first realised he'd been born on the minus side of fortune. He was 'Joe Hughes who always did the impossible. Joe Hughes who believed there was no place he couldn't go and nothing he couldn't do. Joe Hughes in the wheelchair - a truly remarkable man who gave us all courage.')

At the end of that night in the Sloan's, Joe let me wheel him home

– a privilege only allocated by the fiercely independent Joe to his closest friends – and exulted in being tossed out of his wheelchair in Divismore Crescent. We were free-wheeling down the Crescent with me riding on the back of the wheelchair and Joe whooping it up, when the whole shebang went over on its side on the bend. Once we'd dusted off, Joe laughed all the way home. His brother was less impressed when he saw the cut of his mud-spattered sibling at the door.

Meanwhile, further encouraged by the intervention of Joe, we plodded on with the work at 42, always developing new approaches and often amazed by the responses that greeted us. One venture found us in the Mourne Mountains with a mixed group of teenagers, all in the 14-16 age-bracket. Leading the group were myself, Greg Dormani and Ann-Marie Hartigan – Greg's former host who was now sponsored by the Quakers to work full-time at 42. Our goal was the 2,796-foot summit of Donard. Approaching the mountain from Slieve Donard Park, we followed the tumbling Glen River until we were above the tree-line, and then cut straight up the northern face of the mountain. At that juncture, 14-year-old Bernard Logan made a point.

'For fuck's sake Keern,' he said, 'Why do we have to go up there? We can see it from *here*!'

Bernard's was relentless logic, a legacy of the clear thinking that was so much a trait of his mother, Mary. This would most notably manifest itself years later when, after a night at the Sloans', Mary went back to Larry Sloan's house for an after-club party. Later, while in the kitchen, she slipped and broke a leg. Then, a woman in her seventies, full of drink and in severe pain, Mary displayed the most amazing presence of mind.

'Call an ambulance,' Larry said.

'Sh-top!' Mary ordered, finger in the air, 'Firsht, take me out and find a hole.'

In the dead of a winter's night, the other party-goers hoisted Mary aloft and, as per instruction, ferried her around the estate until they found a suitable compensation-sized hole into which Mary could be deposited.

'Now,' Mary instructed, 'Youse can call yer ambulance.'

\* \* \*

By the middle of April 1975, IRA units in Ballymurphy were becoming very dubious about the effects of the ceasefire and the fact that the Incident Centres were being paid for by the British. Many of the Volunteers considered it a low period during which the IRA was beind dragged into a sectarian conflict and compromised by its own lessening of security. In the meantime, the wider situation had become such that it was virtually impossible to know anymore who was most likely to shoot you next. Along with the OIRA/PLA feud, another feud had been raging between the UDA and UVF since mid-March. There was also the continuing sectarian slaughter, with people from both sides being gunned down in the streets and blown up in pubs. And there was the British army's role, which, despite the ceasefire, combined overt killings with its covert surveillance and an anti-ceasefire destabilising programme. In addition, the IRA continued to operate on a low key, retaliating for British violations of the ceasefire, or at times it seems, simply unable to control some of its members. It also engaged, along with every other group, in ongoing punishment shootings carried out against alleged criminal elements.

Yet, despite the times, people did their best to go on with normal life. At 42 the community work and human rights efforts were maintained, and the parties went on. On St. Patrick's Day I had even found myself at a *fleadh cheoil* - a traditional Irish music festival - in Crossmaglen in South Armagh.

Crossmaglen, a village built around a market square, complete with cattle-pens, was then a kernel of republican resistance. Radiating out from the village, IRA units in the South Armagh area had maintained a classic rural guerrilla war since the beginning of the Troubles, regularly attacking local bases and military patrols, and mining the narrow country roads with culvert bombs. So dangerous were the roads that the military bases were serviced by helicopter - even the refuse went out that way. Sometimes, the helicopters too were shot at. Prior to the *fleadh*, I had never been to Crossmaglen but managed, despite the climate of fear, to hitchhike there from one of the final residentials of my Youth & Community Work course which had been held at the Society of African Missions priory in Dromantine, close to Newry.

The residential would be remembered for the shotgun loaned to myself and Tommy Rainey from loyalist East Belfast by one of the monks at the priory - and for the 'hymns'. On the afternoon of the first day, Tommy and I left with the shotgun for a few pot-shots. Ten minutes later, there was a discharge when Tommy aimed rather badly at a crow. Inside the priory, our fellow students were taking bets on who had shot whom. This was only a joke as Tommy and I, though of greatly opposing political beliefs, were good friends: I used to offer to countersign any application he'd like to make for an Irish passport. Give him a reference, so to speak. The 'hymns', however, were another matter.

Late at night, four ruffians from Derry led the rest of us Fenians down the corridors, past the Protestant doors, humming a sort of Gregorian chant. That did Tommy's head in. He later claimed that, as a result of the 'hymns' and the crucifix above his bed, he was having nightmares for the rest of the month. Sandy Woods, another friend of mine from the course, who was a serving member of the Ulster Defence Regiment and a born-again Christian, told Tommy to let it pass: we'd pay for it in Hell.

Arriving in Crossmaglen on the afternoon of March 16$^{th}$, I was surprised to find that the massive military base behind the square didn't prevent the car in which I was travelling from being stopped at an IRA checkpoint just outside the village. Five minutes later, in the square itself, I was approached by a man who identified himself as Irish Republican Army and asked if he could check my rucksack for bombs. The southern accent, however, put him at his ease and he arranged for me to sleep on the floor of a house just off the square. The following day was a great day of denial. Under the gaze of watch-towers and machine gun nests, musicians came from far and near and the village partied like it hadn't a care in the world. Not a Brit was to be seen anywhere. In the afternoon, I ran into Tom Gormley, a mandolin-player and singer from Monaghan, who'd been a long-time friend back in Cork. He was sitting outside a pub along with a big circle of others, half a dozen tins of beer at his side and the mandolin picking away, sending rich clear notes into the Crossmaglen air.

'Tom,' I shouted, 'Give us *The Creggan White Hare*.' And Tom did, as if no years had passed between us. I walked on and never saw him again.

The following day I shared a lift back to Belfast with Eamonn McCann, the Derry socialist writer and civil rights leader who left me with a good grounding in helpful socialist analyses.

By the end of the month, when we had the Day of The Gasmen, even the utility services were pretending that all was normal. Ever since the beginning of the Troubles, when the area had become a no-go zone, the gasmen had been absent. To ensure a steady supply of gas, people had removed the money-box from the meter and had since been rotating the one shilling through the slot. Then, without warning, the gasmen arrived, escorted by military vehicles. Accompanied by two cartoons donated by Pat Burns, *Spotlight* reported the event with its characteristic anarchistic line:

*'The people of the Upper Springfield area, lulled into a sense of security by the ceasefire and the recent low-profile activity of the British army, were rudely awakened by a concerted attack by a seemingly new militant breakaway group... Eye witnesses described the attackers as being dressed in paramilitary uniforms on which the symbols GAS featured prominently.*

*As with previous attacks on this area, a strong contingent of security forces was present, yet made no move to intervene or constrain the assailants. One shocked housewife told our reporter, "They rushed up to my door, demanding money. What could I do? I phoned the Incident Centre but they were away for their tea."*

*Another eye-witness claimed, "I saw it all. One minute all was quiet. The next, a column of armoured cars swooped into our street. Men and women trembled. Little children fled in panic as hundreds of men in uniforms swarmed out of the vehicles, attacked the houses nearest them, jumped back in and were gone in a flash."*

*'... this was obviously a well-drilled flying column and on this evidence, more attacks can be expected in the future. All citizens are asked to be vigilant and to keep an eye out for the Flying Gasmen.'*

By the middle of June, the truce was falling apart, although the British and the IRA seemed to think otherwise, and Merlyn Rees continued to release the Long Kesh internees as part of the overall deal. From where we sat at 42, it was clear that everyone who could fire a gun or prime a bomb was working double time. Then a new conflict broke the surface in Ballymurphy. On the evening of June 16th Frank Cahill called at the house. I opened the door and he walked in with a light in his eyes.

'Hiya Frank,' Cora said, 'Will you have a cup of tea?'

'I will indeed me girl,' Frank said, planting himself down on the settee of my still-functioning, 60-pence three-piece. He took out the fags and passed them around.

'You're looking very anxious,' I said, noticing that Frank was in that state of agitation, broadly described in Ballymurphy as 'yer arse is making buttons'.

'Des is after resigning,' Frank said.

'Resigning!' I said, Resigning from what?'

'The Church,' Frank said, 'He's after resigning from the Church.'

'You're not serious!' Cora said as she and I simultaneously flopped down into the two armchairs, 'What happened?' A couple of weeks earlier, Des had accompanied one of our localised Youth & Community Work training courses to the Servite Priory at Benburb for a residential weekend and there had been no hint of anything of this sort.

'That episode in St. Thomas's was the last straw,' Frank explained, 'It's been a long time coming. But he didn't take any action until his mother died. It would've been too much for her.'

The episode to which Frank was referring had taken place on April 24th at prize-giving night at the school. The headmaster, 62-year-old Seán McKeown, had invited his son, Ciaran, a journalist who would later become one of the central figures of the 'Peace People', to cover the event. He was particularly to cover the speech to be made by our old buddy, Canon Pádraig Murphy, who was chairperson of the school's management committee. When the younger McKeown arrived, however, he was immediately set upon by the Canon. Murphy pulled from his pocket an article, entitled 'Shared Schools', that Ciaran had written for the *Sunday Press* the previous May. The article explored a controversial decision by Bishop Philbin to withhold the sacraments from children attending state schools. (The Vere Foster affair all over again!) To the astonishment of both McKeowns, Murphy then directed Ciaran from the building, pronouncing him 'persona non grata' in 'any Catholic institution'. After eighteen years in St. Thomas's School, eleven of them as principal, Seán McKeown resigned.

This was the culmination of the long saga that had begun back in 1968 when Des Wilson was first confronted with the Catholic hierarchy's attempts to frustrate the civil rights movement. It had been going on ever since, right through the Church's failure to condemn the brutality of Internment Week, Bloody Sunday, the Westrock Massacre, Operation Motorman and the ongoing military campaign of terror against civilans in nationalist areas.

More recently, in 1973, there had been an additional local assault

## Chapter 23

by the Church on 'outsiders'. On September 17th, four Asian nuns, placed in Ballymurphy as an act of solidarity by Mother Teresa's Missionary Sisters of Charity, had vacated their house in Springhill Avenue. The house was immediately occupied by local nuns under the control of Down and Connor. Overseeing the evacuation and reoccupation were Canon Murphy and Fr. George O'Hanlon. The following Sunday, September 23rd, an official statement from Mother Teresa was read out at all masses in St. John's and Corpus Christi churches. In it she claimed that her nuns had left Springhill because their presence elsewhere was 'very necessary ... No one has forced me'.

Nobody in the Upper Springfield believed that the sudden visit by Mother Teresa all the way from Calcutta, the hurried consultation with the Bishop, and the unannounced departure of the nuns in the middle of many successful unfinished projects were unrelated. Then a week later, a draft letter in Mother Teresa's own handwriting turned up in a rubbish bin, expressing anger and bitterness at being forced to leave Springhill. In a last ditch effort to prevent the nuns' decampment, Des Wilson, who was in the Basque country at the time, phoned Mother Teresa from San Sebastian, asking that her sisters stay a little longer so as to minimise the hurt to the community. She replied that if her nuns were wanted in 32 places around the world, why should she stay a day more than necessary in a place in which they were not?

Five days after the loss of Mother Teresa's nuns, the Upper Springfield suffered a further clearance at the hands of Down and Connor. Two nuns from the Society of the Holy Child, Sisters Eileen and Elizabeth, were told to pack their bags and go. They had arrived in Ballymurphy with the Bishop's approval at the beginning of the year, Sister Eileen to specialise in adult education and Sister Elizabeth in family welfare. The two women, who'd shed their habits, had moved into a house in Springfield Park, both finding paid work so that they could be self-supporting. On September 22nd, they were given the clerical boot on the grounds that the Diocese couldn't 'have Sisters roaming around the district on their own and setting up communities'.

'It's no surprise,' Frank said of Des's resignation, 'It's been one thing after another.'

Although the most recent events were seen by the community as the factors that drove the decision, we learned within hours that

Des had actually tendered his resignation on March 2<sup>nd</sup>, and had it accepted by the Bishop on April 25<sup>th</sup>. He had merely kept his silence until June 16<sup>th</sup>.

Within two days the anger that spilled across Ballymurphy had gathered into a coherent form. On the evening of June 18<sup>th</sup>, Cora and I were among 1,500 people who stormed the hall of St. Thomas's School, breaking the locks of the front door as we went. Despite the anger, the impromptu public meeting that followed was a dignified and ordered affair. Frank Cahill was elected chair and, after two hours of heated debate, a Parish Council Steering Committee was formed, with a mandate to fight back on behalf of the people. To the great chagrin of Canon Pádraig Murphy, I ('that Communist up in Ballymurphy') was one of those elected to the new body. The rest he condemned as 'lapsed Catholics'. A couple of days later, Cora appeared on TV on our behalf to further impair the Canon's digestion.

The ensuing struggle became known in Ireland as the 'Holy Watergate', and might well have begun that night, had Frank not dampened down the enthusiasm of some of the angrier women, with the symbolic burning out of Canon Pádraig Murphy. As it was, the Parochial House was put under siege for several hours the following day by a massive spontaneous protest of young people. Over the coming months, the furore and public debate shook the Catholic Church in Ireland to its foundations. One commentator stated that, whereas the millionaire recluse, Howard Hughes, had been given one week to prove that he was still alive, the Irish Catholic Church had been given only slightly longer.

'I didn't know you were that strong on the future of Irish Catholicism,' Donal said when he heard of my appointment. Cora simply threw her eyes towards that final goal of all good Catholics.

Throughout May, June and July, as we picketed, protested and wrote letters to newspapers about the iniquities of the Church, the IRA remained generally inactive against crown forces, although four soldiers were killed on July 17<sup>th</sup> by a remote-controlled milk-churn bomb near Forkhill in County Armagh. The sectarian attacks, however, continued, as did the UDA/UVF feud. The Upper Springfield was generally spared until June 20<sup>th</sup> when a 48-year-old man was wounded from a passing car in an attempted sectarian assassination in Springhill Avenue.

The onset of the long summer days meant preparations again for the usual set of holiday schemes, playschemes and outdoor programmes for the young people of the area. It also brought our friends from various parts of Ireland to the ongoing revelries at 42. Lelia Doolan arrived at the door one afternoon in a sweep of hair and clothes. Lelia had begun her career as an actress and singer before becoming a director and head of entertainment with Radio Telefís Éireann. She went on to become artistic director of the Abbey Theatre and moved from there to Belfast to complete a doctorate in anthrapology and work with women's groups and community and arts projects. She had become a regular visitor to Des Wilson's house. Joe Dennehy turned up with Jamil, a South African of Pakistani extraction who was a friend of Niall's, but with whom Joe now lived, along with five of Jamil's friends (all students in Dublin's College of Surgeons). Jamil, who brought with him a selection of spices the six mothers had sent from South Africa, made us the first curry Cora and I ever tasted, despite having travelled in Pakistan. On another occasion, we arrived home after a few days away to find an Indian man living in the house. He'd arrived in the area looking for a place to stay, and someone had given him the key to 42. Then Joost Van Dommele turned up from Ghent at the head of an energetic young cadre of the Belgian Irish Support Group who crashed on the floors for a week.

We were also joined by Richard Fox, a tall bearded American who managed to convince half of Ballymurphy that he was CIA without ever mentioning the organization. Richard had moved into the area and secured a house when houses were hard to secure. Then one day he was lifted by the Brits and we never saw him again, further fuelling speculation that he was some kind of clever spy.

Looking back at what 42 managed to achieve, some elements stand tall. By bringing large numbers of local young people into community projects, and building together through the informal training programmes, the parties (not to be underestimated), and events like the festivals, it broke the mould identified by Tony Spencer in his survey - that of community organisations dominated by older men. Together we worked hard, unfettered by fear of regulations, and we did it without even a phone! The house in Ballymurphy Road also attracted many outsiders, and friends and families of ours - most of them young - who developed deep friendships with the young people of Ballymurphy, sharing and developing ideas in a time of a global youth revolution and a war in the North. Many of the young outsiders went on to actively support the project and to return again and again. People like Chrit and Annemiek who brought waves of other young 'Dutchies' who stayed with families throughout the district and made films to take back to the Netherlands. People like Joost and his Belgian support group. People like our Niall and Joe Dennehy and Eileen Costigan and Gearóid Mac Allister (who helped me choose my first guitar). People like Harry Bellingham who changed all our worlds in his own unique way.

But, most of all, it brought that small core of unsung stalwarts who had pooled around my father through The Association of Human Rights in the North, and its offspring, *Between*. Without any support from the state in its early days, and often enduring the hostile rebuffs of funding bodies, they battled on year after year. Without them, we couldn't have succeeded as we did. They were our right arm and our most active friends. Financially and with personnel, they supported our community and human rights efforts, defended the dignity of individuals and communities, and provided a holiday scheme for families under duress - more than 10,000 people in all over a 25-year period. By the time their commitment would begin to wind itself down with the release of the last political prisoners, following the signing of the Good Friday peace accord, many of those who first threw their hat in the ring as teenangers were grandparents. Amidst the enduring relationships that developed over that time, there were several North-South marriages.

Down through the years, our Cork friends never buckled despite the constant harassment of the Irish Special Branch. With apparently little else to do, these defenders of the state considered a scheme that gave respite to women and children from both sides of the political divide a threat to national security, and hounded its voluntary workers at home and at work. They even raided our own family home in 1987, looking under the sink for four shiploads of arms that Colonel Muamar Gaddafi had sent from Libya to the IRA! On that occasion, they hadn't reckoned on my mother, Máire. Finding a desk in the house and sure they were on to something big, one of the Branchmen asked, 'What's that for!' My mother calmly explained that it was used for the work of *Between* and the Cork Lupus Support Group. 'What's lupus?' the Branchman asked. 'Oh,' my mother said, 'I have that. It's an incurable, life-threatening disease.' Given the speed with which the Branchmen vacated the house, God help Ireland if it's ever attacked by a 15-minute Iraqi weapon of mass destruction!

\* \* \*

In July, while Cora was in Cork looking after one of the summer camps and Union Jacks littered the North, we answered the call of the

## Chapter 23

Ennis *Fleadh*, a bigger version of the Crossmaglen *fleadh* and part of a national network of such festivals.

We drove there by minibus - Donal, Kieran, 16-year-old Paul Kennedy (a new comer to the work of 42 who lived in Turf Lodge), Pat Burns, Debbie Pickvance from Bristol who was back on a visit, myself, and Greg. Arriving on the Friday afternoon, we sussed out accommodation in a hay barn outside town before heading off to the festivities. We then joined a couple of New Age travellers who'd arrived by horse and cart, and did the obligatory pub crawl of all *fleadh cheoils*. But when we arrived back at our barn in the early hours, there was a slight problem. Greg, who was first in, immediately about-turned.

'Ciarán,' he said as young Paul headed unsteadily towards the barn door, 'Possession is in dispute. There are some people in there. I believe they might be in *flagrante delicto*...'

'Paul...! Paul...!' I called. But it was too late. Paul continued on, disappearing into the dark barn and walking right up to the hay which spilled down in layers to the concrete floor. When he heard a rustling below and mistook it for some of us, he struck a match. As he did, we could hear a woman shriek.

'Oh dear...!' Greg said.

The shriek was followed by an angry male voice.

'Who the fuck are *you* mate?' the voice roared, 'Florence fucking Nightingale!' Anyone would think it was deliberate.

We waited a while for the opposition to vacate the barn, but they didn't, and in the end, we had to sleep on the bus. In the morning we had Guinness for breakfast, rejoined our New Age friends, and started again.

On Sunday, eyes a-bloodshot and hair a-tangle, we left Ennis for the long drive back north, Pat driving and everyone else maintaining the party mood. Greg and Donal were playing guitars and the last of the carry-out was being consumed. Crossing the border, Kieran chucked the bones of a chicken supper out the window.

'Keep Ireland tidy,' he howled, 'Throw it in Britain.'

We continued on north, the seasonal Union Jacks - already prominent on the northern edge of Newry - becoming even more so as we made our way into the village of Loughbrickland.

'Bet you don't climb that pole and rip down that Union Jack,' Pat said as we reached the northern outskirts of the village.

'A flag each?' I said. (Remember: we were in our early reckless twenties.)

'You're on!' Pat said.

Pat stopped the bus beside a set of flagpoles. We both jumped out, and while the men of Loughbrickland were distracted by Sunday dinner, we shinned up a flagpole each and ripped down two flags.

'Up the Murph!' Pat roared at the distracted men of Loughbrickland. It was then that an awful sight unfolded: the smiling, long-haired Debbie was changing places. She was in fact climbing into the driver's seat! As Pat and I stared in disbelief, the minibus took off up the Belfast road, leaving the two of us stuck up flagpoles in loyalist Loughbrickland like coconuts in a shooting gallery!

'Burns,' I said as we broke our previous personal bests, tearing after Debbie and the bus, 'This is the last time I ever listen to you.'

'Yer bum's a plum,' Pat said.

In August, the ceasefire went through a particularly shaky period. On the night of the 8th, three days after the Dutchies, Chrit and Annemiek, had turned up from the Netherlands for a second visit, the annual internment-anniversary bonfires got under way and rioting broke out at the Taggart. Shooting between the IRA and the Brits followed, developing into heavy gun-battles across the west of the city. The rioters at the Taggart pulled back as the IRA put the Taggart, and Fort Pegasus on the Whiterock Road, under siege and wounded an RUC man. The rioting happened again on the 10th, giving way in the afternoon to more gun-battles that began at Divis Flats and spread up the Falls to Ballymurphy and Turf Lodge. On the 11th the shooting spread to the Shankill after an attempted bank robbery was foiled. Then on August 12th the shooting died down. And the rather odd truce was found to be still holding.

Two weeks later, on Sunday, August 24th, I was in the first of two cars that had a lucky escape when driving back from the 42 project's new holiday home in County Cavan. We'd acquired the house the previous summer from the eccentric John Godley, Third Lord Kilbracken of Killegar. The bearded, long-haired John, author and journalist, was a sitting member of the British House of Lords, but had a passion for all things Irish, and was particularly disturbed by events in the North. (In 1972, after the Bloody Sunday massacre, the decorated wartime pilot who'd been the youngest lieutenant commander flying a combat plane, had handed back his medals to the British queen.) On our first meeting with him, he was quick to point out that his family hadn't been planters, but were traders and merchants. John, who had a fondness for the drink, had inherited the Killegar estate in 1950. In 1970, however, much of Killegar House had been destroyed by fire and, although no evidence was ever presented, local rumour had John and the dropeen at the centre of the tragedy. When we arrived down in 1974, after Jim and Norma Lynch had made contact on our behalf, we found the big house still in ruins and 53-year-old John living among the charred remains as he worked on its restoration.

Now, a year later, after a successful season of childrens' holidays at the old teacher's house on the Killegar estate, we were on our way home. Brendan McQuillen, who'd been volunteering in the summer camps since 1973, was driving our car through South Armagh when we encountered two vehicle checkpoints. Both were manned by the Ulster Defence Regiment. We were stopped at the first but the second was still in the process of being set up when we went through. When the second car, driven by Kieran Fagan, arrived some fifteen minutes behind there was only one checkpoint. In the meantime two men on their way home from a football match in Dublin's Croke Park were abducted from their car and machine-gunned by the Protestant Action Force (a cover for the then legal UVF) - the ghost patrol operating the second 'UDR' checkpoint! We had been very lucky: a few minutes later and it doesn't bear thinking about...

By the end of August, the deal between the British and the IRA began to become undone in earnest. A political Convention, set up to try and find an internal solution (without the participation of loyalist or republican forces), was hopelessly deadlocked, as the IRA had foreseen. The IRA now expected a British declaration of imminent troop withdrawal (which, according to the Rev. Arlow, had been promised in the event of failure of the Convention). On August 27th the IRA resumed its bombing campaign in Britain in an attempt to prod the British government into its pull-out declaration. Nothing happened. At the end of September the bombing was resumed in the North, as were full-scale attacks on the British. Still nothing happened - and still the 'truce' officially remained. There was clearly going to be no British withdrawal.

\* \* \*

Towards the end of August, my sister, Emer, turned up from Cork. She stayed a month, fell in love with Donal and went back home to abandon three years study at the top of the UCC medical faculty for a life in the North with Donal. Her month-long stay in Ballymurphy coincided with a week-long break we'd planned for Inis Mór, the largest of the Aran Islands off the coast of County Galway. For Cora and me, it would be the beginning of the end of our first years in Belfast.

I left a day early to attend a court case in Galway. I was to speak on behalf of some young lads from Ballymurphy who'd robbed a petrol station in the city, then hired a taxi to take them to the border. The driver, who'd heard about the robbery, got suspicious and phoned the Gardaí. Bringing along my now-fading wedding suit, I hung it neatly in a bus shelter in Salt Hill late at night while I bedded down on the shelter's bench. The next day I donned the suit, attended court, watched my young friends being sentenced to terms in Mountjoy Jail, packed up the suit and waited in the square in central Galway for the others to arrive. That evening, Frank, Tess, Donal, Emer and Cora arrived in a minibus borrowed from the Association of Youth Clubs. They had also picked up two fashionably scruffy young Dubliners, Tom and David, and convinced them to also come to Inis Mór. Meanwhile I had met a twenty-year-old German student named Joseph with shoulder-length blond hair and a wispy beard who'd also decided to come along.

On Inis Mór we were joined by Micheál Mac Cába, our old friend from Cork and Glaslough days, who was now a teacher on the island. Micheál, who came originally from Carraroe in Connemara, could play half a dozen instruments, was a great old-style shuffle-dancer and was on first-name terms with every poteen-maker from Hag's Head to Killala Bay. His position on the island would, we expected, cloak us in the mantle of respectability we so craved. But, we hadn't reckoned on the Parish Priest.

These were days before tourism had reached the Arans and transport to the islands was a rusty old tub that ran from Galway city to Kilronan Pier, providing some curious side-shows along the way. Our first stop was off the coast of Inis Meán, the second of the islands, where a small community clung precariously to a few hundred yards of rocky coastline. There, we waited for a delivery of swimming cattle. Since the ferry couldn't go close to the island for fear of being holed on the rocks, the fishermen rowed out in tarred-canvas curraghs, with the cattle tethered behind. The cattle were then looped around the belly and hoisted up in the air where they spun wildly, spraying spirals of watery shite all over

## Chapter 23

the deck. As everyone ran for cover, the cattle were lowered into a pen. Then hundredweight bags of cement were dropped from the ferry to the fishermen below who stood ramrod-straight in the bobbing curraghs, catching them in their arms. These men were the descendants of Aran Islanders who'd hunted giant basking sharks from those same flimsy curraghs. They stopped making men like that a long time ago.

We then moved on to Inis Mór, ten miles by three, where visitors were a rarity and where Mícheál was waiting at the pier with advice as to where we could camp.

'There's a bit of a field,' he said, 'near the Parish Priest's house, but you'll have to go to the village for water.' Undeterred by that little detail, we pitched our big green canvas tent near some sycamores in the designated spot, and set off to explore the island.

Inis Mór was stunning. Backing away from the sheltered harbour at Kilronan, where the fishing boats docked in the evening, the land rose gradually in a south-westerly direction. At its lower levels, the island was a patchwork of bare limestone plateaux, and small fields created from seaweed and sand by generations of islanders. Where centuries of rain had carved the limestone into a criss-cross of channels, delicate alpines and small shrubs kept their heads down from the winds that whipped in from the sea. Beyond the web of dry-stone walls that protected the fields, the land rose sharply to a bulwark of sheer cliffs that defended the island's south-western flank against the pounding Atlantic. Far below the rim, gulls floated on the thermals, giving out sharp, lonely cries that echoed off the cliff walls. Down in the waves, there were seals and dolphins.

That evening we lit a fire and sat around drinking beer and whiskey. Donal and Mícheál played music and we sang along. Joseph gave us a couple of German songs and we all swayed as if we were in a beer-hall.

'I've been offered a plot of land on the island,' Mícheál told us between songs, 'It's a rare compliment. The islanders don't sell to strangers. They welcome people but they hold onto the land.'

'Do you think the Parish Priest minds us being here?' Emer asked, 'He hasn't appeared from behind the curtains since we arrived.'

'None of his business,' Mícheál said, 'This isn't his land. But I'm sure he wouldn't mind anyway.'

But it appears he did. While we'd been strolling the island's lanes, the Parish Priest had been taking umbrage. He never appeared from behind the curtains, nor said anything, but he contacted the authorities in Galway about a possible sanitary hazard. Tess was alone and asleep when the boys from Galway turned up.

'Excuse me madam,' one of two pin-striped bureaucrats said, poking his face into the tent, 'Do you mind if I ask where you go to the toilet.'

Tess, whose first instinct was to defend herself against the intruder, reached for the tent mallet. She then realised the nature of the intrusion and let go the mallet.

'What!' she said, 'How dare you wake me up to ask me a stupid question like that. Away and give my head payce!' The boys did as they were told and went back to Galway.

A day later, two strange, thick-necked chaps with short hair and trench coats arrived on the island. They mooched around for a couple of days, hiding in the bushes and the like.

'They're here to spy on us,' Frank said, 'Sent over by some blurt from Fine Gael after the Parish Priest heard the Northern accents.'

'What makes you think that?' Cora asked.

'Special Branch,' Frank said, 'You'd spot them anywhere. Bunch of fuckpots.'

* * *

On our second day on Inis Mór, we followed a dirt track to the western end of the cliffs to visit the prehistoric Dún Aonghusa. According to Mícheál, the clifftop fort was built 5,000 years earlier by the Tuatha Dé Danainn, a mythical people whose ghosts patrol the ramparts of Ireland's ancient places. Secure behind three defensive walls, the fort was protected by the Atlantic precipice and a surrounding minefield of *chevaux de frise*, sharp upright stones buried into the ground at crazy angles to deter any prehistoric landward enemy advance. From its ramparts that evening, we watched an awesome sunset as the god-awful midges moved in; and Mícheál happened to mention that he had a boat.

'I do,' he said, 'I bought an old curragh. It's full of rips and holes but I'm going to get it fixed up in a month or two. It's down on the beach.'

Next afternoon, four of us carried the boat to the sea. We slung it over our heads in traditional style, so that it wobbled down the beach like a headless, eight-legged pantomime horse. Once we had it in the water, Joseph, Emer and I studied the holes and rips. The most serious was an eight-by-two-inch horizontal tear at the front,

## Chapter 23

half way between the floor and gunwale.

'If the three of us sit towards the back,' I said, 'We'll be able to keep the bow clear of the water. We can spread our feet to cover the worst of the other holes.'

'Hang on a minute,' Emer said. She went off up the beach and came back with an empty catering-sized ham-tin. 'For baling,' she said. The three of us then hopped aboard and pushed off from shore. Joseph did the fishing. I did the rowing on a pair of long, slender, half-rotten oars. Emer did the baling. Cora watched from the shore as we became a spot on the horizon, wondering how long before she should call the coastguard.

'By the lording', livin', lovin' lightin' Jaysus!' Mícheál said when he arrived at the beach and saw his curragh a mile offshore, caught in a rip that was pulling hard towards the Galway coast. 'And to think that I was going to waste good money getting that thing fixed!'

Mícheál also had a small motorbike on which we hunted rabbits. After the pubs closed on the third night, we took off around the dirt boreens of the island. Mícheál drove, Cora sat behind him to carry the catch, and I sat behind Cora, ready to chase after any rabbits blinded by the headlight of the bike. We came back with three rabbits, skinned and cooked in a stew by Mícheál the following evening.

On the second night, the slight, 52-year-old Frank replaced Cora in the middle and we set off again down the pitch-black, rocky, dirt lanes of Inis Mór. For the first ten minutes we had no luck. Then a rabbit jumped out of the grass verge in front and took off. Mícheál revved up and gave chase. The rabbit ran into a field and we followed. As we bounced along in the dark, focused on the fleeing tail, the warren for which it was heading was not altogether visible until we slammed into it. The front wheel of the bike sank deep into a hole and the three of us shot in unison out over the handlebars. The last thing I saw before I hit the ground was Frank's glasses sailing in a neat arc through the full beam of the somersaulting bike. We came back with cuts and bruises, and two rabbits donated as a consolation prize by another night hunter who'd fished us out of the warren and had a car-boot full of dead rabbits.

The following morning, Cora and I were down at Kilronan pier, watching the fishing boats leave for the open sea, when a thought bubbled straight out of the water.

'What about another trip?' I said.

## The Year Of The Feuds

'What!' Cora said.

'Around the world. We could leave in the spring. Take the boat to Swansea, hitchhike to London and fly from London to India.'

'What in the name of blazes put that into your head?'

'The sea. It's like a magnet to the rest of the world.'

'I thought you were against flying,' Cora said. Up until then I'd been a dedicated overlander, believing that air travel was a form of cheating. But, there had already been two attempts at India...

'This one time,' I said, 'It's the only way of making sure we get there - unless the plane falls out of the sky. Are you on?'

'I suppose so,' she said, 'But how will we tell people we're just up and leaving? It's all a bit sudden.'

'Dunno,' I said; but as I stared out to sea the horizon filled with desert sunsets, Afghan bandits, camel trains, hashish dens, and semi-naked women in shop windows in Istanbul. And that was how we made the decision. As with the ad in the *Sunday Press*, an instant on Kilronan pier had dropped at our feet a whole new possibility.

On our last night on the island, the drink was flowing in the local pub and the music was bringing the house down when the publican made a sudden announcement.

'Everyone, drink up now and go!' he said, 'The local Garda has been spotted on the prowl.

'How many of them are there?' Tess asked in clearly sceptical tone.

'One,' the barman said, looking puzzled.

'ONE!' Tess roared, her eyes wide with genuine disbelief, 'ONE! For Jaysus' sake, we have twenty thousand British soldiers, fifteen thousand RUC, seven thousand UDR, and you're tellin' us we'll have to go because of *one* Garda! Are you right in the friggin' head!'

\* \* \*

Down in Cork, Niall and Harry Bellingham had gone to sea.

It had been a bright sunny summer's morning. They were both down the docks, dying of thirst and looking for a pub that was serving drink. With no work and no intention of sullying the day with any thoughts of it, they were passing a berthed ship when they saw a guy hanging over the side, painting the steel.

'What are you doing there friend?' Harry asked.

'I've just signed up with this steamer,' the guy answered, 'The captain is short of crew. He still needs a cook and an able seaman.'

Immediately, Niall became a cook of some renown and Harry's

## Chapter 23

maritime history stretched all the way back to Noah. Desperate for the additional crew members, the captain invited the two lads aboard and fed them whiskey and 200 fags each.

'Go home and get your passports lads,' he told them, 'You're hired.' An hour later, Niall and Harry were finding their sea-legs with the help of some more of the whiskey, and the boat was ready to sail.

We'll remember at this stage that Harry bore great antipathy to all things English which included in this instance, the ship's first mate. The first mate was unaware of this, but had a bad attitude anyway. This manifested itself when they were about to sail. Harry was hauling up one of the timbers that protected the hull of the ship from the quay wall when the first mate gave him some advice.

'Bellingham,' he said, 'Drop that and I'll drop you.'

With that, Harry tossed the lot into the river.

'My friend,' he growled at the first mate, 'I've done my part. Now, it's your turn.' Sensibly, the first mate backed off.

There was now a great wrong to be righted. The ship's accommodation was segregated into officers quarters and crew's quarters and the food was similarly doled out.

'There was a great slab of pork,' Niall explained, 'with a fat side and a lean side, and the lean side was supposed to be for the officers. But that got sorted: by the time we got to the first port of call - Arklow - the officers were starving and the crew were fed like kings!'

From Arklow, the ship turned for Hamburg in Germany, and Niall and Harry got back into the whiskey. On the night they were crossing the English Channel, it came Harry's turn for the night watch. This began at 2.00am when the poor man had a ferociously sick head, and was to last to 6.00am. When Harry went up to the wheelhouse, he found the steering locked in place with the peg that was used to secure it during the change of watch. The boat was doing fine, holding its course, so Harry jammed the peg in place and went back to bed. At six in the morning, the cabin door burst open and the first mate came charging through like a madman.

'Bellingham!' he roared, 'Are you out of your fucking mind! We've been drifting all night! We don't know where we are! We're on one of the busiest shipping lanes in the world! We could've crashed into another ship!' At this point, it began to dawn on the captain that he might have erred in his choice of crew.

Eventually, the ship reached Hamburg and Harry went ashore

and got langers drunk. As so often happened when the drink took hold, he began to think of villains, and the chief villain who came to mind was the first mate who had abused him so. Fired up on hard liquor, Harry headed back to the ship to exact vengeance. When he couldn't find the first mate, he decided that the captain would do. In a panic the captain fled and locked himself into his cabin. If he did, Harry got the fire-axe and attacked the cabin door. But the captain managed to raise the alarm and Harry was arrested. Released again as the captain didn't want to go through all the hassle of charging him with attempted murder, he was booted off the boat and woke up later under a concrete stairs somewhere near the docks of Hamburg.

Harry then staggered into the city centre to some square or other where he unleashed his largesse on the street-drinkers of Hamburg. Broke, he then set off for Ireland, making his way to the Hook of Holland by locking himself into train toilets. The 'able-bodied seaman down on his luck' then cadged a lift to Ireland on a tramp steamer.

Back on the original ship, Niall went on strike over the treatment of Harry. He locked himself in his cabin and, plied with food, drink and cigarettes by the rest of the crew, refused to come out again until he'd made landfall back in Ireland.

\* \* \*

As the autumn closed in on the Upper Springfield the sound of blast bombs and gunfire became more frequent, and the killing started again. On September 9$^{th}$ 41-year-old George Quinn of Glenalina Road was killed by loyalist gunmen at the Turf Lodge roundabout. On October 10$^{th}$, 24-year-old Sean McNamee was shot dead at the Whiterock Industrial Estate when he grappled with three Official IRA members during an armed robbery at the Macweld Engineering Plant, owned by himself and his brother.

Then on October 29$^{th}$ the area became engulfed in a new wave of feuding between the Official and Provisional IRAs. It began at about 6pm when the Provisionals launched 31 separate attacks in the space of half an hour against known Officials, several of them in Ballymurphy. One man was killed and 20 were wounded. Immediately Belfast's Officials struck back, and the cycle began, with the Brits staying well in the background. During the next two weeks of inter-street war, people stayed indoors after dark in nationalist areas, something that the years of loyalist terror had

## Chapter 23

failed to achieve.

In the Upper Springfield, the streets were patrolled by armed men. In Whitecliff Parade behind us, both factions were dug in, one at each end of the street. Homes were sniped at and sprayed with gunfire, while cars passed one another in blazing shoot-outs. One night, Cora and I were upstairs in the living-room, listening to music, when we heard lowered voices outside in the back-garden. To make sure that we weren't the targets, we peeked out the bedroom window. Down below in the dark, we could make out two men with guns. But, we weren't in the sights. Instead, they ran up through the garden, kicked in the back door of a house behind and emptied a magazine through the kitchen ceiling.

Along with actual members of both organisations, 'supporters' were also targeted; and that meant almost anyone in the community. In an atmosphere of unparalleled fear, nationalist Belfast watched appalled until eleven people were dead and fifty wounded in hundreds of incidents. Among the dead was a six-year-old girl, struck by a bullet during an attempt on her father's life.

The initial rash of shootings was followed in the Upper Springfield by sporadic sniping, then further casualties. On October 31st, a 15-year-old boy was wounded near the re-built Kelly's bar. Shortly afterwards a burst of shots fired at a group of youths standing in New Barnsley Crescent injured a 16-year-old girl. On November 3rd, 22-year-old ex-internee James Fogarty, a former member of the Officials, was shot dead at his home in Rock Grove in front of his wife and child. Three nights earlier shots fired into his home had narrowly missed his wife, who later took her own life.

On November 7th a bomb was thrown by the Officials at Kelly's Bar in response to the bombing of several Officials' pubs by the Provisionals. On November 8th a pensioner was shot at while getting out of a car in our own street. On November 11th, 19-year-old John McAllister of Ballymurphy Drive was shot dead as he waited for a bus at the top of Springhill Avenue. He was killed because his mother, Ethel, was a prominent member of the Republican Clubs (Officials).

The feud finally came to an end on November 13th, the day after the Officials had killed 28-year-old John Duggan, chairperson of the Falls Taxi Association. The community-based Black Taxis, supported by most residents of West Belfast, formed a huge cavalcade of protest, demanding an immediate end to the shooting and bombing.

Meanwhile, on November 12th, the truce with the British had eventually come unstuck when the telephone links with the Sinn Féin Incident Centres were severed. The war was back in full swing. The British were now ready to move forward with a new judicial framework of jury-less courts, allowing internment without trial to be ended. On December 5th, several men from Ballymurphy were among the last to be released from the internment cages of Long Kesh.

\* \* \*

In the week leading up to Christmas, Santa Claus, in the form of Kieran Fagan, came to 42. After a big trawl for toys and other suitable presents, and the fulsome support again of our Cork crew, several large sacks were filled and the living room became a grotto, complete with Christmas tree, tinsel star, balloons - and the old green bulb again. The entry between our house and Hunters' became the queue. The children and mothers were led in the back door to visit the big bearded ho-ho-hoing man himself and get a Santa parcel for a minimal fee. In the children's faces, it was all magic. One lad, in particular, I will never forget. He was about six and came into the room as enthralled as if he'd just been transferred to the North Pole itself.

'And what would *you* like for Christmas?' Santa asked after the usual ho-ho-hoing and sitting on the knee.

'Santa,' the wee lad said in a whisper, 'I would like an Action Man.' His mother, meanwhile, was indicating to Kieran - no promises.

'Ho-ho-ho,' Santa said, 'We'll see what we can do. Now you go over and get yourself a nice wee present from the bag.'

The little lad went over to the bag, still looking back at Santa, rummaged around and pulled out his parcel.

'Are you going to open it?' his mother asked. He did - and pulled out a brand-new Action Man. There was at least one child in Ballymurphy that Christmas who believed in miracles. Meanwhile, Kieran - who got piddled on at one point - kept his spirits up with a large bottle of whiskey. When he was exhausted, Frank Cahill junior donned the beard and robes but Kieran kept the whiskey.

Just before Christmas, Mags Geaney - an old Cork friend - arrived from Dublin and stayed for our standard anti-Christmas, Christmas party which attracted the usual crowd of anti-Christmas

## Chapter 23

people. Cora, Mags, Kieran, Donal and I then headed for Cork in the Andersonstown Handicapped Association minibus. There, we collected Emer and continued on to the Dingle Peninsula, staying for the New Year in the old cottage where Cora and I had spent our honeymoon. As we drove up into the remote Valley of the Cam (pronounced Cowm) at the back of Mount Brandon, Cora and I were still wondering how we'd break the news of our planned trip to Frank and Tess.

\* \* \*

It was hard news to break. But, when Frank called to the house the day we got back, I bit the bullet.

'Frank,' I said, 'Cora and I are planning to travel again... Something we need to do before we get settled.'

For a moment, Frank had a stunned look on his face.

'So, you're abandoning us...,' he said, a wry smile working its way across his face, 'When are you thinking of going?'

'Easter,' I said, 'We hope to be away by late April.' Frank shrugged his shoulders, took off his glasses and began to wipe the lenses.

'I'm not *very* surprised,' he said after a pause, 'I always had a feeling it would come. But, I also hoped it wouldn't. Lots of people have come through Ballymurphy over the years and made all sorts of contributions; but, apart from Des Wilson's house, not much else compares to what's come out of this house. You'll both be missed.' Coming from Frank, that was probably the greatest accolade Cora or I would ever receive.

'The years we spent here were the best of our lives,' I said.

'But not enough to make you want to stay,' Frank said, a touch of irony in the voice.

'We have to do this,' I said, 'No point in storing up regrets for the future. But, maybe in a few years, when we've laid the travelling bug to rest...'

'Careful you don't make promises you mightn't be able to keep,' Frank said, 'Every step leads to the next... Let's just make the most of the time that's left.'

We did our best. Over the coming months little changed at 42. The community effort and the parties went on unabated while I opened up negotiations with Belfast City Council on getting a resource centre for the Upper Springfield. The talks began between myself and Brendan Henry, Assistant-director of Community Services. The nature of the talks was that, every time I came across Brendan,

I asked him when we were getting our resource centre. At one such meeting, he pleaded, 'Ciarán, will you just leave me alone!' But, in the end it bore results. Brendan worked for us in the background. I was in the house one morning in late February and answered the door to find Dorita Field, the Council's Director of Community Services, standing there. She would've phoned, she explained, if we'd had such a thing in the house.

'So,' she said when she came in, 'You want a resource centre and you want the Council to pay for it?' She sat down, discussed the prospect, and then acknowledged that the need had been proven by 42. 'We'll be considering it over the coming months,' she promised, 'Be hopeful.' Dorita Field was true to her word. The Upper Springfield Resource Centre that grew out of those discussions still operates from the top of the Whiterock Road.

At Frank's behest, we became basket-makers in our final Ballymurphy weeks.

Soaking the rattan in the bath, we'd gather in the evenings - Frank and Tess, Frank junior, Philip and young Seán Cahill, Seán Adams (who, since Glaslough days, had taken to peering around corners in the same way as young Frank), Seán Butler, Cora, Donal and myself. The living-room became the factory where, over several weeks leading up to Easter, we churned out Easter baskets by the dozen. We then raffled them in the local clubs as part of a fund-raising effort aimed at buying the house in Killegar from Lord Kilbracken. At the same time, Cora and I began to focus on Asia.

When news got out that we were leaving, we had many visitors. Sam McCready and Tommy Rainey turned up from East Belfast and were treated to the usual tea and toast - Sam called it Ballymurphy chicken. Lelia Doolin arrived from Dublin to wish us well. By now, Lelia had been around Ballymurphy for a couple of years, on and off, working on various arts-related projects. Brian Smeaton, the eccentric, heavily-bearded, Dublin-born reverend who preached on the Shankill in his thick Dublin accent, dropped in to bless us. As well as being involved in Des Wilson's *People's Theatre* productions, Brian had joined the rest of us in the efforts of the Greater West Community Association to establish common cause across the community divide on community issues.

Among the others to become active in the Association was Sammy Smyth, a prominent UDA member who seemed very old to

## Chapter 23

me when we first met, but was only forty-four. Sammy, an affable grandfatherly figure, brought an interesting UDA perspective to the meetings. Then we heard him one morning on the radio threatening a loyalist war in which no prisoners would be taken. I always found him a little disconcerting after that, but was still shocked when he was shot dead by the IRA at his sister's home in Alliance Avenue on March 10$^{th}$ 1976 at the age of forty-six. Just a few days before, I'd been talking to him in North Belfast. War can be funny like that: it can anaesthetise you until every now and again you feel its wash brush by.

\* \* \*

It was only fitting that the last thing we did before leaving Ballymurphy was organise a final, three-day party. Right through that Friday and Saturday, every incoming train brought revellers from Cork, Dublin, Galway and Derry until the party-goers were billeted across the whole area. Banjo-players, guitar-players, pipers, bodhrán-players, shuffle-dancers, all filed up Ballymurpy Road to the great chagrin of our nearest neighbours. There were parents, grandparents and teenagers, poteen-distillers, clergy, IRA Volunteers, foreign students and everything in between. As usual, Frank Cahill was Master of Ceremonies and as usual (when pressed) he gave us his rendition of *Sweet Sixteen*. Tess sang *Lament for Seán South* and *She Moved Through The Fair*. Donal and his guitar, despite the abundance of musicians, anchored the show as he had done from day one. Kieran, as always, played the whistle. Pat Burns left his banjo at home. And, where close-knit gatherings happened, there were the stories.

There was Bridie Adams who answered the door one day to find the Brits looking for her son, Seán.

'You know, he's a bad boy,' the officer said after they'd searched the house, 'Where is he?'

'I don't know,' Bridie said, poker-faced, 'To tell you the truth sir, we had words and he left.'

'Is that so?' the Brit said, eyeing the overtly deferential Bridie suspiciously, 'Well, if you see him, you can tell him we're looking for him.'

'I will indeed sir,' Bridie said, 'But if you see him first, will you tell him something for me?'

'What should I tell him?' the Brit said, beginning to suspect he was being taken for a ride.

'Come home Seán,' Bridie said, 'All is forgiven.'
And there was Mrs. McGuinness down in Westrock who arrived in to find her house being torn apart in an arms search and several rifle stacked in the corner.

'Say nathin'!' she told the family, 'Nobody open their mouth!'
'Ma...,' her son, Danny, began.
'Say nathin'!' came the order again.
'But ma...'
'I told you, say nathin'!'
'Ma, they belong to *them*...'

'Is Gerry Finnegan after turning into a wino?' Peggy Burns wanted to know. Gerry had brought a load of wine to help refresh the guests and, as far as Peggy was concerned, nobody drank wine for any other reason in those days. Young Frank Cahill's contribution was a more conventional fourteen bottles of Vodka. Jimmy Burns brought his home-made 'Kahlua'. The green light burned day and night for the three days and buckets of water flowed to the loo. Jan McCarthy sang to the Brits in her English accent and black evening gown - same old song about soldiers and hookers. Ann Stone wanted to know of the Brits if they still wore their kinky boots. My cousin, Seán, toppled backwards into a large box of Easter Eggs left over from the basket-making. Rosie Lawlor drove an elbow through one of the papered-over holes in an upstairs stud wall. Our Niall, Joe Dennehy and Mícheál Mac Cába turned out the hot poteens. Mags Geaney, up again from Dublin, had tears in her eyes. And Paul from Turf Lodge did it again.

'I've just walked in on two people in the small bedroom in the back,' he said, mournful eyes to heaven.

'You've a great future ahead of you,' I joked. We both laughed but I was right. After the party I never saw Paul again, although I was to spend many of the coming years in Ballymurphy; but Paul's would be one of the great success stories of the area.

The last thing I knew of him when we left in 1976 was that he planned to go on with his education. I didn't see him or hear from him again for 31 years. Then, in late 2007 I got an email to my work from a man who was trying to get his hands on the most recent edition of *Ballymurphy and the Irish War*. In the email, there was fulsome praise for the earlier versions, and some memories of growing up in the flats above the Bullring and moving to Turf Lodge when the flats were wrecked in the early Troubles. There

## Chapter 23

was also a word of thanks for believing in him when he was sixteen. I stared long and hard at the name at the bottom of the email: Paul Kennedy, Professor of Clinical Psychology and Academic Director, Oxford Doctoral Course in Clinical Psychology, University of Oxford.

Fair play to you Paul.

At one point during the final night of the party the house was so packed that I was afraid the upstairs would come down on the people below. The fourteen musicians had to retreat to the yard for elbow room, leaving no room for the Brits, and Cora eventually went up to Cahill's to get some sleep. By Monday morning the complaints were coming in from as far away as Springhill.

'We'll report this to the Boys,' old John Maguire from two doors up threatened. But, unknown to John, half of 'B' Company had been at the bash.

Young Frank Cahill was the last man standing on Monday morning.

'If you hadn't been at this,' he said as he left, peering furtively up and down Ballymurphy Road, 'you wouldn't believe it happened.'

A day or two later Cora and Donal left for Cork with the furniture we'd inherited from Maggie's so it could be stored in the home of her brothers, John and Nelius, while we were away. There was then one final, 42-based community development training weekend at the old Servite Priory in Benburb, Co. Tyrone, after which Jean drove me to the border, south of Newry.

'I suppose it's the end of something,' she said, 'Now Ballymurphy can go into rehabilitation.'

'That's not very nice,' I said.

'It's about as nice as it gets,' Jean said, 'Will you miss us?'

'With all my heart,' I said and that was the teetotal truth.

'Take this,' she said and handed me an envelope, 'But don't open it until I'm gone... Now, follow your heart.' We embraced and said goodbye and I was swept by the enormity of leaving Belfast and the huge extended family with whom Cora and I had shared so much. No matter where the road would take us, I knew in my soul that being adopted by the people of Ballymurphy was the greatest privelege we would ever have bestowed on us.

With drooped shoulders I walked down the narrow border road to the next bend. Then a last wave to Jean and she was gone, whereupon I opened the envelope. Inside was a 16-page, home-made *bon voyage* full of Jean's drawings and pieces of verse. Two dried mountain primroses, brought back in 1974 from Mussouri in India, were cellotaped to the last page. One of the stanzas read:

*'Where happiness is madness, 'tis wisdom in disguise ...
Where sanity is sadness 'tis folly to be wise.'*

My eyes watered with the thought. It seemed like sound advice.